# Hybrid Computational Intelligence

T0296651

Hybrid Computational Intelligence for Pattern Analysis and Understanding Series

# Hybrid Computational Intelligence

## Challenges and Applications

Series Editors

**SIDDHARTHA BHATTACHARYYA**

**NILANJAN DEY**

Edited by

**SIDDHARTHA BHATTACHARYYA**

**VÁCLAV SNÁŠEL**

**DEEPAK GUPTA**

**ASHISH KHANNA**

ELSEVIER

**ACADEMIC PRESS**

An imprint of Elsevier

Academic Press is an imprint of Elsevier
125 London Wall, London EC2Y 5AS, United Kingdom
525 B Street, Suite 1650, San Diego, CA 92101, United States
50 Hampshire Street, 5th Floor, Cambridge, MA 02139, United States
The Boulevard, Langford Lane, Kidlington, Oxford OX5 1GB, United Kingdom

**Notices**
Knowledge and best practice in this field are constantly changing. As new research and experience
broaden our understanding, changes in research methods, professional practices, or medical
treatment may become necessary.

Practitioners and researchers must always rely on their own experience and knowledge in evaluating
and using any information, methods, compounds, or experiments described herein. In using such
information or methods they should be mindful of their own safety and the safety of others,
including parties for whom they have a professional responsibility.

To the fullest extent of the law, neither the Publisher nor the authors, contributors, or editors,
assume any liability for any injury and/or damage to persons or property as a matter of products
liability, negligence or otherwise, or from any use or operation of any methods, products,
instructions, or ideas contained in the material herein.

**British Library Cataloguing-in-Publication Data**
A catalogue record for this book is available from the British Library

**Library of Congress Cataloging-in-Publication Data**
A catalog record for this book is available from the Library of Congress

ISBN: 978-0-12-818699-2

For Information on all Academic Press publications
visit our website at https://www.elsevier.com/books-and-journals

*Publisher:* Mara Conner
*Editorial Project Manager:* Gabriela D. Capille
*Production Project Manager:* Punithavathy Govindaradjane
*Cover Designer:* Victoria Pearson

Typeset by MPS Limited, Chennai, India

Working together
to grow libraries in
developing countries

www.elsevier.com • www.bookaid.org

# Dedication

*Dr. Siddhartha Bhattacharyya would like to dedicate this book to Dr. Fr George Edayadiyil, Honorable Chancellor, CHRIST (Deemed to be University), Bangalore, India.*

*Dr. Václav Snášel would like to dedicate this book to his wife Božena Snášelová.*

*Dr. Deepak Gupta would like to dedicate this book to his father Sh. R.K. Gupta, his mother Smt. Geeta Gupta, his mentors Dr. Anil Kumar Ahlawat and Dr. Arun Sharma for their constant encouragement, his family members including his wife, brothers, sisters, kids, and to his student close to his heart.*

*Dr. Ashish Khanna would like to dedicate this book to his mentors Dr. A.K. Singh and Dr. Abhishek Swaroop for their constant encouragement and guidance and his family members including his mother, wife, and kids. He would also like to dedicate this work to his (Late) father Sh. R.C. Khanna with folded hands for his constant blessings.*

# Contents

# List of contributors

**Rashmi Agrawal**
Faculty of Computer Applications, Manav Rachna International Institute of Research & Studies, Faridabad, India

**Suyash Agrawal**
Maharaja Agrasen Institute of Technology, Delhi, India

**H. Ashwin**
Department of CSE, Ramaiah Institute of Technology, Bangalore, India

**Siddhartha Bhattacharyya**
Department of Computer Science and Engineering, CHRIST (Deemed to be University), Bangalore, India

**Hrishikesh Bhaumik**
Department of Information Technology, RCC Institute of Information Technology, Kolkata, India

**Susanta Chakraborty**
Department of Computer Science & Technology, Indian Institute of Engineering Science and Technology, Howrah, India

**Suman Deswal**
Deenbandhu Chhotu Ram University of Science and Technology, Sonepat, India

**Sampath Emani**
Department of Chemical Engineering, Universiti Teknologi PETRONAS, Tronoh, Malaysia

**Deepak Gupta**
Department of Computer Science and Engineering, Maharaja Agrasen Institute of Technology, Guru Gobind Singh Indraprastha University, Delhi, India

**Neha Gupta**
Faculty of Computer Applications, Manav Rachna International Institute of Research & Studies, Faridabad, India

**R. Hanumantharaju**
Department of CSE, Ramaiah Institute of Technology, Bangalore, India

**Srinidhi Hiriyannaiah**
Department of CSE, Ramaiah Institute of Technology, Bangalore, India

**Anita Kanavalli**
Department of CSE, Ramaiah Institute of Technology, Bangalore, India

**Ambeshwar Kumar**
School of Computing SASTRA Deemed University, Thanjavur, India

**R. Manikandan**
School of Computing SASTRA Deemed University, Thanjavur, India

**Vishwanath Panwar**
Department of Mechanical Engineering, Rai Technology University, Bangalore, India

**S. Seema**
Department of Computer Science and Engineering, Ramaiah Institute of Technology, Bangalore, India

**Moolchand Sharma**
Maharaja Agrasen Institute of Technology, Delhi, India

**Chetan Shetty**
HCL Technologies, Bangalore, India

**Gagan K. Shetty**
Department of CSE, Ramaiah Institute of Technology, Bangalore, India

**Siddesh G.M.**
Department of ISE, Ramaiah Institute of Technology, Bangalore, India

**Kaushik Singh**
Department of CSE, Ramaiah Institute of Technology, Bangalore, India

**B.J. Sowmya**
Department of Computer Science and Engineering, Ramaiah Institute of Technology, Bangalore, India

**A.M.D. Srinivas**
Department of CSE, Ramaiah Institute of Technology, Bangalore, India

**K.G. Srinivasa**
Department of Information Management & Coordination, NITTTR, Chandigarh, India

**Pramod Sunagar**
Department of CSE, Ramaiah Institute of Technology, Bangalore, India

**Seshu Kumar Vandrangi**
Department of Mechanical Engineering, Universiti Teknologi PETRONAS, Tronoh, Malaysia

# Preface

There has been increased popularity of hybrid computational intelligence over the last decade, mainly due to the extensive success of these systems in a wide range of real-world complex problems. This is affected by the increased capabilities of hybrid computational intelligence technology. Another reason for this extensive success is the synergy derived by the hybrid computational intelligent components, such as neuro-fuzzy, rough-neuro, rough-fuzzy, fuzz-rough, fuzz-evolutionary, neuro-evolutionary, neuro-fuzz-evolutionary, ensemble methods, expert system, deep learning, and heuristics to name a few. Each of these constituent methodologies gives rise to hybrid systems with complementary reasoning and searching methods that allow the use of domain knowledge and empirical data to solve complex problems.

This volume covers the basics of computational intelligence. It brings together many different aspects of the current research on intelligence technologies such as neural networks, support vector machines, fuzzy logic, and evolutionary computation, and covers a wide range of applications and implementation issues from pattern recognition and system modeling, to intelligent control problems and biomedical applications. This book is also enriched with the definition and description of hybrid computational intelligence. In addition, it briefly explains the most popular varied applications of hybrid computational intelligence.

The book contains nine well-versed chapters written by the leading practitioners in the field.

The study and analysis of human behavior using a computer modeling approach is known as opinion mining or sentiment analysis. Data mining, Web extraction, text mining, etc. are the key areas of opinion mining. Social media platforms are gaining popularity and are becoming essential components people's lives. Various social networking websites, such as Facebook, Twitter, and WhatsApp are generating huge amounts of data and the mining of these data helps in discovering hidden and useful information of high potential. Calculation and evaluation of average inclination of any opinion/sentiment toward any entity helps both the organization and the individual to obtain the correct opinion about ongoing trends or unfamiliar things. Various computational intelligence techniques are also used to analyze the sentiments of users. In Chapter 1, Application and techniques of opinion mining, the authors cover the fundamental concepts of opinion mining and sentiment analysis. The chapter also includes various techniques of opinion mining, along with various tools used to analyze opinion. Some key areas related to feature extraction, ontologies, and deep learning have also been discussed. Toward the end of the chapter research and future directions and references for further study are given.

Data generated from social media and travel blogs signify vital travel behavior and information about destination resources. Due to the increasing use of social media and technological advances in smartphone segment and internet connectivity, "big data" can be accessible now at a low cost. Tourism industries have been adopting innovations in information and communication technologies, where smart tourism is a newer approach that has evolved in recent years. Big data is becoming the new frontier for managing information. Big data has showcased the need for technological infrastructure that brings out tools to capture, analyze, and store for visualizing massive amounts of structured and unstructured data to enhance potential growth with regard to both business and travel experience. In spite of all this, big data analysis for tourist destinations remains limited. Semantic analysis explores the pattern of movement of tourists and inclinations within the tourist destination. Chapter 2, Influence of big data in smart tourism, discusses the impact of big data analysis in enabling smart tourism. The chapter focuses on global information systems, which provide a visual division of the origins of bloggers. Emotional examination of the underlying information indicates tourists' satisfaction levels, while content examination explores more severely disgruntled characteristics of tourist experiences. The results should help in providing plans for improving planning, designing, and services at tourist destinations.

There is a huge amount of digital information including images, audio, and video in addition to the textual data that is accessible to everyone and anywhere due to the advances in the Internet and smartphones. Multimedia data are accessible and huge in number because of the high-resolution cameras that are available in smartphones. Multimedia platforms and social media gather these data and facilitate storage, analytics, and management of the data. In particular, video data are used in areas such as education, broadcasting, entertainment, and digital libraries. The applications that use video data should be efficient to retrieve the videos as quickly as possible and analyze the information that is embedded in it. Most of these applications are based on indexing and searching, that is, the texts associated with the video are used for the retrieval.

Content-based video retrieval (CBVR) techniques are efficient techniques for video retrieval. Chapter 3, Deep learning and its applications for content-based video retrieval, outlines the techniques for video retrieval using CBVR with an experiment on a data set for retrieval.

The explosion in smartphones has led to major changes in the perception of news, which has led to the use of social media to propagate fake news and system-generated content without proper validation. The existing solutions to this problem employ the use of technologies like machine learning. The identification of unverified articles is a classification problem where given a document, the system classifies it as either "fake" or "valid". This process involves the collection of large amounts of text corpus of both valid and fake news articles. The issue with these existing systems is the validity of the data aggregated from different sources. This can lead to the problem of human bias in labeling the articles collected. As an initial step to reduce this bias, Chapter 4, A computationally intelligent agent for detecting fake news using generative adversarial networks, proposes a fake news detection framework, which uses a generative modeling technique, which employs a generator—discriminator (G—D) setup. The G—D model is extended from the SeqGAN model. The generator generates new data instances, while the discriminator evaluates them for authenticity. When the models train competitively, the generator becomes better at creating synthetic samples and the discriminator gets better at identifying the synthetic samples. Thus, a data set is synthesized by merging the real articles with the articles generated by the generator, which is trained using the G—D setup. This data set is then used to train the agent (classifier) to identify the articles as "fake" or "valid."

Healthcare is an accomplished domain, which incorporates advanced decision-making solutions, remote monitoring systems, healthcare, operational excellence, and recent information systems. To address and deal with the complexity of the healthcare problem computational intelligence has been implemented. Chapter 5, Hybrid computational intelligence for healthcare and disease diagnosis, and Chapter 6, Application of hybrid computational intelligence in health care, present detailed surveys of healthcare logistics and highlight the application of hybrid intelligence in healthcare analytics. Several medical imaging modalities and segmentation techniques used for healthcare improvement have been discussed. In addition, the effectiveness of deep learning techniques, such as convolutional neural networks or recurrent neural networks, for segmenting medical images is also touched upon.

Agriculture is the backbone of India, not only in terms of feeding the population, but also accounting for the largest part of the gross domestic product. The prominent concern in agriculture is diseases in plants that impact food production and the livelihoods of humans and animals. There are no efficient methods to detect these diseases at their outset. The task of detection of different kinds of diseases in plants is still carried out with the naked—eye perception methods. This is a tedious process that consumes a great deal of time without great accuracy, and so automation of this process is required. Image processing is often used as an effective solution for plant disease detection. It takes into consideration features which may not be detected by the naked eye. By the application of these techniques, such as enhancing the image and extracting the features, the type and severity of disease in a plant can be identified. Chapter 7, Utility system for premature plant disease detection using machine learning, illustrates some notable works related to automatic disease detection in plants, specifically with respect to the use of techniques including image processing and modeling techniques, such as neural networks with the help of drone technology. The chapter also presents a new system capable of detecting any disease irrespective of plant species employing support vector machine and image-processing techniques.

In the past few decades, several research attempts have strived to utilize artificial intelligence (AI) in solving computational fluid dynamics (CFD)-related problems; translating into AI/CFD systems. This increasing trend has been motivated by documentation illustrating that AI/CFD systems are better placed and promising relative to their successful application to some of the well-formulated CFD problems that require pre-enumerated solution selection or classification. However, some scholarly observations contend that when CFD tasks are formalized or understood poorly, the application of AI technology leads to a large investment of effort and long system development times, with payoff unguaranteed. Given this dilemma, it becomes important to examine some of the AI/CFD or AI-based CFD approaches that have been applied to different CFD tasks, as well as some of the factors affecting the success of the perceived approaches. Chapter 8, Artificial intelligence-based computational fluid dynamics approaches, examines some of the AI-based CFD approaches that have gained application relative to the setup and solution of CFD problems. These include the use of the Elman neural network (ElmanNN) as an AI in CFD's hull form optimization, the use of genetic algorithm (GA)-based CFD multiobjective optimization, the implementation of fluid flow optimization using AI-based (convolutional neural networks) CFD, the use of coupled AI (via ANN) and CFD in predicting heat exchanger thermal—hydraulic performance, and the use of ANNs in CFD expert systems.

For the last two decades, video shot segmentation has been a widely researched topic in the field of content-based video analysis (CBVA). However, over the course of time, researchers have aimed to improve upon the existing methods of shot segmentation in order to gain accuracy. Video shot segmentation or shot boundary analysis is a basic and vital step in CBVA, since any error incurred in this step reduces the precision of the other steps. The shot segmentation problem assumes greater proportions when detection is preferred in real time. A spatiotemporal fuzzy hostility index is proposed in Chapter 9, Real-time video segmentation using a vague adaptive threshold, which is used for edge detection of objects occurring in the frames of video. The edges present in the frames are treated as features. Correlation between these edge-detected frames is used as a similarity measure. In a real-time scenario, the incoming images are processed and the similarities are computed for successive frames of the video. These values are assumed to be normally distributed. The gradient of these correlation values are taken to be members of a vague set. In order to obtain a threshold after defuzzification, the true and false memberships of the elements are computed using a novel approach. The threshold is updated as new frames are buffered in, and is referred to as the vague adaptive threshold (VAT). The shot boundaries are then detected based on VAT. The effectiveness of the real-time video segmentation method is established by an experimental evaluation on a heterogeneous test set, comprising videos with diverse characteristics. The proposed method shows a substantial improvement over existing methods.

The objective of this book is to bring a broad spectrum of emerging approaches on the application of hybrid computational intelligence to solve real-world problems. This volume is expected to benefit undergraduate students of information technology and computer science for a greater part of their advanced studies curriculum.

**Siddhartha Bhattacharyya, Václav Snásel,**
**Deepak Gupta and Ashish Khanna**
*India and Czech Republic*
September, 2019

# CHAPTER 1

# Application and techniques of opinion mining

## Neha Gupta and Rashmi Agrawal
Faculty of Computer Applications, Manav Rachna International Institute of Research & Studies, Faridabad, India

## 1.1 Introduction

Various researchers have worked in the field of opinion mining—the initial research was carried out by Nasukawa and Dave in 2003. Because of the explosive growth of the World Wide Web and the use of various data-mining techniques, researchers are more inclined toward the analysis and mining of user sentiments. Opinion mining refers to the study of sentiments, opinions, attitudes, emotions, etc. that are analyzed and obtained from various written sources. We usually make a perception about a particular product or situation based on the beliefs and views of others. As people are very active on social media platforms and express their views using Facebook or Twitter, so organizations are working on analyzing the sentiments of people related to various issues to help them analyze the product/situation more accurately.

Nowadays, opinion mining is one of the most active research areas that include the concept of natural language processing (NLP) and data mining. Various opinion-mining tools, such as NLTK, WEKA, and Rapid miner, are used to mine the opinions of users. Opinion is mainly classified as positive or negative. NLP algorithms are used to track the mood of the public about a particular product. Opinion mining is widely used in various business applications to decide the utility of a particular product or a process based upon the sentiments/reviews of users.

## 1.2 Fundamentals of opinion mining

Over the last two decades, data-mining techniques in computer science have evolved significantly. The latest buzzword in this mining era is opinion mining, which has gone to a deeper level of understanding the behaviors of

*Hybrid Computational Intelligence*
DOI: https://doi.org/10.1016/B978-0-12-818699-2.00001-9
1

people in relation to particular events [1]. Opinion mining examines the feelings of people in a given situation by looking at opinions, emotions, or sentiments that are posted on social media. These opinions can be either positive or negative. Although a lot of research has been carried out by various researches on sentiment analysis, the term opinion mining was first introduced by Nasukawa and Dave in 2003. Since then research in this field has boomed at an exponential rate. The main reason for this growth is the expansion of the World Wide Web (www).

There are also various other factors that contribute to the ever-increasing demand of opinion mining and these factors are:

1. Evolution and expansion of various machine learning techniques to extract the information and to process any language.

2. Because of the dramatic growth of social networking sites and expansion of www, data sets used by machine learning algorithms can be easily trained.

People are now able to conveniently communicate with each other via various Internet channels that include email, Facebook, WhatsApp, LinkedIn, etc. This communication is happening because of the recent development of technology and social media and is generating a huge amount of data which are a gold mine to discovering hidden and useful information. In this chapter we use the terms "opinion mining" and "sentiment analysis" interchangeably. Let us first understand the meaning of two key terms: "opinion" and "sentiment."

## 1.2.1 Defining opinion

Our decisions are dependent upon the opinions or sentiments of others. We are usually influenced by the opinions of others and take decisions accordingly. Opinion is a subjective statement as it describes the thinking or the beliefs of a person about a particular thing. Opinion can be defined as a judgment or a belief that lacks absolute conviction, certainty, or optimistic knowledge. It concludes that certain facts, ideas, etc. are likely to be true or are true.

Alternatively, "it is an estimation of the quality or worth of someone or something" [2].

## 1.2.2 Defining sentiments

Sentiments are central to almost all human activities [3] and act as key influencers of our behaviors.

Sentiments an individual has with objects in context are how they formulate an opinion. Sentiments are defined as "an attitude toward something; refined or tender emotion; manifestation of the higher or more refined feelings." It is a thought influenced by a proceeding from feeling or emotion [3]. Sentiments analysis can be classified as positive, negative, or neutral [4]. The techniques which classify the sentiments into labels can be supervised as well as unsupervised techniques.

The *Supervised learning technique* uses machine learning algorithms. These algorithms take a training data set to make a classifier and the accuracy of the classifier is checked by the test data set. The different supervised learning techniques are:

1. Naïve Bayes algorithm
2. Decision tree induction
3. Support vector machines
4. Linear regression
5. *K*-nearest neighbor

Choosing an appropriate set of features is an important but basic task. For this classification, common features include the presence of terms [3] and their frequency, phrases, parts of speech, negations, and opinion words.

*Unsupervised learning techniques* are also known as clustering. This is also used to label the data. In this technique there are no training data. The data are labeled by the Euclidian distance. Here clusters are formed and each cluster is given a label. Then the new data arrive for labeling. These are labeled according to the cluster in which the data point lies. This approach involves comparing the text against the word lexicons or sentiment lexicons [3]. These sentiment lexicon values are determined prior to the sentiment analysis. The expression and collection of words [3] that are used to express views, opinions, and people feelings are what ultimately define a sentiment lexicon. The words in the text are identified as positive or negative word lexicon. Based on the lexicon it is determined to be positive or negative.

The different unsupervised techniques are:

1. *k*-Means
2. *k*-Meloid (an object-based algorithm)
3. Dictionary-based approach
4. Corpus-based approach

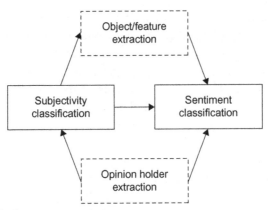

**Figure 1.1** Task of sentiment analysis.

### 1.2.3 Task of opinion mining

The task is to gather nuggets of useful information from the huge amount of data that are subjective in nature. We can represent an opinion using sentiment polarity. The task is to find whether the opinion reflects positivity, negativity, or is neutral in nature. This can be applied in many areas, such as movie reviews, product reviews, health, medicine, and business intelligence. Opinions do not only provide useful information by mining useful information, they answer many unanswered question and summarize data. The subtask of opinion mining is to find information about aspects of the data (see Fig. 1.1).

### 1.2.4 Representation of opinion

The representation of opinion is classified as:
1. Basic representation
2. Detailed representation
*Basic representation*: In this representation, a basic conclusion is taken out of a statement in context. It is divided into three main components:
- *Opinion holder*: This represents a person or an organization that is expressing his opinion about a particular subject or situation (e.g., person, place, product, event, or organization) [3].
- *Opinion target*: This represents the object (thing or person) about which an opinion is expressed. For example, airline services (may represent one single entity, group of entity, etc.) [3].

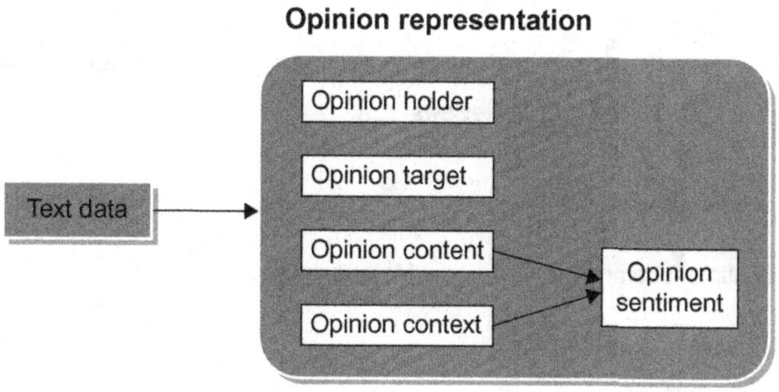

**Opinion representation**

Figure 1.2 Representation of opinion.

- *Opinion content*: This represents the text or statement of expression, for example, a descriptive or brief paragraph or article about the object [3].

  *Detailed representation*: In this representation, a better or detailed conclusion is extracted from the statement or text under consideration. It is divided into two main components:
- *Opinion context*: This represents the situation under which the opinion was expressed (e.g., place, duration).
- *Opinion sentiment*: This represents the feelings of the opinion holders. Opinion holder feelings can be positive or negative, satisfaction or dissatisfaction, etc. [3] (Fig. 1.2).

## 1.3 Feature extraction and its impact on opinion mining

Feature extraction is a fundamental step of opinion mining. Feature extraction can be defined as the extraction of people's opinions depending upon the characteristic of a particular product. The features of a particular product or object are extracted based on the comments of the customers about that product. For example, a company xyz launched a water purifier and people started giving their opinion about this water purifier by mentioning its water quality, size, water wastage, etc., so here water quality and size can be defined as the features of the water purifier and based upon the comments of the people we can predict and classify the sentiments or opinions about the water quality of the purifier.

The various steps of feature-based opinion mining are:
1. Extraction of a particular feature;
2. Prediction of sentiments;

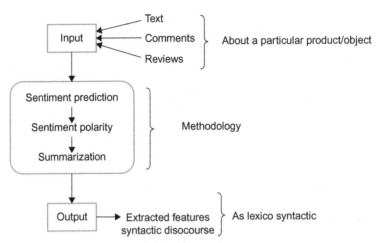

**Figure 1.3** Feature extraction and mining process.

3. Classification of sentiments (positive, negative, or neutral);

4. Summarization of sentiments based on extracted features (lexico syntactic, syntactic, or discourse).

The steps are illustrated in Fig. 1.3.

Features are extracted and classified based on the following steps that also include various mining techniques:

1. Analyzing text and fact reviews;
2. Analysis and classification of features;
3. Analysis and categorization of sentiments.

## 1.3.1 Analyzing text and fact reviews

Reviews given by customers can be both subjective as well as objective. Subjective reviews describe the feelings, views, or reactions of the customer about a particular context, while objective reviews represents realistic information about a context. These reviews are mined using mining techniques which include support vector machine (SVM), naive Bayes classifiers, etc. The workings are illustrated in Fig. 1.4.

### 1.3.1.1 Analysis and classification of features

In this step features are extracted using a numerical parser and with a set of predefined rules. The parser will help in recognizing the applicant information module. This module is reviewed based on the previous context as some of the nouns or noun phrases are missed because of the limitations of parser morphology. New phrases or text are added to the parser.

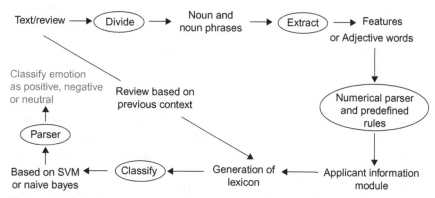

**Figure 1.4** Flowchart representing the feature extraction process. *SVM*, support vector machine.

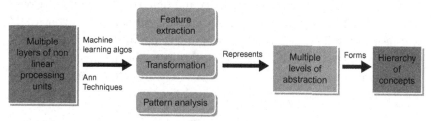

**Figure 1.5** Representation of deep learning.

### *1.3.1.2  Analysis and categorization of sentiments*

This step categorizes the extracted feature as an emotion. In this step a parser is added to classify the emotion as positive, negative, or neutral [4] based on the predefined rules.

## 1.4  Deep learning and its relation to opinion mining

Learning the data representations using various machine learning algorithms is known as deep learning. This learning of data can be represented using supervised, unsupervised, or partially supervised approaches. Deep learning can be represented as illustrated in Fig. 1.5.

Deep learning is used to extract and transform features and to analyze patterns by processing multiple layers of nonlinear information using various machine learning approaches that may be supervised or unsupervised to form a hierarchy of concepts. These hierarchies contain multiple levels of abstraction to simplify the complexity of the relationship among data. Deep learning uses artificial neural networks and is mostly based on unsupervised learning. Deep learning generates statistical models that represent multiple levels of concepts where lower level concepts are defining higher level concepts and vice versa [5].

It works on multiple layers of neural networks and produces unpredictable results. The results are far better than previous machine learning algorithms. Neural networks works on multiple layers. It exploits the learning power capacity of neural networks and consists of neurons, that is, information-processing units arranged in layers carrying some weight and by applying some bias to a particular function producing results. Neurons are connected by weights to other neurons. They are also known as feedforward neural networks in which there is one input layer and one or more output layers. They are known as shallow neural networks (with one or two layers).

However, deep neural networks have multiple layers of nonlinear processing units. They extract features and transform them. The lower level/ layer near to the input learns simple features, while upper layers seek difficult features extracted from lower layer features. The architecture is hierarchical in nature and represents a powerful feature. Here learning can be supervised, unsupervised, or semisupervised (Fig. 1.6).

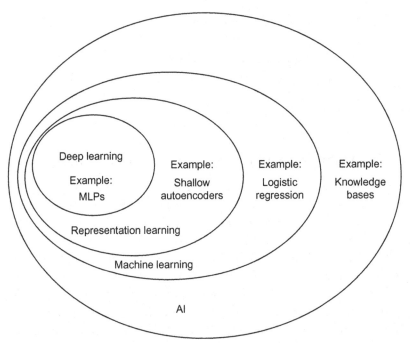

**Figure 1.6** Deep learning overview. *MLP*, multilayer perceptron; *AI*, artificial intelligence.

Convolutional neural networks, recurrent neural networks, and long short-term memory models are supervised learning models.

## 1.4.1 Opinion mining with deep learning

SVM is better than naive Bayes and other classifiers. It supports a multiclass classification process. However there remain many shortcomings in SVM. Convolutional neural networks perform a lot of work in language processing. They can do POS, part of speech tagging, extraction, and identification of semantics of sentiment analysis [5].

Recursive neural networks (RNNs) are used for showing movie reviews. Deep learning for opinion mining often provides advanced functions in lexicon-based methods and NLP techniques [5]. The most important and basic algorithms used in opinion mining and sentimental mining are SVM, RNN, and convolutional neural network (CNN) [5] (Fig. 1.7).

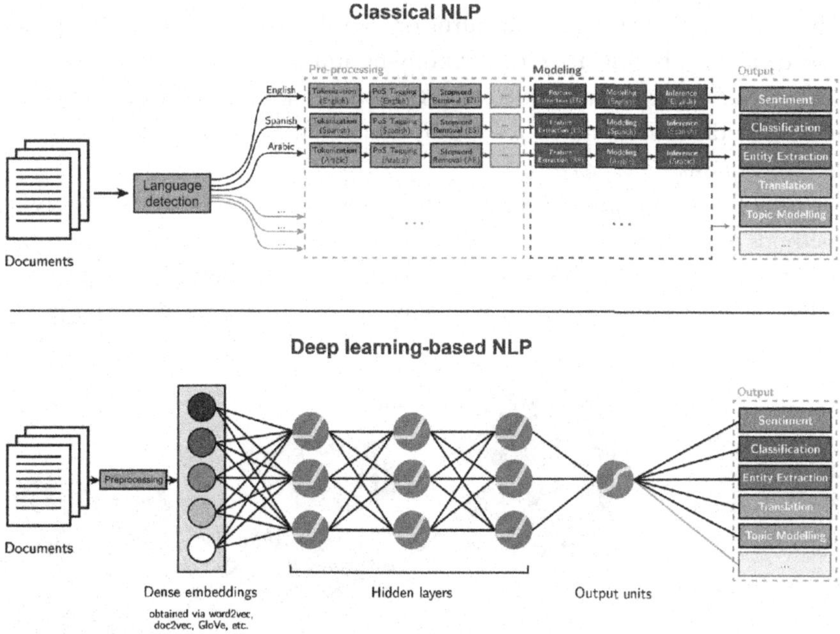

**Figure 1.7** Comparing classical natural language processing (NLP) and deep learning-based NLP.

## 1.5 Techniques of opinion mining

### 1.5.1 Lexicon-based approach

One of the approaches or techniques of semantic analysis is the lexicon-based approach. This technique calculates the sentiment orientations of the whole document or set of sentence(s) from semantic orientation of lexicons. Semantic orientation can be positive, negative, or neutral. The dictionary of lexicons can be created manually as well as automatically generated. The WorldNet dictionary is used by many researchers. First of all, lexicons are found from the whole document and then WorldNet or any other kind of online thesaurus can be used to discover the synonyms and antonyms to expand that dictionary.

Lexicon-based techniques use adjectives and adverbs to discover the semantic orientation of the text. For calculating any text orientation, adjective and adverb combinations are extracted with their sentiment orientation value. These can then be converted to a single score for the whole value (Fig. 1.8).

The different approaches to lexicon-based approach are:

1. *Dictionary-based approach*

In this approach, a dictionary is created by taking a few words initially. Then an online dictionary, thesaurus or WordNet can be used to expand that dictionary by incorporating synonyms and antonyms of those words. The dictionary is expanded till no new words can be added to that dictionary. The dictionary can be refined by manual inspection.

2. *Corpus-based approach*

This finds sentiment orientation of context-specific words. The two methods of this approach are:

*Statistical approach*: The words which show erratic behavior in positive behavior are considered to have positive polarity. If they show negative

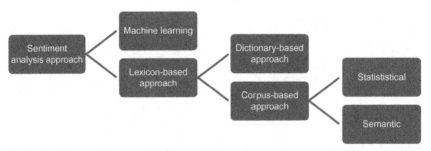

**Figure 1.8** Types of lexicon-based approach.

recurrence in negative text they have negative polarity. If the frequency is equal in both positive and negative text then the word has neutral polarity.

*Semantic approach*: This approach assigns sentiment values to words and the words which are semantically closer to those words; this can be done by finding synonyms and antonyms with respect to that word.

## 1.5.2 Naive Bayes classifier

Naive Bayes is one of the classification techniques of data mining. Naive Bayes classifies the data into classes by building a classifier (function) based on training data. The accuracy of the classifier is checked using testing data. Naive Bayes classifier is dependent on the statistical probability of the words. The theorem is:

$$P(A|B) = (P(B|A) * P(A))/P(B) \qquad (1.1)$$

Naive Bayes classifier is used to classify the sentiments into classes, whether positive or negative. For example, if we want to calculate the review of a particular movie naive Bayes classifier can be used. We should have supervised data for this. This technique performs very well in many cases (Fig. 1.9).

## 1.5.3 Support vector machines

Support vector machines are the supervised classification technique for data mining. They are a linear classification/regression algorithm, and find a hyperplane which divides the training set of data into classes/labels which fit the data. The support vector machine performs well in sentiment mining. Many researchers have proves that SVM is a better technique as compared to naive Bayes (Fig. 1.10).

## 1.5.4 Decision trees

A decision tree is also a classification technique. Decision trees perform well in the classification of sentiments. A C4.8 classifier is used nowadays.

**Figure 1.9** Naïve Bayes classifier.

**Figure 1.10** Support vector machines.

It is represented as the J48 classifier in WEKA. This approach creates decision trees based on set criteria. It can create prepruned as well as postpruned trees. The accuracy of this classifier is high. It uses a greedy technique and top-down approach.

## 1.6 Tools of opinion mining

Nowadays, industries are offering widespread tools for opinion mining [6] for the purposes of data preprocessing, classification, clustering, sentiment analysis, etc. Some of the most popular tools are:
- Gate
- NLTK
- WEKA
- Apache OpenNLP
- Opinion Finder
- Stanford CoreNLP
- Pattern
- LingPipe

The following section covers WEKA and Apache OpenNLP, which are the most commonly used tools in opinion mining.

### 1.6.1 WEKA

WEKA, which was developed in the University of Waikato (New Zealand), is written in Java language and uses the general public license (GNU) [6]. WEKA can be embedded as a library in any application as it has a general application programming interface (API). The WEKA is an inquisitive nature flightless bird found only in New Zealand.

WEKA is an assortment of machine learning algorithms for performing data-mining jobs. The algorithms of machine learning are applied directly on to data sets. It encompasses almost all tools which are used in data preprocessing, classification, regression, clustering, association rules, and visualization. It is also appropriate for evolving novel machine learning patterns.

### 1.6.1.1 Features of WEKA

1. Platform independent
2. Open source and free
3. Easy to use
4. Offers a wide variety of data preprocessing tools
5. Flexibility of scripting experiments
6. Graphical user interface
7. Provides different machine learning algorithms

### 1.6.1.2 Installation of WEKA

WEKA can be downloaded from http://www.cs.waikato.ac.nz/ml/weka/. The following commands are executed at the command prompt which is required for WEKA environment variable in Java.

setenv WEKAHOME /usr/local/weka/weka-3-0-2
setenv CLASSPATH $WEKAHOME/weka.jar:$CLASSPATH

After completion of the download, run the exe file and choose the default set-up.

### 1.6.1.3 WEKA application interfaces

WEKA provides five application interfaces. These are Explorer, Experimenter, Knowledge flow, Simple CLI (command line interface), and workbench. Explorer is WEKA's main application interface. It is the graphical interface to perform data-mining tasks on raw data. Experimenter allows users to execute different experimental validations on various data sets. Knowledge flow is an explorer with drag and drop functionality. It supports incremental learning from previous results. Simple CLI provides a command line interface which is a simple interface for providing commands from a terminal. Workbench is an application interface which combines all user interfaces into one. Fig. 1.11 shows the WEKA explorer which contains six tabs, these are:

1. Preprocess
2. Classify
3. Cluster
4. Association
5. Select attributes
6. Visualize

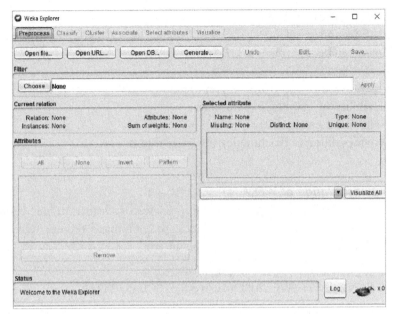

**Figure 1.11** WEKA explorer.

Without completing the initial preprocessing of the data set a user cannot move between the different tabs. There are three methods for data preprocessing:

1. Open URL
2. Open file
3. Pen database

Fig. 1.12 shows a screenshot of data preprocessing in WEKA.

WEKA supports various file formats through which data can be imported. The most common data formats are attribute-relation file format (ARFF), comma separated values (CSV) and database using open database connectivity (ODBC). Fig. 1.13 shows the use of an ARFF file in WEKA.

## 1.6.2 Apache OpenNLP

One of the most common tools for NLP is Apache OpenNLP which is based on Java. It provides efficient text-processing services by tokenization, POS tagging, named entity recognition (NER), and many other components used in text mining.

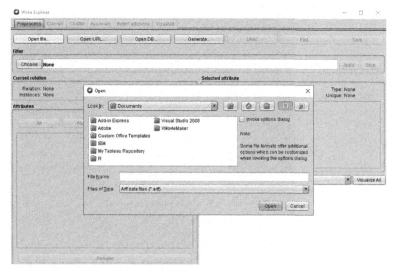

Weka Explorer
Preprocess
Open file...
Open URL...
Open DB...
Generate...
Filter
Choose
None
Current relation
Relation: None
Instances: None
Attributes
Selected attribute
Type: None
Unique: None
Open
Look In:
Documents
Add-in Express
Adobe
Custom Office Templates
IBM
My Tableau Repository
R
Visual Studio 2008
XMovieMaker
Invoke options dialog
Note:
Some file formats offer additional options which can be customized when invoking the options dialog.
File Name:
Files of Type:
Arff data files (*.arff)
Open
Cancel
Visualize All
**Figure 1.12** Data preprocessing in WEKA.

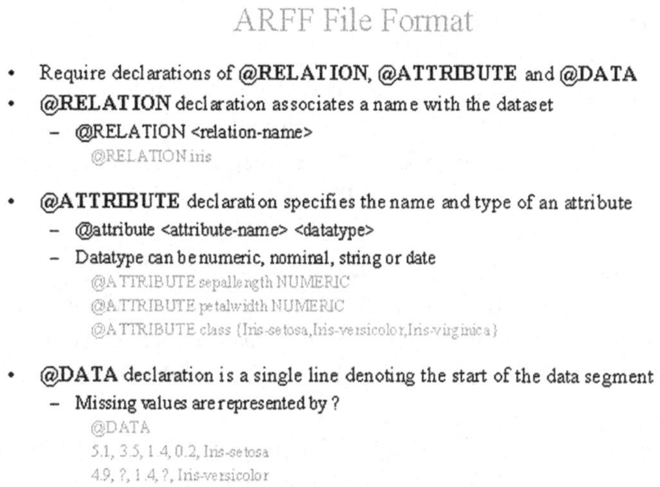

ARFF File Format
Require declarations of @RELATION, @ATTRIBUTE and @DATA
@RELATION declaration associates a name with the dataset
@RELATION <relation-name>
@RELATION iris
@ATTRIBUTE declaration specifies the name and type of an attribute
@attribute <attribute-name> <datatype>
Datatype can be numeric, nominal, string or date
@ATTRIBUTE sepallength NUMERIC
@ATTRIBUTE petalwidth NUMERIC
@ATTRIBUTE class {Iris-setosa,Iris-versicolor,Iris-virginica}
@DATA declaration is a single line denoting the start of the data segment
Missing values are represented by ?
@DATA
5.1, 3.5, 1.4, 0.2, Iris-setosa
4.9, ?, 1.4, ?, Iris-versicolor
**Figure 1.13** Example of an attribute-relation file format file.

Noteworthy features of OpenNLP are:

1. Natural language generation
2. Summarize
3. NER
4. Tagging (POS)

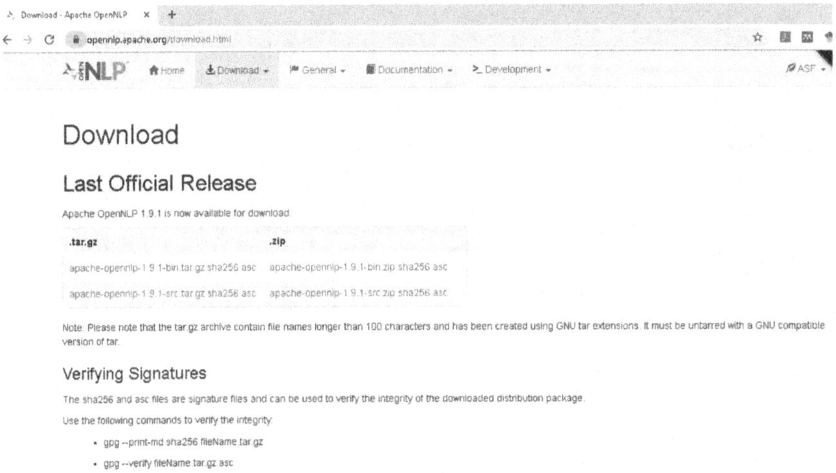

**Figure 1.14** OpenNLP.

**5.** Searching
**6.** Translation
**7.** Feedback analysis
**8.** Information grouping

The Apache OpenNLP library provides classes and interfaces to perform various tasks of NLP. In addition to a library it also provides a CLI, which enhances the functionality. To perform a set of tasks, a predefined model is provided by the OpenNLP which can be downloaded from the website as shown in Fig. 1.14.

The various steps of using OpenNLP are:

**1.** *Sentence detection*: To detect the given text, SentenceModel class is used which belongs to the package *opennlp.tools.sentdetect*. To identify the position of a sentence in the given text sentPosDetect() method is used.

For example, "Hello Mohan. Where are you going?" is segmented into two sentences: Hello Mohan and where are you going [6].

Sentence detection is a challenging task due to difficulty in identification of the sentence separator as apart from the end of sentence, period (.) can occur in various places in a sentence.

**2.** *Tokenization*: Tokenization refers to the splitting of a sentence into its smaller parts which are known as tokens. A tokenizer tokenizes a sentence into its root form that is known as the morphological form. For example, "this is my book" is tokenized to "this," "is," "my," "book,"

**Table 1.1** Part of speech tags (POS tag).

| POS tag | Description |
| --- | --- |
| VBD | Verb, past tense |
| DT | Determiner |
| VB | Verb, base form |
| NNP | Proper noun, singular |
| VBZ | Verb, third person singular present |
| TO | The word "to" |
| IN | Preposition or subordinating conjunction |
| NN | Noun, singular or mass |
| JJ | Adjective |

where four tokens are generated from one sentence. Three types of tokenizers available in OpenNLP are *SimpleTokenizer*, *WhitespaceTokenizer*, and *TokenizerME*. These classes contain methods *tokenize()* and *sentPosDetect()*.

3. *Named entity recognition*: In NER the aim is to discover the named things like things, places, and name of the person in a given text. The class for performing his in OpenNLP is *TokenNameFinderModel* class and belongs to package *opennlp.tools.namefind*. Methods used here are *find ()* and *probs()* which are used to detect the names and probability of the sequence, respectively.

4. *Tagging*: Parts of speech tagging was conferred in Ref. [7]. OpenNLP provides the part of speech tags given in Table 1.1

POS tagging can be understood with the following example.

"Ram had an enemy named Ravan."

   a. "Ram"—NNP (proper noun);
   b. "had"—VBZ (verb);
   c. "an"—DT (determiner);
   d. "enemy"—NN (noun);
   e. "named"—VBZ (verb);
   f. "Ravan"—NNP (proper noun);
   g. "."—period.

5. *Lemmetization*: After the part of speech tagging we get the tokens of a sentence. In order to further analyze the text, lemmatization is applied. Lemmatization is a technique of finding the base form of a word.

For example, in the sentence: "Ram had an enemy named Ravan," the base form of named is name.

There are two types of lemmatization in OpenNLP: statistical and dictionary based. In statistical lemmatization a model is built using the training data, whereas in dictionary-based lemmatization a dictionary is required to discover all valid combinations of a word.

6. *Parsing*: Parsing technique was deliberated in Ref. [8] in which the syntactic structure of a sentence is analyzed using context free grammar. The *ParserModel* and *ParserFactory* class which belong to the package *opennlp.tools.parser* and *ParserTool* class which belongs to package *opennlp.tools.cmdline.parser* are used to parse the sentence.

7. *Chunking*: One of the essential components of chunking is POS information. Chunking can be defined as dividing or grouping the sentence into meaningful word groups, like noun groups and verb groups. The following example illustrates chunking.

> *"He"—noun phrase*
> *"played"—verb phrase*
> *"Very well"—Adjective phrase*
> *"the teacher"—noun phrase*
> *"will teach"—verb phrase*
> *"to"—preposition phrase*
> *"students"—noun phrase*

## 1.7 Ontology-based opinion mining

The fundamental research in opinion mining is focused around two areas: sentiment analysis and property-level opinion mining. In general, in sentiment classification the documents (reviews) are classified as positive, negative, or neutral [4], but these results are considered to be too vague and broad. Recurrently it has been found that the same sentence contains positive and negative sentiments. For example, "I was hurt by the behavior on that day but he is a good friend of mine." To overcome the ambiguity of sentiment analysis, ontology-based opinion mining is preferred. Ontology is referred as an unambiguous comprehensive learning of perceptions. It defines a common terminology for researchers who work in that field. It includes properties of each concept, their limitations, and relationship with other concepts. Jalota and Agarwal [9] presented a study on ontology-based opinion mining.

To represent opinion mining as a model, an opinion can be articulated as any node or attribute of a node where components are represented as nodes and each node may have certain attributes. Opinions are expressed as quintuple, and quintuple is processed to three levels of sentiment analysis which are: (1) document level, (2) sentence level, and (3) aspect level. Document level is the simplest form of sentiment analysis where it is assumed that only one subject has been described in the document. Subjectivity classification, sentiment classification, opinion helpfulness prediction, and opinion spam detection are examples of document-level sentiment analysis. Opinion summarization through sentence-level sentiment analysis is performed by extracting key concepts from the various sentences [10]. When the researcher assesses other finer details like the attributes or features of an entity, various approaches are used to perform aspect-level sentiment analysis. The crucial resource for sentiment analysis is the sentiment lexicon, which is used to represent linguistic knowledge. Sentiment Lexicon, SentiWordNet, and Emotion lexicon are some of the public domain sentiment lexicons.

As discussed above, ontology is the representation of detailed concepts. It has been proved that ontology can serve the purpose of domain knowledge representation as well as helping the information extraction process [11]. The following are the advantages of using ontology:

1. It enables regaining of domain knowledge.
2. It separates the domain knowledge from operational knowledge.
3. It provides a common understanding of the information structure.
4. It facilitates knowledge modeling.
5. It provides ease of communication across entities.
6. It facilitates computational inference.
7. It enables querying and browsing by creating metadata.

Based on domain dependence, the ontologies can be classified as shown in Fig. 1.15.

Domain ontology construction is the process of defining terminologies and the relationship between these terminologies. Ontologies can be constructed using any methodologies (Fig. 1.16).

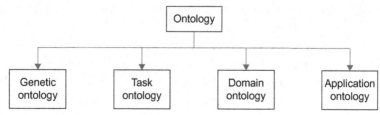

**Figure 1.15** Classification of ontology.

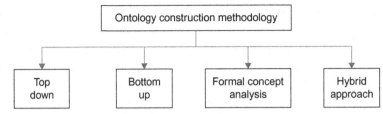

**Figure 1.16** Construction of ontology.

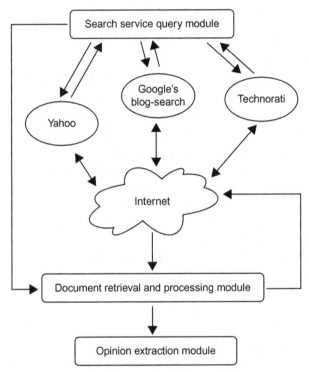

**Figure 1.17** General structure of an opinion miner.

In the top-down approach, ontologies are constructed with high-level ontological concepts, whereas the bottom-up approach is completely the reverse of the top-down approach.

Fig. 1.17 represents the structure of a general opinion miner which illustrates the working of any opinion-mining system implemented by tools of opinion mining. Fig. 1.18 represents the ontology of a mobile phone given in Ref. [12]. The researcher conducted a prestudy on three mobile phones and after extracting opinions from the reviews, the

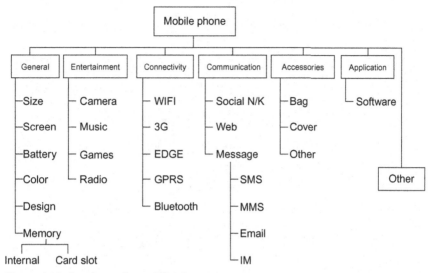

**Figure 1.18** Ontology of a mobile phone.

ontology was presented. A refined ontology was given in Ref. [13] after incorporating the missing features in the ontology given by Yakuub. These missing features are highlighted in Fig. 1.19. Further work was done in this and ontology for wet and dirty mobile phones were also presented in Ref. [13].

## 1.8 Applications of opinion mining

There are various fascinating applications of opinion mining as nowadays, with the complexity handling of NLP by machine learning algorithms, we can easily identify and analyze the data sets which store structured as well as unstructured data. Some of the applications of opinion mining are listed below.

Opinion mining is mainly used to improve the quality of a product or service by identifying people's opinions regarding that product or service, and its quality being improved accordingly. With the help of opinion mining and sentiment analysis policy makers take the views of the public toward the formulation of any new policy. Thus it is used for policy making. In business, it is used for augmenting the customer experience. One of the popular applications of opinion mining in business is brand brisking. Opining mining can also be used to develop q recommendation system. Opinion mining can be applied to obtain improved surveys. In the hotel

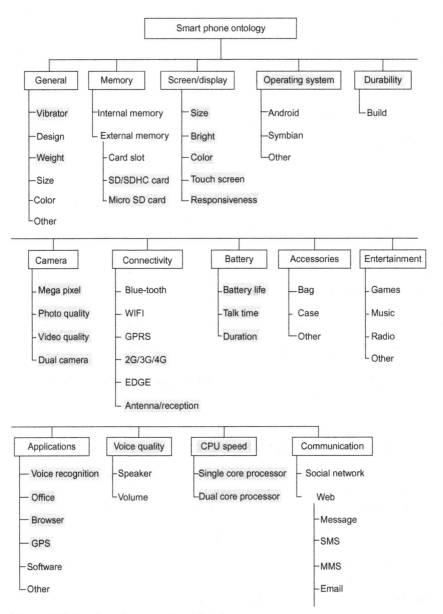

**Figure 1.19** Ontology for a smart mobile phone.

trade it can be used to find guest preferences, their behavior for a particular property, and making operational enhancements with capital expenditure. Opinion mining can be significantly used in marketing research. Opinion spam detection is also one of the important applications of this field.

## 1.9 Conclusion

Although a lot of work has been done in this area, there remain some open research challenges. The domain-dependent nature of sentiment words provides room for researchers working in this area. Various NLP overheads create interference in analysis, hence much work can be still carried out in this area. The development of fully a automatic opinion-mining tool, successful handling of polarity in statements, and generating lexicons for opinion mining are the future directions for research.

## References

[1] R. Agrawal, N. Gupta (Eds.), Extracting Knowledge From Opinion Mining, IGI Global, 2019.
[2] B. Pang, L. Lee, Opinion mining and sentiment analysis, Found. Trends Inf. Retriev. 2 (1—2) (2008) 1—135. Available from: https://doi.org/10.1561/1500000011.
[3] A. Seth, K. Seth, Fundamental of opinion mining, Extracting Knowledge From Opinion Mining, IGI Global, 2019, pp. 1—19.
[4] T.K. Das, Business intelligence through opinion mining, in: S. Trivedi, S. Dey, A. Kumar, T. Panda (Eds.), Handbook of Research on Advanced Data Mining Techniques and Applications for Business Intelligence, IGI Global, Hershey, PA, 2017, pp. 142—161. Available from: http://doi.org/10.4018/978-1-5225-2031-3.ch008.
[5] I.R. Vanani, M. Amirhosseini, Deep learning for opinion mining, in: R. Agrawal, N. Gupta (Eds.), Extracting Knowledge From Opinion Mining, IGI Global, Hershey, PA, 2019, pp. 40—65. Available from: http://doi.org/10.4018/978-1-5225-6117-0.ch003.
[6] N. Gupta, S. Verma, Tools of opinion mining, in: R. Agrawal, N. Gupta (Eds.), Extracting Knowledge From Opinion Mining, IGI Global, Hershey, PA, 2019, pp. 179—203. Available from: http://doi.org/10.4018/978-1-5225-6117-0.ch009.
[7] J. Camacho-Collados, M.T. Pilehvar, R. Navigli, Making sense of word embeddings. A unified multilingual semantic representation of concepts, in: Proceedings of the Association for Computational Linguistics, 2015, pp. 741—751.
[8] E.H. Huang, R. Socher, C.D. Manning, A.Y. Ng, MaxMax: A graphbased soft clustering algorithm applied to word sense induction, in: Proceedings of the 14th International Conference on Computational Linguistics and Intelligent Text Processing, 2012, pp. 368—381.
[9] C. Jalota, R. Agrawal, Ontology-based opinion mining, Extracting Knowledge From Opinion Mining, IGI Global, 2019, pp. 84—103.
[10] V. Kalra, R. Agrawal, Challenges of text analytics in opinion mining, Extracting Knowledge From Opinion Mining, IGI Global, 2019, pp. 268—282.
[11] S.K. Jolly, R. Agrawal, Anatomizing Lexicon with natural language Tokenizer Toolkit 3, Extracting Knowledge From Opinion Mining, IGI Global, 2019, pp. 232—266.
[12] R. Yaakub, M. Li, Y. Feng, Integration of opinion into customer analysis model, in: proceedings of Eighth IEEE International Conference on e-Business Engineering, 2011, pp. 90—95.
[13] S.Z. Haider, An ontology based sentiment analysis: a case study (Master Degree Project in Informatics, University of Skovde), 2012.

# CHAPTER 2

# Influence of big data in smart tourism

**Pramod Sunagar[1], R. Hanumantharaju[1], Siddesh G.M.[2], Anita Kanavalli[1] and K.G. Srinivasa[3]**
[1]Department of CSE, Ramaiah Institute of Technology, Bangalore, India
[2]Department of ISE, Ramaiah Institute of Technology, Bangalore, India
[3]Department of Information Management & Coordination, NITTTR, Chandigarh, India

## 2.1 Introduction to smart tourism

### 2.1.1 Introduction

Smart tourism is associated with the development of innovative tools by applying information and communication technology in tourism. It involves collecting and using the data derived from organizational sources, social connectedness, physical infrastructures, and improved technologies to boost efficiency, experiences, and sustainability. Tools and technologies like Internet of Things (IoT), mobile communication, cloud computing, and artificial intelligence are used for data gathering, analysis, and decision making for smart tourism. To provide smart tourism opportunities, these tools are combined with the existing infrastructure.

The main aims of smart tourism are to improve tourism experiences and the effectiveness of resource administration, and to increase the competitiveness of destinations by emphasizing their sustainable aspects. This information can be used to facilitate the efficient allocation of required resources for tourism. Smart cities can boast of having the required infrastructure where one can install big data systems to collect, store, and analyze it. They are observed to be effective in technologically advanced destinations such as smart cities. "Mobiles application," "augmented reality," and "near-field communication" are a few examples of smart tourism tools.

The United Nations World Tourism Organization defines tourism as a cultural, social, and economic phenomenon which demands that people travel outside their natural surroundings for personal or business reasons [1]. The application of the smart concept to tourism requires information-rich

*Hybrid Computational Intelligence*
DOI: https://doi.org/10.1016/B978-0-12-818699-2.00002-0

data and has a high reliance on information communication technologies (ICTs). There is a logical progression of smart tourism from conventional tourism to e-tourism. The foundation for this was positioned early with the adoption of ICT in tourism. Web-based technologies have paved the way for the emergence of e-tourism in the form of reservation systems. This, in turn, led to the extensive adoption of social media and mobile tourism. The evolution of ICT in tourism has been mainly due to smart tourism.

The organization of the tourism industry has been transformed yet again. Working toward the process of traveler experiences is different in traditional tourism compared to smart tourism. Smart tourism engages the support of ICTs to improve the traveler's experience.

## 2.1.2 Smart cities are leading the way for smart tourism

Everything is branded as smart today; from smartphones, smart watches, smart TV, smart cars, smart homes and smart hotels. Smart cities are becoming the perfect places to live and work sustainably. Since the smart city has a high end infrastructure in place, it can help smart tourism to prosper. By collecting details of user preferences, the tourism sector can provide better services. This association is yet to be explored fully.

The Smart Cities Council labels a city as a smart city if it has cutting-edge technology rooted at all junctions. In their Smart Cities Readiness Guide, the council takes a complete, comprehensive view that "includes the entirety of human activity in an area, including city governments, schools, hospitals, infrastructure, resources, businesses and people."

There is an increase in the number of destinations adopting a smart city approach. The following are examples:

- Malta is a smart city island.
- Singapore is a smart city now.
- The Smart City Challenge in the United States saw seven finalists: Austin, Columbus, Denver, Kansas City, Pittsburgh, Portland, and San Francisco.
- Masdar City in Abu Dhabi is projected to be the world's smartest city.
- India aims to convert at least 20 cities throughout the country into Smart Cities.

ICT tools help a smart city to collect and gauge the environment around roads, buildings, transportation, water, and the air. Sensors are installed throughout the city to observe and accumulate data for air quality, water quality, energy flow, traffic movement, and the movement of people in busy junctions. With the help of wired and wireless connections, the collected data are then transmitted through the Internet of Everything (IoE). All these systems are interrelated in the IoE. These collected data are then processed and analyzed to enable improved decisions to be made by decision-makers in government or business [2].

## 2.2 Introduction to big data

Due to the modern information system and technologies like Cloud Computing and the IoT, a colossal amount of information is generated daily. Social network giants Facebook, Instagram, Twitter, and WhatsApp have been the main contributors to generating such mammoth amounts of data in terms of text, images, and videos.

### 2.2.1 What is big data?

According to Wikipedia, big data is a field to analyze and extract information and to work with data sets which are huge and intricate. Traditional data-processing applications will not be able to work with such intricate data sets. The task is to assemble, arrange, process, and gather insights from large data sets. Modern computer systems have the capabilities to store, process, and extract useful information from large data sets.

### 2.2.2 Big data systems are different

The elementary necessities for functioning with big data sets of any size are the same. Significant challenges arise when designing solutions for data which are enormous in scale, the speed with which it is generated, and during the processing of such data. The objectives of big data systems are to exhibit insights and associations from massive volumes of dissimilar data. This task would not be possible using conventional methods. Big data is characterized by the "three Vs of big data" [3] as shown in Fig. 2.1. However, there are now other Vs being added to the list for the generation of massive data.

- *Volume*: The big data systems are defined by the sheer scale of the processing of information. The data sets considered for big data applications are of a large scale compared to old-fashioned data sets. The processing of data sets cannot be handled by a single computer. This

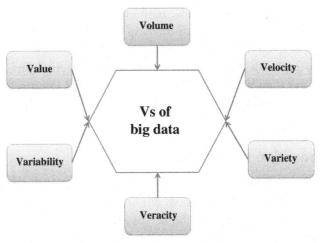

**Figure 2.1** Different Vs of big data.

task requires pooling, assigning, and coordinating resources from groups of computers.

- *Velocity*: Big data systems are equipped to efficiently handle moving information with speed compared to other traditional data systems. Data flow regularly into the big data system from numerous sources. These data are processed at real time to gain insights from the data sets. Because of this, big data analysts are moving toward a real-time streaming system from a batch-oriented approach.
- *Variety*: Data can be gathered from different applications; server logs, social media feeds, and physical device sensors. These data are unique and, because of the different sources from where they are generated, the quality of the data differs. Big data systems should be able to handle potentially valuable data irrespective of their source.
- *Veracity*: One of the challenges faced by big data analysts is to process complex data coming from a variety of sources. Another challenge is evaluating the quality of such complex data.
- *Variability*: Disparity in the quality of the data set is affected by the variations present within it. Extra resources need to be added to detect, clean, and process low-quality data to make them more useful.
- *Value*: The end result of big data processing is to bring value to the data set. It can become difficult sometimes to extract the actual value of the data using the big data systems and the different processes.

### 2.2.3 Types of big data

The following are the different forms of big data:

- *Structured*: The data which can be accumulated, processed, and regained in a fixed format are called structured data. Structured data are extremely prearranged data that can be readily and flawlessly stored and accessed from a database by a simple query. For example, imagine a car database where the car number, model, registration year, and price are stored in a structured manner.
- *Unstructured*: The data which have no fixed format are known as unstructured data. Working with an unstructured data set is very difficult as it requires one to convert the unstructured data to structured data first to process. This is not only time consuming but also a tedious job. Unstructured data can be from social media data such as Facebook, Twitter, Instagram, and Web logs.
- *Semistructured*: Semistructured data contain both structured and unstructured data. Data which contain valuable information but are not classified as structured or unstructured are considered as semistructured data.

### 2.2.4 Life cycle of big data

Big data analysts have used different approaches when dealing with data sets. Those steps which are commonly used when working with those data sets are highlighted:

- capturing the data,
- storing the data,
- preprocessing the data,
- analyzing the data, and
- visualizing the results.

### 2.3 Applications of big data

Big data applications can help companies to make better business decisions by analyzing large volumes of data and discovering hidden patterns. These data sets might be from social media, data captured by sensors, website logs, customer feedbacks, etc. Organizations are spending huge amounts on big data applications to discover hidden patterns, unknown associations, market style, consumer preferences, and other valuable business information [4]. The following are domains where big data can be applied:

- health care,
- media and entertainment,
- IoT,
- manufacturing, and
- government.

## 2.3.1 Health care

There is a significant improvement in the healthcare domain by personalized medicine and prescriptive analytics due to the role of big data systems. Researchers analyze the data to determine the best treatment for a particular disease, side effects of the drugs, forecasting the health risks, etc. Mobile applications on health and wearable devices are causing available data to grow at an exponential rate. It is possible to predict a disease outbreak by mapping healthcare data and geographical data. Once predicted, containment of the outbreak can be handled and plans to eradicate the disease made.

## 2.3.2 Media and entertainment

The media and entertainment industries are creating, advertising, and distributing their content using new business models. This is due to customer requirements to view digital content from any location and at any time. The introduction of online TV shows, Netflix channels, etc. is proving that new customers are not only interested in watching TV but are interested in accessing data from any location. The media houses are targeting audiences by predicting what they would like to see, how to target the ads, content monetization, etc. Big data systems are thus increasing the revenues of such media houses by analyzing viewer patterns.

## 2.3.3 Internet of Things

IoT devices generate continuous data and send them to a server on a daily basis. These data are mined to provide the interconnectivity of devices. This mapping can be put to good use by government agencies and also a range of companies to increase their competence. IoT is finding applications in smart irrigation systems, traffic management, crowd management, etc.

### 2.3.4 Manufacturing

Predictive manufacturing can help to increase efficiency by producing more goods by minimizing the downtime of machines. This involves a massive quantity of data for such industries. Sophisticated forecasting tools follow an organized process to explore valuable information for these data. The following are the some of the major advantages of employing big data applications in manufacturing industries:

- high product quality,
- tracking faults,
- supply planning,
- predicting the output,
- increasing energy efficiency,
- testing and simulation of new manufacturing processes, and
- large-scale customization of manufacturing.

### 2.3.5 Government

By adopting big data systems, the government can attain efficiencies in terms of cost, output, and novelty. Since the same data set is used in many applications, many departments can work in association with each other. Government plays an important role in innovation by acting in all these domains.

Big data applications can be applied in each and every field. Some of the major areas where big data finds applications include:

- agriculture,
- aviation,
- cyber security and intelligence,
- crime prediction and prevention,
- e-commerce,
- fake news detection,
- fraud detection,
- pharmaceutical drug evaluation,
- scientific research,
- weather forecasting, and
- tax compliance.

## 2.4 Use of big data in the travel sector

The travel industry is seeing an unprecedented growth of data due to smartphone affordability, faster Internet access at cheaper rates, and the influence of social media. Over the last few years, the mobile travel space has seen rapid growth. Major online travel websites have launched mobile apps to help customers plan for their travel—from booking flights to booking hotels with the necessary information regarding the hotel and places to visit. These mobile apps are providing instantaneous travel plans, hotel preferences, location tracking, ticket booking, price comparisons, and gathering feedback. Because of such technology, consumers have more power to search and decide on their travel plans based on their flexibility. Travelers are also now knowledgeable about the different services from various providers at competitive rates. Travelers can demand better quality of services from service providers. Due to such technology, the customer is reaping the benefits of competition. However, the travel sector is facing difficulties in utilizing this technology effectively to boost their operations. These service providers are now using big data analytics to increase their business, get recognition from customers compared to their opponents.

A prospective traveler will be responsible for generating a large quantity of data at different phases including searching, planning, price comparison, booking, cancellation, and feedback. Service providers are now targeting novel ways to power this information to target a greater audience and to serve them better. Travel service providers are gaining an in-depth understanding of the markets to devise their strategy to anticipate market inclinations and customer travel plans. The travel sector has acknowledged the power of big data analytics to explore hidden business insights. Many companies in the travel domain have already executed big data analytics for quick and customized travel experiences for targeted customers.

Some of the points which travel sectors target to improve business via big data analytics include [5]:
• personalized customer experience,
• customer recommendations,
• better pricing strategy,
• improvising system, and
• targeted marketing and sales optimization.

Thus big data can restructure the travel sector. An efficient big data analytic strategy is crucial to discovering consumer inclinations, travel behavior, business style, and prospects. Due to the rapid digital revolution, it is obvious that those who adapt quickly to the new technology will dominate the industry by providing the best service. Technology is moving forward with improvements in wearable devices, complex analytics, and improved reality enabled by the IT industry. It is expected that the travel sector will see more innovative changes in the near future. Using big data and analytics will help also to devise solutions to large-scale problems in health care, retail, banking and finance, agriculture, and education.

## 2.5 Big data is transforming the travel industry

Big data is changing the way companies manage their operations. Data are generated due to customer interactions with mobile applications or website applications for shopping, booking cabs, searching for the nearest restaurants, or booking a holiday. Companies can analyze these data to understand traveler preferences and to provide improved services. Like any other industry, the travel industry can get remarkable benefits by adapting to big data systems. By exploring how big data is transforming the travel industry, one can see how other business could gain benefits from its use [6]:

- customized user experience,
- unique differentiation,
- pricing strategies,
- improvement of business operations,
- real-time travel assistance,
- insight into people's needs,
- competitive differentiation, and
- loyalty programs and improved marketing strategies.

Although, we are able to list the advantages of big data to improve the travel experience, there is the possibility of customers being unwilling to share their details. One of the causes of such a phenomenon is the misuse of personal details. The collection of data by companies must be done through legitimate means and used only to improve the traveler's experience and not for any other use. When travel companies gain insights into customers' travel patterns, spending patterns, and related information, customized tours can be created for the customers. The use of big data in the travel industry not only helps companies to make more profit by attracting customers but also help customers to obtain a personalized experience.

## 2.6 Key findings for the travel sector

### 2.6.1 Benefits of big data to tourism businesses

Big data analysis is becoming a driving force for changes in almost all the major industries. It is also changing the way of doing business for the hospitality and travel sectors. The data involved here include searching for hotels, booking flights, hotels, cabs, preferences of travelers for the location of hotels, etc. Due to advancements in the computing technologies, the big data analysis platform has become cheaper to procure and work with. This helps to gain business insights to boost the revenue of the sector. In addition, there are substantial changes for big data because the costs of data analytic tools are becoming cheaper. Big data can be used to target a specific audience with tailor-made advertisements to boost company revenues. The prospective for big data in tourism is huge. Tourism organizations should not undervalue its importance for profit generation. With big data analysis, the travel sector can learn a lot about customer inclinations. This can help to build a strong connection with travelers to use the same system for such plans in the future. The following are points that will be revamped by applying big data to boost the travel sector [7]:

- consumer behavior,
- feedback mechanisms,
- greater personalization,
- unique differentiation,
- improvement of business operations,
- real-time travel assistance, and
- the ability to meet future needs.

## 2.7 Tools for big data analysis for smart tourism

There are large numbers of big data tools accessible currently for data analysis. The data analysis process consists of inspecting, cleaning, transforming, and modeling data with the objective of discovering valuable information, suggesting conclusions, and supporting decision making [7].

### 2.7.1 Open source data analytics tools

- *KNIME*: An analytical platform consisting of thousands of modules, integrated tools, and built-in support for algorithms to extract hidden patterns in the data set.

- *OpenRefine*: Works with untidy data, it is the best tool if the data set is large.
- *R*: It is a not only a language but also a platform. Used for statistical computing and visualizing.
- *Spyder*: Powerful tool coded in Python for data investigation. Supports analysis, debugging, data assessment, and visualization abilities.
- *Orange*: Tool with interactive workflow and used for analyzing and to visualize data.
- *RapidMiner*: Open source visual programming tool used for analyzing and modeling data.
- *Pentaho*: Platform to prepare and unify any data and supports a wide range of tools for analysis life cycle.
- *Talend*: Open source integration tool for data-intensive streaming processes.
- *Weka*: Open source software with user friendly graphical user interface, implemented in java, supports machine learning algorithms.
- *Gephi*: Open source software, written in java, helps to perform network analysis and data visualization.
- *Datawrapper*: Online data visualization tool for developing interactive charts such as bar graphs and line graphs.
- *Solver*: Tool for preparing financial reports, budgets, and analysis with the given data set.
- *Qlik*: Tool to create visualizations, dashboards, and applications.
- *Tableau Public*: Tool to visualize the data set, explore insights, and validate the hypothesis.
- *Google Fusion Tables*: Tool used for analyzing, visualizing, and mapping using the data set.
- *Infogram*: Tool which supports a large set of interactive charts and maps for data visualization.

## 2.7.2 Demonstration of R, Spyder, and Jupyter Notebook

Data set used: "Visitors to Taiwan by Residence."

This is a part of the Taiwan tourism data set. This data set, which has been taken from kaggel.com, contains the number of visitors on a monthly basis to Taiwan. It also consists of details of the number of people visiting Taiwan from different countries and continents as shown in Table 2.1. The data include the number of visitors every month from 2011 to 2018. Following is a snapshot of the data set used.

**Table 2.1** Visitors to Taiwan by residence.

| Residence | Region | Subregion | Total | Period |
| --- | --- | --- | --- | --- |
| Hong Kong, Macao | Asia | | 177,057 | 2017-12 |
| Others, Africa | Africa | | 441 | 2017-12 |
| United States | America | | 41,329 | 2018-01 |
| Canada | America | | 9752 | 2018-01 |
| Others, Asia | Asia | | 1128 | 2018-01 |
| Others, Southeast Asia | Asia | Southeast Asia | 1945 | 2018-01 |
| Vietnam | Asia | Southeast Asia | 25,401 | 2018-01 |
| Thailand | Asia | Southeast Asia | 23,329 | 2018-01 |
| Philippines | Asia | Southeast Asia | 30,927 | 2018-01 |
| Indonesia | Asia | Southeast Asia | 13,026 | 2018-01 |
| Unstated | | | 1882 | 2018-01 |
| Malaysia | Asia | Southeast Asia | 31,359 | 2018-01 |
| Middle East | Asia | | 1715 | 2018-01 |
| India | Asia | | 2579 | 2018-01 |
| Korea, Republic of | Asia | | 129,355 | 2018-01 |
| Japan | Asia | | 161,912 | 2018-01 |
| Mainland China | Asia | | 218,648 | 2018-01 |
| Hong Kong, Macao | Asia | | 106,441 | 2018-01 |
| Mexico | America | | 344 | 2018-01 |
| Singapore | Asia | Southeast Asia | 31,314 | 2018-01 |
| Argentina | America | | 159 | 2018-01 |
| Others, America | America | | 970 | 2018-01 |

### 2.7.2.1 Using Spyder and R

We are trying to discover the highest number of visitors. By using the Spyder and R tools, we have generated graphs to display the highest number of visitors by country and continent. The data set has to be cleaned first before applying analysis to it. Usually the data set will have some missing values or null values. The data analyst can update such values to clean the data set. Once it is cleaned, the data set can be loaded to the big data tools and analyzed. Using the Spyder tool, we have shown in Fig. 2.2 that Asia accounts for the highest number of visitors to Taiwan compared to other continents. Fig. 2.3 indicates the number of visitors from different countries.

Using the Spyder tool the graph shown in Fig. 2.2 has been generated and plt.title() has been used to plot the title of the $X$ and $Y$ axis, and to label the axes using plt.xlabel() and plt.ylabel(). Different data frames were read with different column names. Finally, we have the statistics for

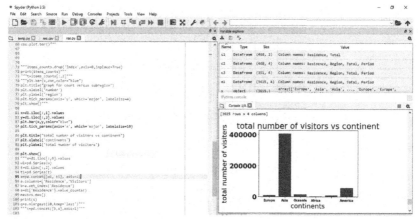

**Figure 2.2** Displaying the total number of visitors from different continents using Spyder.

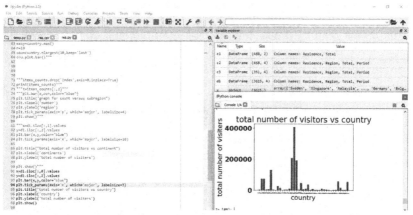

**Figure 2.3** Displaying the total number of visitors from different countries using Spyder.

tourists who visited Taiwan, with around 400,000 tourists from Asia alone visiting. Fig. 2.3 indicates the number of visitors from different countries.

Using the R tool, we have shown in Fig. 2.4 that Asia accounts for the highest number of visitors to Taiwan compared to other continents. Similarly, Fig. 2.5 indicates the number of visitors to Taiwan from various countries. The R tool provides support for visualizing the results. In Fig. 2.6 we have shown graphically that Asia accounts for the highest number of visitors to Taiwan compared to other continents. In

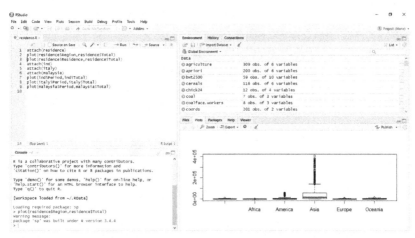

**Figure 2.4** Displaying the total number of visitors from different continents using R.

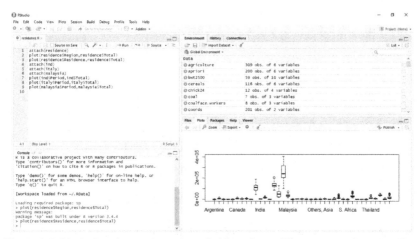

**Figure 2.5** Displaying the total number of visitors from different countries using R.

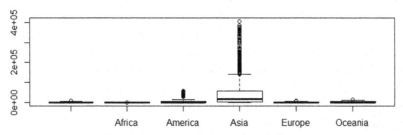

**Figure 2.6** Visualizing the total number of visitors from different continents using R.

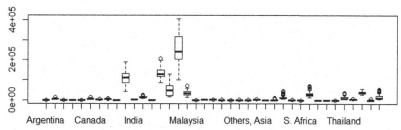

**Figure 2.7** Visualizing the total number of visitors from different countries using R.

Fig. 2.7 we have shown graphically the number of visitors to Taiwan from various countries.

Fig. 2.5 shows the statistics for people from different countries visiting Taiwan using the R tool. It shows that most tourist were from Malaysia. If the Spyder tool is used, then data are read from the data set in the form of data frames which are then able to be plotted on the graph. However, in the case of R, the data are read in the form of a table (a combination of rows and columns) and the graph is plotted directly using plot (). The graphs or the analysis we obtain from both tools regarding tourists to Taiwan are the same. When comparing the performance of both analyses, R gives better performance due to a lower time requirement for fetching the data set.

Figs. 2.6 and 2.7 show graphical representations of the total number of visitors to Taiwan and total number of visitors from different countries using the R tool.

Fig. 2.8 illustrates the number of visitors to Taiwan from India in the years 2016, 2017, and 2018, with the number of visitors increasing year on year. This can help the travel industry in Taiwan to attract the Indian travelers by setting up Indian food stalls, shopping complexes, etc. Figs. 2.9 and 2.10 illustrate the numbers of visitors to Taiwan from Italy and Malaysia, respectively, in the years 2016, 2017, and 2018. There is a dip in the number of travelers from 2017 to 2018. Taiwanese tourism therefore can take measures to improve this number by discovering the reasons for this drop through surveys.

### 2.7.2.2 Using Jupyter Notebook

Jupyter Notebook is an online, open source tool to work with data sets to implement machine learning algorithms. We have implemented linear regression model using the Jupyter Notebook on the data set in Figs. 2.11 and 2.12.

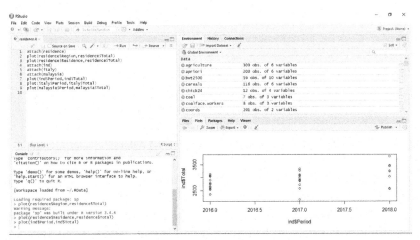

**Figure 2.8** Displaying the total number of visitors from India in the years 2016, 2017, and 2018 using R.

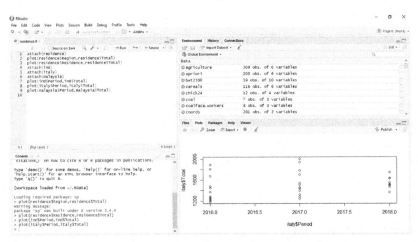

**Figure 2.9** Displaying the total number of visitors from Italy in the years 2016, 2017, and 2018 using R.

### 2.7.3 Analysis of the tourism data set

When the travel sector implements big data applications and analyzes such a data set, they can change some of the operations to increase their business. Using Spyder and R we have found that the highest number of visitors to Taiwan is from Asia. The travel sectors can change the menus in

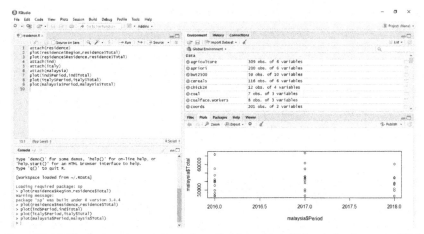

**Figure 2.10** Displaying the total number of visitors from Malaysia in the years 2016, 2017, and 2018 using R.

**Figure 2.11** Linear regression model using Jupyter Notebook.

hotels by offering more Asian foods. The highest numbers of visitors are from China, therefore, by establishing Chinese hotels, and providing local guides who are fluent in the Chinese language, visitors will feel comfortable in visiting the same places repeatedly.

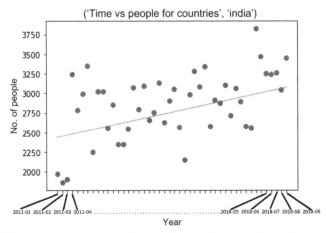

**Figure 2.12** Linear regression model using Jupyter Notebook for visitors from India.

## 2.8 Applying PROPHET and ARIMA prediction models

The "Visitors to Taiwan by Residence" data set is a time series data set where the visitor counts from various countries and continents have been arranged by month from the years 2011 to 2018. The tourism industry would like to predict the number of visitors for a particular time period from a country or continents and use it to prepare the concerned industries like hotels, entertainment, food, and travel. If the visitor count is decreasing, the tourism industry should take the necessary steps to attract more tourists. Here we are predicting the number of visitors for the next year by applying the *PROPHET* and *ARIMA* models using R language.

### 2.8.1 PROPHET model

The PROPHET model is the one of the quickest forecasting model and is available both in R studio and Python Analytics platforms. The PROPHET model gives strong results even with missing values, longer trends, and larger outliers in the data set. The PROPHET model is one of the optimized open source software from Facebook to forecast values. PROPHET works well and forecasts better when a data set consisting of the time, daily, weekly, yearly, trends, and seasonality.

### 2.8.2 ARIMA model

The ARIMA model is a set of statistical models for analyzing and forecasting time series data. The ARIMA model also considers both trends and seasonality for forecasting. ARIMA is an acronym for autoregressive integrated moving average. It is a generalization of the simpler autoregressive moving average and adds the notion of integration.

### 2.8.3 Analysis of the prediction models

We have applied the ARIMA and PROPHET model on the data set as depicted in Figs. 2.13 and 2.14. We found that the forecast for the future dates has minimal variations in the results from both models. While the PROPHET model predicted an increase in the number of visitors from 2019 to 2022, the ARIMA model predicted a decrease in the visitor count. We also found that the predicted values from the PROPHET model are better and the error values of the PROPHET model in forecasting the future values is much less as compared to other time series techniques and models. In our data, ARIMA is modeled based on *pdq* values (*p*: no. of autoregressive terms; *d*: no. of nonseasonal differences needed for stationarity; and *q*: no. of lagged forecast errors in the prediction equation) and seasonality values where these values are inserted by cross-checking with many sample values and checking the error value. However, as observed in this sampling, making seasonality stationary, which is required to maintain a trend in the prediction, has failed. In contrast, PROPHET has been designed to automodify the data while applying the model. PROPHET checks for trends and seasonality with a special concept as it includes holidays and has some change points.

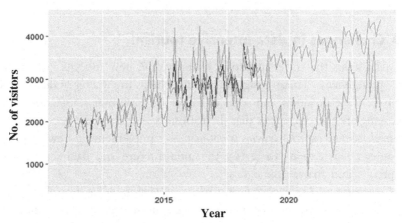

**Figure 2.13** Prediction of the numbers of visitors using the PROPHET and ARIMA models.

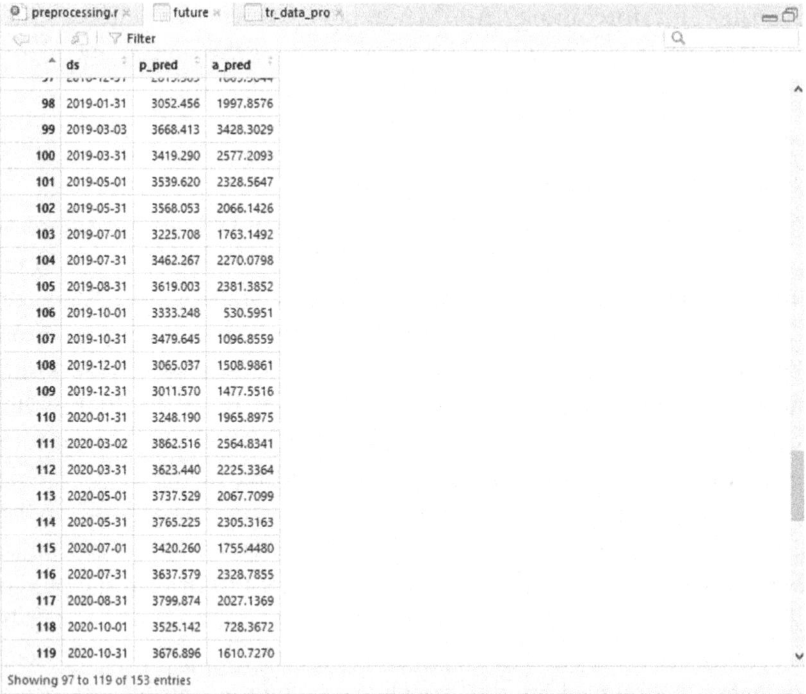

| | ds | p_pred | a_pred |
|---|---|---|---|
| 97 | ~~2018-12-31~~ | ~~2019.303~~ | ~~1003.3044~~ |
| 98 | 2019-01-31 | 3052.456 | 1997.8576 |
| 99 | 2019-03-03 | 3668.413 | 3428.3029 |
| 100 | 2019-03-31 | 3419.290 | 2577.2093 |
| 101 | 2019-05-01 | 3539.620 | 2328.5647 |
| 102 | 2019-05-31 | 3568.053 | 2066.1426 |
| 103 | 2019-07-01 | 3225.708 | 1763.1492 |
| 104 | 2019-07-31 | 3462.267 | 2270.0798 |
| 105 | 2019-08-31 | 3619.003 | 2381.3852 |
| 106 | 2019-10-01 | 3333.248 | 530.5951 |
| 107 | 2019-10-31 | 3479.645 | 1096.8559 |
| 108 | 2019-12-01 | 3065.037 | 1508.9861 |
| 109 | 2019-12-31 | 3011.570 | 1477.5516 |
| 110 | 2020-01-31 | 3248.190 | 1965.8975 |
| 111 | 2020-03-02 | 3862.516 | 2564.8341 |
| 112 | 2020-03-31 | 3623.440 | 2225.3364 |
| 113 | 2020-05-01 | 3737.529 | 2067.7099 |
| 114 | 2020-05-31 | 3765.225 | 2305.3163 |
| 115 | 2020-07-01 | 3420.260 | 1755.4480 |
| 116 | 2020-07-31 | 3637.579 | 2328.7855 |
| 117 | 2020-08-31 | 3799.874 | 2027.1369 |
| 118 | 2020-10-01 | 3525.142 | 728.3672 |
| 119 | 2020-10-31 | 3676.896 | 1610.7270 |

Showing 97 to 119 of 153 entries

**Figure 2.14** Total number of visitors predicted using the PROPHET and ARIMA models.

This may be an advantage which gives PROPHET better accuracy than ARIMA.

## 2.9 Challenges in data-intensive tourism

Big data helps the travel industries by providing new insights into travelers' preferences. These insights can also help the travel industries to improve their products and services for better customer satisfaction. The following are the challenges that the tourism sector may face:

- *Implementing big data systems is not that easy*: Implementing new technologies needs experts to set up the infrastructure and data scientists to process and analyze the data set.
- *Companies need to migrate from a relational database to big data*: The ever-growing tourism industry needs to scale the storage size to accommodate real-time as well as huge volumes of data. Big data technologies give the necessary requirements.

- *Acquisition of new tools, storage devices, servers, and other related software*: Setting up the infrastructure to capture and store data related to tourists will not be easy. Small firms may not be able to afford the cost of setting up such an infrastructure.
- *Gathering and storing of structured and unstructured data*: The data can be collected using surveys, logs, etc., which will be either in structured or unstructured formats.
- *Processing unstructured data*: Processing unstructured data is the biggest challenge in big data analytics. Nearly 80% of the data exists in unstructured format. Finding hidden and useful patterns in such data requires skillful data scientists.
- *Exploring hidden patterns which can boost business*: By analyzing big data, data scientists need to explore hidden patterns which can help improve the business by making changes to the business.
- *Privacy of customer details*: Preserving the important details of customers is very important. Misusing customer details will affect the business.
- *Predicting the vacation periods and attracting travelers with discounts*: Probable vacation periods, like festival times or summer holidays, can be predicted to attract customers. Offering discounts to customers on ticket bookings or hotel bookings will also attract customers.
- *Retaining customers*: Providing a good travel experience to customers will help in retaining them. This can be done by either customizing the services to their needs or by providing discounts for the next trip.
- *Proficient data analysts who can extract the useful insights from the big data*: Data scientists are in demand now due to the exponential growth of big data. Real-time analysis and accurate prediction can help industries to greatly increase their profits.

## 2.10 Conclusion and future scope

Due to the digital age, a great deal of data is generated on a daily basis. Improved smartphones, faster Internet connectivity, social media giants, etc., are the main sources of data being generated at a rapid pace. The tourism sector can reap high benefits by employing big data in their systems. Since the data generated for the travel industry is generally from social media, such as Facebook, Twitter, Instagram, and Web logs, they are of an unstructured nature. Data analysts need to convert these unstructured data into structured data and explore hidden insights which will help the tourism sector to modify their operations and services to attract more customers. Working with big data is not an easy task. The company should invest in setting up the infrastructure to collect, store, and process the big data. To beat the competition, the company should have the required expertise in the big data domain to analyze the data and extract useful information that companies can use to improve their services. Lot of tools and frameworks are available for working with big data. A data-driven tourism sector can change the customer experience and generate more profit.

Data related to tourism can be pooled among different sectors, such as the food industry, hotel industry, travel industry, and shopping industry to create a travel-friendly system. Mobile apps, where travelers make holiday bookings will generate a great deal of data [8]. Big data analysis can help to create an environment with different industries to enable a network to support the needs of tourists. Prediction models can be applied to foresee an increase or decrease in the number of visitors from a particular country and to revise the strategy to attract more customers.

## References

[1] <https://en.wikipedia.org/wiki/Smart_tourism>.
[2] <https://www.hotelmanagement.net/tech/how-smart-cities-are-leading-way-to-smart-tourism>.
[3] <https://www.digitalocean.com/community/tutorials/an-introduction-to-big-data-concepts-and-terminology>.
[4] <https://www.edureka.co/blog/big-data-applications-revolutionizing-various-domains/#Big_Data_in_Manufacturing>.
[5] <https://www.happiestminds.com/blogs/how-big-data-analytics-is-redefining-the-travel-industry/>.
[6] <https://insidebigdata.com/2017/06/30/big-data-transforming-travel-industry/>.
[7] <https://bigdata-madesimple.com/top-30-big-data-tools-data-analysis/>.
[8] H. Yin, Y. Zhu, The influence of big data and informatization on tourism industry, in: 2017 International Conference on Behavioural, Economic, Socio-cultural Computing (BESC), Krakow, 2017, pp. 1−5.

## Further reading

<https://www.newgenapps.com/blog/how-big-data-is-taking-the-travel-industry-to-places>.
G. Chareyron, J. Da-Rugna, T. Raimbault, Big data: a new challenge for tourism, in: 2014 IEEE International Conference on Big Data (Big Data), Washington, DC, 2014, pp. 5−7.
M.B. Dezfouli, M.H. NadimiShahraki, H. Zamani, A novel tour planning model using big data, in: 2018 International Conference on Artificial Intelligence and Data Processing (IDAP), Malatya, Turkey, 2018, pp. 1−6.

U. Gretzel, et al., Smart tourism: foundations and developments, Electron. Mark. 25 (3) (2015) 179—188.

U. Gretzel, L. Zhong, C. Koo, Application of smart tourism to cities, Int. J. Tour. Cities 2 (2) (2016).

C. Koo, S. Shin, U. Gretzel, W.C. Hunter, N. Chung, Conceptualization of smart tourism destination competitiveness, Asia Pacific J. Inform. Syst. 26 (4) (2016) 561—576.

G. Liu, et al. Path analysis on big data in promoting intelligent tourism implementation, in: 3rd International Conference on Management Science, Education Technology, Arts, Social Science and Economics, Atlantis Press, 2015.

S. Shafiee, A.R. Ghatari, Big data in tourism industry, in: 2016 10th International Conference on e-Commerce in Developing Countries: With Focus on e-Tourism (ECDC), Isfahan, 2016, pp. 1—7.

H. Song, H. Liu, Predicting tourist demand using big data, Analytics in Smart Tourism Design, Springer, Cham, 2017, pp. 13—29.

CHAPTER 3

# Deep learning and its applications for content-based video retrieval

Srinidhi Hiriyannaiah[1], Kaushik Singh[1], H. Ashwin[1], Siddesh G.M.[2] and K.G. Srinivasa[3]
[1]Department of CSE, Ramaiah Institute of Technology, Bangalore, India
[2]Department of ISE, Ramaiah Institute of Technology, Bangalore, India
[3]Department of Information Management & Coordination, NITTTR, Chandigarh, India

## 3.1 Introduction

Data mining is one of the key areas in the computer science field that involves exploring and analyzing large volumes of data and finding patterns in it. The core of data mining has come from statistics and artificial intelligence, along with database management. The main goal of data mining is the classification or prediction of data based on hidden patterns in the data. The applications of data mining include search engines, recommendation systems, digital advertising, etc. The main concern of the techniques of data mining is the growing volume of data and its varied sources. The sources have spread from normal text to audio, video, and other multimedia sources. In this regard, data-mining techniques should be scalable to multimedia management systems. The advancements in mobile technology and its solutions, multimedia data containing audio, video, and text has flourished in wide areas of computing. Valuable data can be found in sources such as YouTube, Twitter, Facebook, and Instagram. The volume of the data uploaded in these multimedia social network sites is growing daily. For example, Instagram users have uploaded over 20 billion photos, 100 videos are uploaded every minute of every day in YouTube, there are 500 million tweets daily on Twitter, and 500 + terabytes of new data are ingested into the databases of Facebook every day. The different types of research that are being conducted in the area of multimedia systems are related to capture, storage, indexing, retrieval, and mining of multimedia data.

*Hybrid Computational Intelligence*
DOI: https://doi.org/10.1016/B978-0-12-818699-2.00003-2
49

In multimedia systems, visual analytics is an emerging research area with a focus on the exploration and analytics of video data. It involves a management system providing a seamless integration of analysis, interaction, and visualization of multimedia data. The era of smartphones helps in acquiring data that are dynamic and heterogeneous in nature. Content-based visual analytics is one such areas where multimedia data related to video helps in analyzing the context-based information in the video. For example, a video related to a topic on "Searching techniques in C" can include binary search and linear search. The user watching the video might be interested in only linear search. Content-based video retrieval systems (CBVRS) will help in this regard to extract the content related to only linear search.

The ongoing innovations in the field of video creation have conveyed the requirement for better handling of video contents. Video retrieval is one of the most vital and fastest developing research areas in the field of multimedia media revolution. Content-based image retrieval (CBIR), also described as query by image content and substance-based visual data retrieval (CBVIR), is the method which uses computer vision for the video retrieval problem, that is, the problem of searching for appropriate video in substantially large databases. "Content" in this scenario refers to shapes, surfaces, figures, or other information which can be retrieved from the image itself, without the reference of the video content. CBVRS help in assisting the user to retrieve a video from a large database of videos. A video may contain text, audio, and images. A CBVRS needs to extract the features from the video and then align it with the query of matching it to find the video from the large database. In this chapter, the focus is on CBVR and its techniques for computational systems.

## 3.2 Video retrieval techniques

With the amount of data available in today's information superhighway, video data accessible by the public is growing daily. The need to index these data is becoming increasingly important. These videos can be segmented into parts and retrieved. The retrieval of these segments can be done by segmenting using different methods. There exist various techniques for querying for video, and some methods such as video, motion, and textual query have been specified. In this section, the different types of retrieval techniques for video are summarized [1].

## 3.2.1 Feature-based video retrieval

Video semantic recognition for the most part experiences the imprecation of dimensionality and the nonattendance of enough high-caliber labeled occurrences, subsequently semisupervised feature determination increases expanding considerations for its productivity and conceivability. The greater part of the past techniques expect that videos with close separation (neighbors) have comparable marks and portray the inborn nearby structure through a graph of both labeled and unlabeled data. Be that as it may, other than the parameter tuning issue hidden in the development of the graph, the proclivity estimation in the first feature space for the most part experiences the scourge of dimensionality. Moreover, the determined graph isolates itself from the method of feature choice, which may prompt minimized execution for video semantic recognition. In this chapter, the aim is to propose a novel semisupervised feature determination strategy from another point of view. The essential supposition fundamental to the model is that the examples with comparative names ought to have a greater likelihood of being neighbors. Rather than utilizing a foreordained similarity graph, we fuse the determination of the neighborhood structure into the technique of joint feature determination in order to become familiar with the ideal graph at the same time [2].

## 3.2.2 Spatial analysis

Data mining, which is of the spatial type, is the process of finding intriguing, valuable, nontrifling examples from substantial spatial data sets. Spatial data mining is the utilization of various data retrieval methods for spatial data. The goal of data retrieval and spatial data mining techniques is to discover relevant designs in data for it to be used as topography. Currently, geographic information systems and data mining have existed as two different advancements, each one with its own methods and techniques, customs, and procedures to deal with data investigation and perception [3].

Automatic detection of spatial relations and salient features in videos for a substantially large video database systems have picked up popularity because of quickly developing large amounts of multimedia features and data with the purpose of performing effective ordering, recovery, and investigation of relevant data. A drawback of databases which consist of multimedia is the need to process and manipulate the data for relevant labeling and feature extraction before analysis. A large quantity of data makes it hard to complete this assignment physically. An appropriate method for the automatic detection of relevant objects, and determination of the spatiotemporal relationship between the objects in video can be made. This framework expects to diminish the work for labeling of objects altogether by following the salient objects and distinguishment subsequently, needing to put the label for each item once inside each shot as opposed to indicating the labels for each article in each frame as they show up.

### 3.2.3 Spatiotemporal querying in video databases

A video data model that permits proficient and successful portrayal and questioning of spatiotemporal properties of objects is introduced. This data model is centered around semantic type contents of videos. The objects are of fundamental interest for querying in video databases. A model which underpins fuzzy spatial inquiries including questioning spatial relationships among objects and questioning the trajectories of objects is considered. This model is sufficiently adaptable to characterize new spatial relationship models between the objects without causing any change to the fundamental data model. A prototype of the proposed model can be executed. The prototype permits different spatiotemporal questions alongside the fuzzy ones and is inclined to actualize compound inquiries without significant changes to the data model [4].

### 3.3 Video querying

In recent times, the retrieval of video for certain aspects and parts of it can be done by querying the video. For example, if we want to view the part of the video that involves all the scenes where a certain character appears in a movie, we will have to query about the particular character. The on-demand part of the video is retrieved by the service. But when such a query is posed, it can pose several interpretations such as below [4]:
- If the character occurs in a few frames out of all the frames, should only the particular subsegment be retrieved or should the entire segment be retrieved.
- In the case where the user specifies that he/she would like to retrieve only a segment in which the character appears, the user would want to view only a small portion of the retrieved part and reserve to view the remaining parts whenever they wish to.

- There could be multiple segments where the particular character may appear. Therefore the user should be allowed to decide whether to view all or any number of segments they wish.

### 3.3.1 Visual query

Query can be done using a visual content such as a picture, diagram, or a small piece of film. By using such visuals, certain aspects of the video can be retrieved based on the preference of the user. When a picture is used, a segment of the video that consists of the particular queried shot can be retrieved. It could also find segments of video that contain shots similar to the one in the specified visual. It could also find all the segments that consist of entities that are found in the specified visual.

For example, we can take into consideration the problem of searching for people who own a cell phone that called 40 other cell phones on a specified date.

The first task to accomplish this is to create a query structure. This structure represents the relationships we are looking for in the data. It consists of one or more types, links, and entities. In the above example the structure consists of 10 types:

- An entity of type person.
- Two cell phone entity types. These are labeled cell_phone1 and cell_phone2.
- Link between person and cell_phone1.
- Link between cell_phone1 and cell_phone2.

The next task is to constrain the search by using relevant conditions such as date and number of calls made. The conditions can be altered by which the relevant queries can be retrieved. Hence, by using appropriate visual query languages, the visual contents can be retrieved based on the requirements of the user.

### 3.3.2 Motion query

Motion is a method of representing the temporal information which is contained in a video. Motion-based queries are attractive features of a video search engine that represents the motion in some fashion. The representation of the motion information and solving the problem based on the formulation of the query need to be executed in parallel. The different types of approaches for motion query that can be used are as follows:

- *Query by shot*: The motion query can be represented using the whole video shot in this method. However, it is computationally expensive.
- *Query by clip*: A clip in the video can be used for the motion query rather than the entire video shot. The video shot might not be useful because it may not represent the adequate data of the entire context.
- *Query by faces and texts*: Faces and texts can be used for the motion query using the frames for a particular set of faces and texts. The data have to be cut with the matched faces and the text in the query.

A video search engine like JACOB [5] is a color- and motion-based search engine. In this the user selects a global motion orientation of each frame for a quadrant. VideoQ [6] is another motion-based search engine in which the user represents the query by giving a description about each frame in a shot, which is combined with colors and keywords to query the database to retrieve the video.

### 3.3.3 Textual query

Using a content-based retrieval technique, the pictures can be used as a query to retrieve significant videos from the database of videos. However, it is limited by the motion of the video data. A textual query offers a characteristic interface and a better methodology for querying. Textual annotations are difficult to create automatically using a video. It requires a lot of analysis around the context of the video and other related hyperparameters with it. However, it can be done with the help of collaborative filtering that improves the confidence of the querying in the video systems. Textual querying offers the flexibility of the query interface to be embodied with the motion videos.

### 3.3.4 Feature clustering

It is generally trusted that a picture in any form is worth in excess of thousands of expressions. There has been rapid development in the field of digital and image gathering. Within numerous zones of business, the scholarly community, government, and hospitals, substantial accumulations of images in digital form are being made. A significant number of these accumulations are the result of digitization of existing accumulations of simple graphs, illustrations, photographs, works of art, and prints, with a tremendous amount of data out there. Be that as it may, we cannot access or make utilization of the data unless it is composed in such a way as to permit productive browsing, looking, and retrieval. Recovering an image from such huge accumulations is a testing issue, and hence techniques for arranging a substantially large database of images and for effective retrieval of relevant content are critical. In a content-based retrieval framework, images are categorized by content and accordingly, with the help of database management frameworks, it is used to perform image retrieval. In any case, two noteworthy problems exist when the span of image gathering is substantially large. One is the tremendous amount of work required to manually explain an image and the other is the outcome of human recognition, that is, for a similar image content, distinctive individuals may be seen in an unexpected way. To defeat such issues, CBIR has been proposed. Rather than being physically explained by content-based catchphrases, images can be recorded in their own visual content, for example, shading, surface, and so on. CBIR is an innovation that looks at the digital image using its visual features and contents. The framework distinguishes the diverse districts present in an image based on their similarity in shading, design, surface, shape, and so forth, and chooses the similarity of two images by recalculating the closeness of the distinctive locales of the images.

CBIR is a technique for recovering images on the basis of automatically inferred features, for example, shape, color, and texture. To scan for a particular image, the client can provide question terms of type, image file/link, and keyword, and the framework will return an image "comparable" to the inquiry. The similarity used for determining criteria could be color distribution in images, meta labels, region qualities, etc. in CBIR framework images are physically commented by content-based keywords, when we inquire using a keyword as opposed to looking into the contents of the image, this framework coordinates the question to the keywords present in the database. It is, by all accounts, difficult to comment on them from an enormous collection of image database. The features present in an image cannot be depicted by a keyword totally, and therefore a new technique has been advanced called CBIR. This technique utilizes the visual content, like color, texture, and shape to recover the image from an enormous database. It is a tedious procedure to look through all images from expansive collections, and so to overcome this issue we use $k$-means clustering algorithm to form a cluster or a gathering of images with a comparative feature and continue to search for the ideal image. In this method color is used as a visual feature for looking through an image. Color is used as a visual feature because it is generally used for image similarity retrieval. Color space is the fundamental part of color feature extraction. A color space is a multidimensional space in which the various dimensions speak to the distinctive categories of color. The color features are mostly three dimensional. In this case RGB is the color space, which initializes to every pixel a vector with three components for the three primary colors—red, green, and blue—giving its color intensities. The space spread over by the R, G, and B depicts the colors which are visible, which are described as vectors in the color spaces of #D RGB. It gives a helpful start to the color features of images. Hence feature clustering has a step-by-step method using $k$-means clustering to execute this.

### 3.3.4.1 Method

There are numerous strategies for clustering created for a large assortment of motivations. $k$-Means is the algorithm used for clustering used to decide the normal gatherings in a data set. This determines the quantity of clusters in the data. The $k$-means algorithm arbitrarily finds the cluster centers in multidimensional space. Each pixel in the image is then assigned to the cluster whose mean vector is nearest. The algorithm continues until there is no change in the position of the class mean vector between progressive iteration of the algorithms. Because the $k$-means algorithm is iterative, the computational time is serious and connected to the image of the video as opposed to the entire scenes it can now be treated as an unsupervised region. The $k$-means algorithm [7,8] gathers the image into clusters based on the color content and then for iteration we near the objective image. As a result of the clustering techniques we can channel most images in the first iteration, as introduced here:

Stage 1: Input the image.

Stage 2: Perform the $k$-means clustering and form a cluster considering the color features.

Stage 3: Apply the quantity of cluster guess $k$.

Step 4: Randomly generate the $k$ cluster and decide the cluster center.

Stage 5: Reassignment of points to the nearest cluster center takes place.

Stage 6: Therefore the center claims a set of points.

Stage 7: A centroid for this set of points is calculated for each center.

Stage 8: Recomputed the new cluster centers.

Stage 9: Repeat stages 5—8 until the required criteria are met. With a single $k$-means clustering algorithm we need to scan through the entire database. Progressive clustering with $k$-means together gives a more precise outcome in a period with the above proposed strategy.

Various leveled clustering helps in quicker image content retrieval and permits scanning for almost all applicable images in substantially large image data sets [4,7,8].

## 3.4 Deep learning for video analysis

Recent applications of deep learning have achieved very good results and accuracy in the field of video analysis. The hierarchical representation of the data helps in achieving promising results. The necessity for this video retrieval arose from the need to retrieve and classify video. It had many smaller aspects in it, such as image classification, face recognition, detection and tracking of objects, and scene labeling. The video that can be used for processing could be a movie, or the data from a surveillance camera or a security camera. Data from these sources are extremely large and contain all sorts of data. It may have information irrelevant to the topic of search and also data that are not required as per the query posed by the user. To carry out the designated task, machine learning algorithms can be employed to collect from such large data. These methods tend to learn from experience based upon the given input and result. The supervised learning technique creates a mapping function for the specified input and output values. However, this technique completely relies on labeled data. This could adversely affect the process of adding extra manual work. There could also be uncertainties and ambiguities in these labels, which could lead to wrong outputs. Shallow learning algorithms, however, have this drawback. In contrast, deep learning algorithms aim to extract a hierarchical representation of data. Nonlinear transformations are done with the help of multiple layers of deep architecture models. By using this technique, higher accuracy is achieved more easily. It happens to achieve better execution values than using handcrafted features or pixel values. The most popular such deep architecture model is the convolutional neural network (CNN). The CNN has been able to achieve great results in fields of computer vision and speech recognition [9].

### 3.4.1 Convolutional neural network for content-based video retrieval

With the improvement of technology, video is everywhere on the Web. What's more, video retrieval strategies have turned into a critical test these days, which means locating those most important videos from a data set for a query video in an effective and precise way. Rather than images, videos give different and complex visual patterns comprising of low-level visual substance in each frame just as high-level semantic contents over frames, which makes video retrieval more difficult than picture retrieval.

With the fast improvement of deep learning, more techniques dependent on deep learning have given us the possibility of proficient and exact video retrieval. Deep learning can procure high-level semantic features by consolidating lower-level visual features and deep CNNs have ended up being adaptable for image portrayal devices with proper speculation capacities, which makes CNNs a crucial part of proficient video retrieval strategies. As of late, enlivened by the achievement of deep learning in image acknowledgment, a few video retrieval strategies have fused hash functions into deep learning designs [9,10]. For instance, Liong et al. [9] applied three-layer progressive neural networks to learn a discriminative projection matrix, expecting the video pairwise data to be accessible. According to this strategy it does not consider the upside of deep exchange learning, as it makes the binary code less powerful. In addition, Zhang et al. [10] proposed a framework of deep encoder—decoder, where a double-layer long short term memory unit pursued by a layer of binarization can specifically encode the video features into binary hashing codes.

In this section, we propose an engineering of deep CNNs intended for video retrieval, as shown in Fig. 3.1. In the training stage, this design acknowledges input videos in a triplet form. Three sets of video frames are chosen arbitrarily from the three input videos and each set has a similar

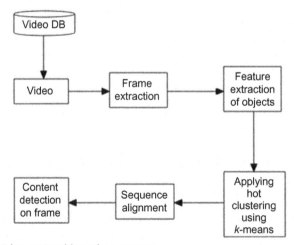

**Figure 3.1** Video retrieval based on content.

number of frames of video. Given three sets of frames of video, the pipeline of the suggested engineering contains three sections:

1. The brought together feature representations of each input frame are separated from the deep CNN, and after that the video frame features of each set are combined into video features by weighted normal so as to simplify the complexity of the network.
2. The primary fully connected layer is trailed by a sigmoid layer intended to learn similarity-preserving binary-like codes, and the second fully connected layer has $k$ nodes, which are equivalents to the number of classifications.
3. The last part is loss function consolidated by arrangement loss and triplet loss. In the recovering stage, binary hashing codes are created by binarization which maps the binary-like yields into 0 or 1. At that point an exclusive-or task is directed on the binary codes of the query video and the binary codes of the videos stored in datasets to get the corresponding Hamming separation and discover the video with the highest similarity (Fig. 3.2).

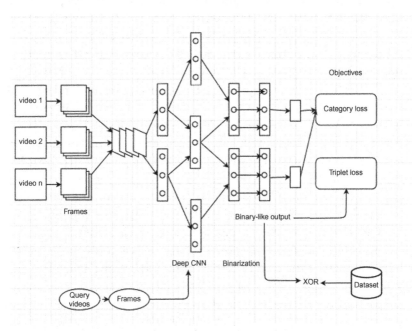

**Figure 3.2** Deep convolutional network.

### 3.4.2 Feature analysis using convolutional neural network for video data

Here we clarify the detailed aspects of the essential operations of 3D ConvNets. We also break down various structures for 3D ConvNets, and express how to prepare them on vast scale datasets for feature learning [11].

Spatiotemporal feature learning can be done using 3D ConvNet. Unlike 2D ConvNet, 3D ConvNet displays the temporal data better with regard to 3D convolution and 3D pooling. Convolution and pooling operations are performed spatiotemporally in 3D ConvNets, while they are done only spatially in 2D ConvNets. Fig. 3.1 outlines this distinction, 2D convolution connected to a picture will output a picture, 2D convolution connected to various pictures by regarding them as various channels which then additionally results in a picture. Later, 2D ConvNets lose temporal data of the input flag directly after each convolution activity. The temporal data of the input bringing about an output are jammed by the 3D convolution.

The more ideal answer for 3D ConvNets would be a homogeneous setting with convolution kernels of $3 \times 3 \times 3$. With a large scale dataset, one can tarin 3D ConvNet with $3 \times 3 \times 3$ kernel with respect to the machine memory cutoff and computation cost. A 3D ConvNet having eight convolution layers, five pooling layers, trailed by two fully connected layers, and a softmax output layer with current GPU memory is structured for this purpose. The system engineering is displayed in Fig. 3.3. The 3D convolution neural network is also called C3D. All 3D convolution channels are $3 \times 3 \times 3$ with stride $1 \times 1 \times 1$. All 3D pooling layers are $2 \times 2 \times 2$ with stride $2 \times 2 \times 2$ aside from pool1 which has a piece size of $1 \times 2 \times 2$ and walk $1 \times 2 \times 2$. It also has the expectation of saving the temporal data in the early stage. Each fully connected layer has 4096 output units.

Our analysis sees that C3D begins by concentrating on the appearance in the initial couple of frames and tracks the remarkable motion in the next few frames. Fig. 3.4 depicts deconvolution of two C3D conv5b feature maps with the highest activations anticipated back to the image space. In the first example, the feature centers around the entire individual and after that it tracks the motion of the pole vault performance over whatever remains of the frames. Also, in the second example it initially centers around the eyes and after that tracks the motion occurring around the

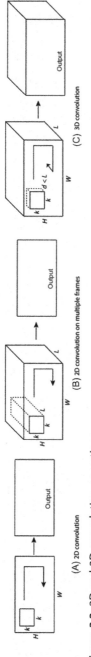

(A) 2D convolution

(B) 2D convolution on multiple frames

(C) 3D convolution

**Figure 3.3** 2D and 3D convolution operations.

| Conv1a | Conv2a | Conv3a | Conv3b | Conv4a | Conv4b | Conv5a | Conv5b | fc6 | fc7 |
|--------|--------|--------|--------|--------|--------|--------|--------|------|------|
| 64 | 128 | 256 | 256 | 512 | 512 | 512 | 512 | 4096 | 4096 |

**Figure 3.4** Architecture for C3D.

eyes while applying cosmetics. Along these lines C3D contrasts from standard 2D ConvNets in that it specifically takes care of both motion and appearance.

```
def extract_features(input_dir, output_dir, model_ty-
pe = 'inceptionv3', batch_size = 32):
"""

Extracts features from a CNN trained on ImageNet classification from
all
videos in a directory.
Args:
input_dir (str): Input directory of videos to extract from.
output_dir (str): Directory where features should be stored.
model_type (str): Model type to use.
batch_size (int): Batch size to use when processing.
"""

input_dir = osf.path.expanduser(input_dir1)
output_dir = osg.path.expanduser(output_dir1)
if not osf.path.isdir(input_dir1):
sys.stderr.write("Input directory '%s' does not exist!\n" %
input_dir)
sys.exit(1)
# Load desired ImageNet model
# Note: import Keras only when needed so we don't waste time revving up
# Theano/TensorFlow needlessly in case of an error
model = None
input_shape = (224, 224)
if model_type.lower() == 'inceptionv3':
from keras.applications import InceptionV3
model1 = InceptionV3(include_top = True, weights = 'imagenets')
elif model1_type.lower() == 'xception':
from keras.applications import Xception
model2 = Xception(include_top = True, weights = 'imagenet')
elif model2_type.lower() == 'resnet50':
from keras.applications import ResNet50
model1 = ResNet50(include_top = True, weights = 'imagenet')
elif model1_type.lower() == 'vgg16':
from keras.applications import VGG16
model1 = VGG16(include_top = True, weights = 'imagenet')
elif model1_type.lower() == 'vgg19':
from keras.applications import VGG19
model1 = VGG19(include_top = True, weights = 'imagenet')
else:
sys.stderr.write("'%s' is not a valid ImageNet model.\n" %
model_type)
sys.exit(1)
```

```
if model_type.lower() == 'inceptionv3' or model_type.lower
() == 'xception':
shape = (299, 299)
# Get outputs of model from layer just before softmax predictions
from keras.models import Model
model = Model(model.inputs, output = model.layers[-2].output)
# Create output directories
visual_dir = os.path.join(output_dir, 'visual') # RGB features
#motion_dir = os.path.join(output_dir, 'motion') # Spatiotemporal
features
#opflow_dir = os.path.join(output_dir, 'opflow') # Optical flow
features
for directory in [visual_dir]:#, motion_dir, opflow_dir]:
if not os.path.exists(directory):
os.makedirs(directory)
```

## 3.5 A multitier deep learning-based video classification using C3D

Video data are high-volume and high-value data. They are, in fact, the cause of around 70% of the traffic on the Internet. It is almost impossible—both too expensive and too slow—to rely on human and manual inspection of large-scale video information. Therefore the issues related to automated analysis are important to answer these queries. When inputting an image or video, a variety of computer vision methods can extract valuable semantic information about objects and their occurrence. In this section, a multitier deep learning-based video classification using C3D is discussed.

### 3.5.1 Data set

In order to achieve complete convergence in the domain of spatiotemporal attributes, we upskill our C3D on the Sports-1M data set, which is classified and renowned as the largest video classification and categorization standard. The data set contains 1.1 million sports videos. Every video has a place within one of the special 487 sports classifications. Contrasted with UCF101, Sports1M has multiple times the quantity of classes and grows exponentially larger in terms of the number of videos [12].

The video-retrieval evaluation technique is a multiyear, worldwide effort to promote study in the field of content-based retrieval for videos. The system every year advances itself to obtain better results in the field of video retrieval [13]. During 2001, 12 hours of video that were publicly available and were based on educational or informational data in MPEG-1 format were used as the data set. In 2002, 73 hours of video were used. This was majorly from the Prelinger Archive that consists of movies based on US culture. The data set also consists of open-source video. Some parts of it were also taken from BBC archives. The Prelinger video consists of digitized versions of advertising, industrial, educational, and amateur films developed between the 1930s and 1970s. In 2003, 133 hours of video were used. This consisted of US newscasts from 1998 and some of it was from the C-SPAN. The C-SPAN data consisted of speeches in the US Congress, public forum discussions, and press conferences [13].

### 3.5.2 Methodology

The methodology for the experiment is followed by training the data set as follows:

*Training*: Training is achieved using the Sports-1M train split as our primary concern. Since Sports-1M has a substantial quantity of videos that exceed our specified time range, we obtained 5.2-second timed clips from each video present on that realm. The size is modified to our convenience by following the dimensions specified, that is, $128 \times 171$. For the main purpose of upskilling and tutoring we snip the clips taken as process material into $16 \times 112 \times 112$ for spatial and temporal jittering. Along similar lines, a complete turnaround of the material is done to achieve 50% likelihood. Upskilling is finished by stochastic gradient descent (SGD) with a minibatch size of 30 exemplar samples. The initial understanding and knowledge acquiring rate is 0.003, and is partitioned into two each 150K streamlined repetitions. The streamlining is halted at 1.9 M repeated cycles (around 13 epochs).

### 3.5.3 Experiment and results

Table 3.1 displays the aftereffects of the presently achieved C3D crisscrossed grid contrasted and DeepVideo and Convolution pooling. We utilize just a single crop for every snippet and run it alongside the interlinked nodes. In regard to video forecasts, 10 clips are extracted from the video. It is significant that there are some setting contrasts between the strategies. DeepVideo and C3D utilize smaller-sized snippets, while Convolution aggregation utilizes any larger-sized clips. DeepVideo considers a significantly more varied estimation of snips in the range of four crops for each snip and 80 resizes for every video contrasted and one and

**Table 3.1** Classification results for Sports1-M.

| Method | Number of networks | Clip hit at 1 | Video hit at 1 | Video hit at 5 |
|---|---|---|---|---|
| DeepVideo's multiframe + Multire | 3 | 42.4 | 60 | 78.5 |
| DeepVideo's slow fusion | 1 | 41.9 | 60.9 | 80.2 |
| Convolution pooling on 120-frame clip | 3 | 70.8 | 72.4 | 90.8 |
| C3D (trained from scratch) | 1 | 44.9 | 60 | 84.4 |
| C3D (fine tuned from I380K pre-trained) | 1 | 46.1 | 61.1 | 85.2 |

10 utilized by C3D, individually. The C3D interlinked domain initially yields a precision of 84.4% and the tweaked model gives a precision of 85.5% with top5 exactness. Both C3D networks beat DeepVideo's networks [12].

In the wake of upskilling and training, C3D can be utilized as an attribute-derived aspect for several retrieval objectives in a multitude of areas. Hence, to retrieve C3D attributes, a video is split into 16 frame-long clips with an eight-frame overlap between two back-to-back clips. The results in Table 3.1 are compared against the previous results discussed in the following paragraphs and tables.

For the educational and the information data [13], the search task given to the system was based on the statements given in terms of text to the system as shown in Table 3.2. The textual representation of the video clipping of the topic should be mentioned. This could also have an optional video clip, an image, or/and an audio clip as an example of what the query would expect as the outcome. It could be people, places, location, objects, or even a combination of these. It also had to detect the shot boundary and to determine if a shot had a boundary that was either abrupt or gradual.

During 2002, new features were added. A higher level of feature extraction was made possible as shown in Table 3.3. More detection features, like outdoors, cityscapes, overlay, monologue, instrumental sound, text overlay, and face were added. It consisted of real-time retrieval queries like videos of named or generic people, places, events, or combinations of these.

During 2003, more analysis and am interactive query system were proposed as shown in Table 3.4. In order to accommodate the results of

**Table 3.2** 2001 Evaluation.

| Task | | Test data | | Measures | Runs |
|---|---|---|---|---|---|
| Shot boundary determination | | 45 videos 5.79 h 595,174 frames, 3179 transitions | | OT10.3 measures including precision and recall | 13 |
| Search (interactive, automatic) | Known item | Shot boundary data + 43 videos | 38 topics | Precision and recall | 10 |
| | general | 5.4 h 2.96 GB | 36 topics | Precision | 11 |

**Table 3.3** 2002 Evaluation.

| Task | Training data | Test data | | Measures | Runs |
|---|---|---|---|---|---|
| Shot boundary determination | 2001 shot boundary data | 18 videos 4.799 h 545,102 frames, 2100 transitions | | Precision and recall frame-precision and frame-recall | 54 |
| High-level feature extraction | 96 videos 22.96 h 7886 standard shots | 23 videos 5.02 h 1848 standard shots | 10 features | Precision, recall, average precision | 19 |
| Search (interactive, manual) | | 176 videos 39.98 h 14,389 standard shots | 29 topics | Average precision, precision, recall, + elapsed time for interactive runs | 14I 28M |

**Table 3.4** 2003 Evaluation.

| Task | Training data | Test data | | Measures | Runs |
|------|---------------|-----------|---|----------|------|
| Shot boundary determination | 2001, 2003 shot boundary data | 13 videos 6 h 596,054 frames, 3734 transitions | | Precision and recall frame-precision and frame-recall | 80 |
| Story segmentation and typing | 115 30-min videos | 105 30-min videos | | Precision and recall new precision and news recall | 41 |
| High-level feature extraction | Extraction | 113 videos | 17 features | Precision, recall, average precision | 60 |
| Search (interactive, manual) | 133 videos 35,067 standard shots | 32,318 standard shots | 25 topics | Precision, recall, average precision + elapsed time | 37I 38M |

extraction and mining of frequently occurring features, the size of the result sets was increased substantially [13].

# References

[1] S.S. Cheung, A. Zakhor, Efficient video similarity measurement with video signature, IEEE Trans. Circ. Syst. Video Technol. 13 (1) (2003) 59–74.

[2] J. Fan, W. Aref, A. Elmagarmid, M. Hacid, M. Marzouk, X. Zhu, Multiview: multilevel video content representation and retrieval, J. Electron. Image 10 (4) (2001) 895–908.

[3] J. Calic, B.T. Thomas, Spatial analysis in key-frame extraction using video segmentation, in: Workshop on Image Analysis for Multimedia Interactive Services, 2004.

[4] J. Meng, J. Yuan, J. Yang, G. Wang, Y.-P. Tan, Object instance search in videos via spatio-temporal trajectory discovery, IEEE Trans. Multimedia 18 (1) (2016) 116–127.

[5] E. Ardizzone, M. La Cascia, D. Molinelli. Motion and color based video indexing and retrieval, in: Int. Conf. on Pattern Recognition (ICPR'96), Vienna, Austria, 1996.

[6] S.-F. Chang, W. Chen, H.J. Meng, H. Sundaram, D. Zhong. VideoQ — an automatic content-based video search system using visual cues, in: ACM Multimedia Conference, Seattle, WA, 1997.

[7] V.S. Murthy, et al., Content based image retrieval using hierarchical and $K$-means, Int. J. Eng. Sci. Technol. 3 (2010) 209—212.

[8] V.G. Tonge, Content based image retrieval by $K$-means clustering algorithm, Int. J. Eng. Sci. Technol. (IJEST) (2011) 46—49.

[9] V.E. Liong, J. Lu, Y.P. Tan, et al., Deep video hashing, IEEE Trans. Multimedia 19 (6) (2017) 1209—1219.

[10] H. Zhang, M. Wang, R. Hong, et al., Play and rewind: optimizing binary representations of videos by self supervised temporal hashing[C], Proceedings of the 2016 ACM on Multimedia Conference, ACM, 2016, pp. 781—790.

[11] A. Krizhevsky, I. Sutskever, G.E. Hinton, Imagenet classification with deep convolutional neural networks[C], Adv. Neural Inf. Process. Syst. (2012) 1097—1105.

[12] D. Tran, L. Bourdev, R. Fergus, L. Torresani, M. Paluri, Learning spatiotemporal features with 3d convolutional networks, in: Proceedings of the IEEE International Conference on Computer Vision, 2015, pp. 4489—4497.

[13] A.F. Smeaton, W. Kraaij, P. Over, TREC video retrieval evaluation: a case study and status report, in: Proceedings of RIAO 2004, 2004.

CHAPTER 4

# A computationally intelligent agent for detecting fake news using generative adversarial networks

**Srinidhi Hiriyannaiah[1], A.M.D. Srinivas[1], Gagan K. Shetty[1], Siddesh G.M.[2] and K.G. Srinivasa[3]**
[1]Department of CSE, Ramaiah Institute of Technology, Bangalore, India
[2]Department of ISE, Ramaiah Institute of Technology, Bangalore, India
[3]Department of Information Management & Coordination, NITTTR, Chandigarh, India

## 4.1 Fake news

Fake news is parading around everywhere, predominantly in your social media feeds, often giving the false impression that it is credible. Fake news is stories generally created to confuse or give a false impression to the targeted audience. The reason why people are susceptible to fake news is that it often looks like websites that are trustworthy, or they use names that are associated with reputable news organizations.

"Fake news" was not a such a big problem a couple of years ago, however it is currently considered to be one of the most prominent hazards to democracy and free dialogue. Being a frequently used term by Donald Trump, it was also 2017's word of the year, causing tensions among nations and resulting in the regulation of social media.

### 4.1.1 What is fake news?

Fake news is a form of content that contains misinformation, either crafted to deceive the readers or purely a misinformed perspective, that is spread via print, news, or social media.

Fake news is generally crafted with the intention of misleading the target audience in an effort to harm an organization or person, or to gain financially or politically.

Fake news is becoming a big problem in politics. One of the characteristics of fake news is that it attracts viewers with false content, often

*Hybrid Computational Intelligence*
DOI: https://doi.org/10.1016/B978-0-12-818699-2.00004-4

better than we can with real content. Media outlets often exploit this feature to attract viewers and increase their advertisement revenue, or spread false propaganda to hurt a competitor's viewership.

Fake news also has the potential to steal the limelight from legitimate news content which makes it more difficult for journalists to cover important news stories. For example, an analysis from BuzzFeed shows that during the 2016 US presidential election, the top 20 fake news stories about the election were much more popular than the top 20 election stories from 19 major media outlets [1].

The word fake news was also misused to dispute legitimate news as well. This tactic, called the lying press, is used to question any form of comments that opposes a particular view point. For example, Donald Trump popularized the term "fake news" to describe the news coverage that showed negative press coverage of him.

Fake news is not only used for financial or political gain. Areas such as nutrition and vaccination are also plagued by fake news. The recent outburst of "vaccines cause autism" is creating significant problems, resulting in parents choosing not to vaccinate their children under the assumption that vaccines cause more harm than good. We must also consider the intent of fake news. Often, fake news might be just a caricature or a satire to amuse viewers rather than to convey a false message.

## 4.1.2 Reasons for the emergence of fake news

Fake news has been around for a long time, but it has gained a lot of traction only recently. Traditionally, we used to consume media only from trusted sources, where the journalists were expected to follow strict rules and guidelines while writing stories and articles. With the advent of Internet media, many people have access to new methods of publishing articles that are often not checked for authenticity and who follow very little regulation or editorial standards.

Many people have access to this unregulated news content on social media sites and find it very difficult to judge the credibility of the news. Some people lack an understanding of how the Internet works and this has also contributed to the outburst of fake news stories.

The primary reason why content creators do so is for profits from advertising revenue. Fake news has the potential to go viral, and stories that go viral create more revenue. The ease of publishing content on social media just makes it easier for them to achieve this.

### 4.1.3 Effects and dangers of fake news

Dating back to 2013, experts at the World Economic Forum [2] discussed potential "digital wildfires" that can be caused due to unreliable information being disseminated online and considered them a catastrophic threat faced by society.

Whenever we discuss fake stories, we generally refer to them with respect to politics. However, fake news also has a huge impact on society in general. Fake news has the potential to cause trouble between communities, religions, and castes by spreading false rumors.

For some people in rural areas, WhatsApp, Facebook, and Instagram are often the main sources of online media. However, these forms of media have the potential to transmit fake news that people may believe to be true.

In recent times, many Indian actors, media, and politicians have been affected by fake news. For instance, during 2017, some media outlets published fake news articles about the author Arundhati Roy, claiming that she had been critical of the Indian army regarding their actions in Kashmir. Even though she did not make any comments regarding the issue, some nationalists branded her as a traitor.

Fake news can also affect international relationships between countries. For instance, in May 2017, Qatar's news agency was hacked and fake comments were published as being made by the Emirates criticizing aspects of US and Arab Gulf foreign policy toward Iran. This incident made the neighboring countries sever diplomatic ties with the country, even though the news agency acted quickly to label the comments as false.

Celebrity scandals are another type of news stories that are plagued by fake news. Most readers find it difficult to distinguish between real stories and fake stories, even though many of them seem so far-fetched that many would realize that they are obviously fake.

These fake scandals are sometimes more believable than the truth. This can cause a lot of damage to reputations. For instance, a recent story published by BuzzFeed about a jewelry shop replacing real diamonds with fake ones led to a fall in the value of the brand's stock by 3.7%.

One of the biggest factors behind the success of fake news stories is their high level of social engagement. Social networks connect us with other people who are generally like-minded peers, who share our beliefs and values, be they social, economic, or political. We share information on these sites which help us define who we are and what we believe. We have access to information shared by people who share the same beliefs that we do. This gives us access to content that is similar to that which we share, indirectly reinforcing our idea and beliefs. Therefore if the belief was flawed, we would likely not come across evidence that discredits our belief because everything we see is similar to what we believe in. We are also far more likely to spread those ideas that we agree with.

India's Supreme Court had recently mulled a petition which challenged a government decision to deport 40,000 refugees who were fleeing persecution in Myanmar. Fake images and videos which depicted the refugees as having attacked Hindus spread on social media causing a great deal of outrage.

There were rumors about a gang of men, allegedly abducting children, on WhatsApp. This caused mayhem, eventually leading to the murder of seven innocent people by mobs in Jharkhand.

In another instance, messages claiming that an immunization drive for measles and rubella in Kerala was a conspiracy to reduce population, made several rounds on social media like WhatsApp and Facebook.

In India, WhatsApp has been used to spread false rumors that have led to numerous mob killings. False messages which portray people as child abductors may be forwarded to their friends and family out of a sense of duty to protect them.

This widespread problem of fake news has a major impact on people's trust in the media. A survey in 2016 shows that the percentage of Indians who trust the media hit an all-time low and still remains at under 50%. Trust in companies has also taken a hit. Around 42% of Indians have lost trust in many different brands. Around two-thirds of Indians get their news from social media, however, they don't always believe it to be true.

For many people, social media is the first source for news. Unfortunately, social media is also the first stop for fake news. Many viral stories don't reflect real news. Regardless of the level of truth behind a post, social media activity is critical for gauging when a story has momentum.

The people decide the authenticity of the news by relying on unreliable pointers such as who sent it to them. With this kind of judgment, messages from friends and family are often blindly trusted.

Solving the problem of fake news is most certainly a difficult challenge for everyone, however, with the use of new technologies, we can get one step closer to controlling the problem.

## 4.2 Deep learning

There has been a lot of interest lately in the tasks that machines are capable of performing, quite possibly better than humans. While technology is evolving rapidly, terms such as artificial intelligence (AI) and deep learning can still be confounding to many. In this section, we discuss deep learning and its applications.

### 4.2.1 What is deep learning?

Deep learning is just a subfield of a broader family of machine learning methods based on learning data representations. Deep learning is mainly concerned with algorithms which are inspired by the structure and functioning of the brain.

When we talk about deep learning, the first thing that comes to mind is a neural network. A neural network is a system of hardware and/or software patterned after the operation of neurons in the human brain. It is inspired by the functioning of the brain and closely resembles it.

A neural network is made up of a huge number of processing units that work in parallel and stacked as layers of units. The first layer of units perceives the real-world data (input)—similar to the task of optic nerves that a play major role in our visual perception. Each successive layer of units in the stack uses the output from the previous layer—similar to the way the information is transferred from optic nerves to the neighboring neurons. The last layer of units provides the output of the entire system.

The main advantage of a neural network is that it automatically learns a good feature representation. This does not mean we do not need to hand engineer features at all, however, we do not have to deal with feature transformation like in a machine learning setting. Instead, we have to fine tune the hyperparameters of the neural networks, such as the network architecture (number of layers, hidden units, and so on), learning rate, etc.

Deep learning algorithms can be applied to unsupervised learning tasks as well. This is very appealing as there is a lot more unlabeled data available as compared to labeled data. One example of such a network is the deep belief networks (DBN).

### 4.2.2 Introduction to neural networks and gradient descent

A neural network is a massively parallel distributed processor with simple units that can store important information and make it available for use.

Typically, neural networks are comprised of layers; an input layer, some hidden layers, and finally an output layer. Each layer will learn to transform its input data into a slightly more abstract and composite representation, which is generally a better representation of the data for the given task. The data can be in various forms. For example, in an image recognition application, the raw input may be a matrix of pixels. The layers of the neural network are trained to represent the pixels of the image. For instance, the first representational layer may learn to encode the spatial structuring of the edges; the second layer might represent arrangements of edges; the third layer may identify the presence of human face components such as eyes and nose; and the fourth layer may identify that the image might be of a human face.

Each layer of a deep neural network has an enormous number of processing units called neurons. Each neuron has its own representation of knowledge that it has learned during the processing of training till now. These layers are completely connected to the preceding and succeeding layers, that is layer $L$ is connected to both $L-1$ and $L+1$ layers. The final/output layer can contain any number of units depending on the function of the system. One of the main features of neural networks is that they are adaptive. Neural networks can adapt their synaptic weights to any change in the world. This property is also useful while training the network. The neural network will adapt its weights to provide a better representation of the information about the world. In a practical context, a neural network is trained on huge data sets. The process of training involves providing the input samples to the network and teaching the network what the desired output should be. For example, in order to train a neural network to identify the faces of actors, one might train it by using it in samples which contain labeled data of actors and nonactors to predict the labels of the input samples. Providing the desired labels to the network enables the model to improve its knowledge by adjusting its weights, eventually improving its output.

The most common algorithm used for updating the weights of the neural network is the gradient descent algorithm [3]. According to the gradient descent algorithm, we update the weights of the network based on the gradient of the loss function with respect to the weight. The intuition behind this is that, if we plot a graph of the loss function vs. the weight, we get a curve representing the value of the loss with respect to the weight. Since our goal is to minimize the loss function, we need to find the set of weights such that the loss is minimum, that is, the weight corresponding to the lowest point of the curve. To obtain such a graph however, we need to have calculated the loss for a huge number of weights, which is impractical. Instead, we take an arbitrary value for the weight, initially, and compute the derivative of the loss with respect to the weight. This gives us the slope of the curve at that point. The slope will give us an intuition of the direction in which we need to update the weight. Using this, we can update the weights in that direction instead of random updates. However, we still do not know the magnitude of the update. For this purpose, we use the hyperparameter called learning rate. The learning rate controls how big a step we take toward the minimum value of the loss function. Learning rate plays a very important role while training a neural network.

## 4.2.3 Deep learning architectures

There are many different architectures that are used for deep learning. This section explores some of the best-known architectures.

### 4.2.3.1 Recurrent neural networks

A recurrent neural network (RNN) is one of the basic architectures. Many of the advanced architectures today are inspired by RNNs. The key feature of an RNN is that the network has feedback connections, unlike a traditional feedforward neural network. This feedback loop allows the RNN to model the effects of the earlier parts of the sequence on the later part of the sequence, which is a very important feature when it comes to modeling sequences [4].

There are many different architectures for RNNs. One of the key differences in the architectures is the feedback within the network. Typically, RNNs can be "unfolded" in time and trained using back-propagation through time, where the same set of weights is used for a layer across multiple timesteps and updated using the gradients similar to the back-propagation algorithm. A generic structure of an RNN is as shown in Fig. 4.1.

### 4.2.3.2 Long short-term memory/gated recurrent unit

The concept of long short-term memory (LSTM) was introduced by Hochreiter and Schimdhuber in 1997 [5]. It is basically a type of RNN architecture, commonly used in various applications and products such as speech recognition systems.

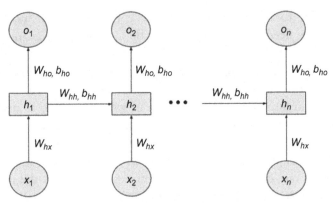

**Figure 4.1** A recurrent neural architecture.

A typical LSTM network has something called a memory cell. The memory cell can retain some information about the sequence, basically allowing it to remember the important features at the beginning of the sequence that might have an effect on the later parts of the sequence, instead of computing the output based on just the previous time step. For instance, if we were to predict the last word of the sentence "I was brought up in France. I speak fluent French." A regular RNN might realize that the word that comes after fluent must be a language. But in order to realize that the language is French, it needs to remember the context. This is where the LSTM comes in. LSTMs do not suffer from this long-range dependency problem.

The main components of the LSTM are its gates. There are three gates in an LSTM: the input gate, the forget gate, and the output gate. The input gate will control the inflow of new information into the cell. The forget gate will control the content of the memory, that is, the forget gate will decide if we want to forget a piece of information so we can store new information. The output gate will control when the information is used in the output from the cell. A gated recurrent unit (GRU) is a simplification of an LSTM. Unlike an LSTM, a GRU has just two gates. This kind of setup ultimately makes the execution faster as there is a lower number of weights to learn [6].

The two gates in the GRU are the update gate and the reset gate. The update gate is used to indicate the extent of previous cell knowledge that is to be retained. The reset gate defines how to incorporate the new input with the previous cell contents. We can think of an RNN as a GRU with the reset gate set to 1 and the update gate set to 0. Compared to LSTM, the GRU is simpler and faster to train but has less modeling capacity. With more data and computation power, an LSTM can be better than a GRU.

### 4.2.3.3 Convolutional neural network

A convolutional neural network (CNN) is a neural network architecture that was inspired by the biological visual cortex in animals [7]. CNNs are widely used for image-processing applications. Early efforts at designing an efficient CNN were mainly focused on handwritten character recognition. One of the most successful architectures for this task was LeNet.

LeNet [8] is a CNN architecture made up of several layers which basically performs the feature extraction followed by classification. The feature extraction layers are the convolution and pooling layers, while the fully connected layers perform the classification task. Initially the image is fed into the convolution layer, which extracts features from the image. These features are then fed to the pooling layer, which can be considered as a method of dimensionality reduction of these features (through downsampling). Then, another layer of convolution and maximum pooling is applied to the features and then it is connected to the fully connected layer. The fully connected layer will classify the image to its respective labels. The network is trained through back-propagation.

The use of layers in this fashion opened many doors to various deep learning applications. Video processing [9], natural language processing (NLP) [10], etc. also make use of CNN. For instance, recent applications of CNNs and LSTMs lead to real-time models that can create captions for images and videos [11,12]. These are systems where an image or video can be briefed about using the natural language. CNNs are used in this context to process the video or the image to give an intermediate output, which is then converted to the final output of the system by another model (perhaps an RNN or an LSTM).

### 4.2.3.4 Deep belief networks

The DBN is a multilayer network where each pair of connected layers is basically a restricted Boltzmann machine. A DBN can be represented as a stack of restricted Boltzmann machines [13].

In a typical DBN, the input layer will learn abstract representation of the raw input and the output layer is responsible for classification of the inputs. Unlike regular neural network training, we train the DBN in two steps: unsupervised pretraining and supervised fine-tuning.

The unsupervised pretraining makes the DBN learn to reconstruct its input. The result of this reconstruction is then fed to the next layer and then appears as an input to the next layer. The next layer learns to reconstruct its input and the result is fed to further layers. This process continues until each layer is pretrained. After the pretraining is completed, labels are applied to the output nodes and learning takes place through back-propagation or gradient descent.

### 4.2.3.5 Deep stacking networks

A deep stacking network (DSN) is different from a deep learning framework because it is a deep set of individual networks with their own hidden layers, unlike one big deep neural net [14]. As the network size grows, training the network gets harder. As a response to this, DSN views training as a set of individual training tasks rather than one single training task.

The DSN consists of a set of units, each one being a subnetwork in the hierarchy of the DSN. For instance, consider a DSN with two modules, each module containing an input, a hidden layer, and an output layer. These modules are stacked on top of one another, effectively making the output of the first unit as the input to the second unit. The second module also receives the original input vector. This allows the network to learn more complex representations of the task that a single network could not learn.

Coming to the problem of training such a big network, the DSN allows for training of each module independently. This allows for isolation of tasks and parallelization of the training, effectively making the problem of training a deep network easy.

## 4.2.4 Applications of deep learning

### 4.2.4.1 Computer vision

Humans can sense the world around them using visual perception through their eyes. Enabling a computer to do this as well is one of the main goals of computer vision.

Deep learning plays a major role in modern computer vision tasks. One of the most recent breakthroughs in the field of computer vision was the task of restoring pixels in an image. Given an image with a low pixel density, the deep learning model is supposed to guess what the image looks like at a higher resolution. Google brain researchers were able to build a system using a method called the "Pixel Recursive Super

Resolution," which was able to significantly improve the resolution of photos of human faces [15].

Photo OCR is another major application of deep learning models in computer vision. Given an image which contains text, the goal of the deep learning model is to retrieve the text from the image. Most state-of-the-art models use techniques like CNN and LSTM [16,17].

### 4.2.4.2 Speech recognition

Speech recognition is a part of our everyday lives. We can find it almost everywhere, from home automation gadgets to simple watches. Speech recognition has always been around, but deep learning has made it possible to recognize speech accurately enough to use it outside a controlled environment.

So how exactly does deep learning accomplish the task of speech recognition? Let us break down the steps for this purpose. The first thing we need to consider is the input to the system. The input of speech is nothing but sound waves. These sound waves are one dimensional, generally represented as a spectrogram. At every moment in time, this spectrogram will have a single value, which is the height of the wave. This can be modeled as a sequence input and thus we need a network that is capable of modeling sequences. LSTMs are quite capable of modeling sequences and have contributed greatly in mapping the spectrogram signals to words [18].

### 4.2.4.3 Natural language processing

NLP is the capability of a system to process human spoken language. Traditionally, humans communicate with machines through programming languages which are precise and unambiguous, unlike the natural language that we use to communicate with each other.

Current research on NLP is mainly concentrated on enterprise search. Enterprise search allows users to query data sets by posing questions in human-understandable language. The task of the machine is to understand the query as a human would and return an answer. NLP can also be used to interpret and analyze text, and extract useful information from it. Text data can include a patients' medical records, a president's speech, etc.

One of the main use cases of NLP is sentiment analysis [19]. Sentiment analysis helps data scientists assess comments on social media to evaluate the general attitude toward a business brand, or analyze the notes from customer service teams to improve the overall service.

NLP models are used in some of the core technologies for machine translation [20]. The models help convert the text in one language to another.

So how does one work with NLP? Current approaches are mainly based on deep learning techniques such as RNNs, LSTMs, etc. The main hurdle for deep learning-based NLP is the availability of data. Deep learning models require large data sets to work with and generalize well.

Earlier approaches to NLP were mainly rule-based. Rule-based approaches mainly involved algorithms with strict rules to look for certain phrases and sequences and perform operations based on these rules. This makes it very rigid and less robust to changes in the nuances of the language and also required a lot of manual intervention. Deep learning techniques allow for a more flexible approach and lets the model learn from examples.

There are many vague elements that appear in human language. For instance, consider the statement "Cloud computing insurance should be part of every service level agreement (SLA). A good SLA ensures an easier night's sleep—even in the cloud," the word cloud refers to Cloud computing and SLA stands for service level agreement. With the help of deep learning techniques, we can effectively train models that can identify such elements.

One of the main advantages of improvements in NLP is the types of data that can be analyzed. A lot of the data being generated day to day is natural language data. Advances in NLP make it possible to use these data and learn from it.

## 4.3 Generative adversarial networks

Before discussing generative adversarial networks (GANs), one should understand the concept of adversarial training. Adversarial training in machine learning is a training procedure in which multiple models are trained to learn competing goals. This is an interesting mode of training due to the semisupervised effects of training.

### 4.3.1 What are generative adversarial networks?

A GAN, as the name suggests, is a neural architecture that is used to train generative models using adversarial training. Generative adversarial neural networks were first introduced by Ian Goodfellow et al. [21] in 2014 as a class of AI models that are trained as a set of two neural networks defined as elements of a zero–sum framework. Through their paper, they proved how we can train a neural network to generate pictures that seem at least superficially original to human viewers. The pictures generated by a model trained in such a manner usually have many realistic characteristics like natural features of a human face, such as the nose, eyes, ears, and hair, even though in tests, human observers can distinguish generated pictures from real pictures in many cases.

In a GAN, one network generates samples (generator) and the other identifies them (discriminator). On a high level, the generator network learns to map a latent space of a particular data distribution of interest, while the discriminator tries to distinguish the samples from the true data and the samples generated by the generator network. The generator's goal is to increase the discriminator's error rate and the discriminator's objective is to find the samples generated by the generator accurately.

In a practical perspective, a target data set is used to pretrain the discriminator. Training a discriminator network involves providing it with samples from the data set until a level of accuracy is achieved. The generator is seeded with a random input, usually sampled from a standard data distribution like a multivariate normal distribution. After this, the samples generated by the generator network are classified by the discriminator. The output of the discriminator is back-propagated to both networks in order to train the generator to produce better samples and the discriminator is trained to classify the samples more accurately. In the case of images, a generator is typically a deconvolutional neural network, whereas the discriminator is usually a convolutional neural network.

The idea to train models in a competitive environment was first proposed by the trio of Li, Gauci, and Gross in 2013 [22]. Their method was intended for behavioral inference.

It was called Turing learning [22] as it was similar to a Turing test [23]. In Turing learning, a generalization of GANS, models need not be just neural networks. Moreover, the discriminator models in Turing learning are set up as active interrogators in a Turing test by allowing them to influence the way a data set is obtained. The proposal of adversarial training dates back to 1992 by Schmidhuber [24].

## 4.3.2 Why should we use generative adversarial networks?

As will be discussed in further sections, GANs are exceptionally effective in generative modeling and can help in training discriminators in a semisupervised setting to help in eliminating the human involvement in data labeling. Moreover, GANs help in situations where the data have unbalanced classes or underrepresented samples. In cases like that, generative modeling has proven to be helpful in generating samples as close as possible to the actual data distribution [21].

### 4.3.3 Applications of generative adversarial network

In recent times, GANs have reportedly been used to produce samples of very realistic pictures in order to visualize new architectural designs, fashion elements [25], and computer graphic assets. Facebook has claimed to use these networks for internal purposes. GANs have also been used to model patterns in video for basic motion aspects [26]. They were also used to remap 3D representations of objects from 2D images [27]. In 2017, a fully convolutional neural network was trained for the automated process of texture synthesis through perpetual loss, which can be useful for image enhancement. The system resulted in generating images with higher quality at high magnification [28]. A painting called "Edmond de Belamy," which was created by a GAN, was sold for $432,500.

GANs have received a lot of recognition in the gaming community for uses in modding games. Many old video game textures are of low quality and difficult to use while modding games. Using GANs, we can upscale these low-quality images and create an ultrahigh resolution. This can then be down-sampled for the game's resolution quality. With proper training, GANs have been proven to generate images that are clearer and sharper than those the original developer intended, and yet preserve the game's original level of detail. Games such as "Final Fantasy VIII," "Resident Evil Remake HD Remaster," and "Max Payne" are well-known examples where GANs were extensively used.

### 4.4 A case study on generative adversarial networks

### 4.4.1 Basics of generative adversarial networks

Before we start discussing GANs, let us first understand what a generative model is. Generative modeling is a technique used to describe the phenomena in data, effectively allowing computers to understand the distribution of the data. In simple terms, we are teaching the computer to generate data from given sample data by understanding the distribution of the sample data.

So what is the point of modeling the data? Well, first of all, the model learns the true distribution of the data. Second, the model can generate previously unseen data.

And what exactly is the goal of a generative model? Simple, to generate realistic content. By realistic content, we mean content as close as possible to the true distribution of the data. An ideal generative model would generate content so similar to the real distribution of the data that it would be impossible to distinguish it from the real data.

When we talk about generating content similar to real data, we are not trying to make the generator learn an identity function. Instead, we try to learn the probability distribution of the real data. We will say that if we have a parameter $W$, we wish to find the parameter $W$ that maximizes the likelihood of real samples. While training the model, we find the $W$ that minimizes the distance between the estimate of real data and the generated samples.

Now that we know what to do, how do you quantify the distance? A proven metric to compare two data distributions is the Kullback−Leibler divergence (KLD) [29]. This works on the principle that maximizing the log-likelihood is equivalent to minimizing the KLD. Hence, to create a good generative model, we have to minimize the KLD between the actual data and the synthetic data generated by the model. With this note, we can explore two types of generative models:

1. *An explicit distribution generative model* is based on an explicitly defined generative model distribution. Through training on data samples, it then refines the explicitly defined model distribution. For example, consider a variational auto-encoder (VAE). A VAE needs a prior distribution and likelihood distribution to start with. With these two distributions, the VAE will be trained to arrive at a variational approximation to actual data.

2. In contrast to the above models, *implicitly distributed generative models* do not use a predefined approximation for model distribution. Such models are usually trained by sampling data from parameterized distribution indirectly. A GAN falls under this category.

### 4.4.1.1 The architecture

As discussed earlier, GANs are made up of two components, a generator (G) and a discriminator (D). These two networks work as adversaries pushing the performance of one another.

### 4.4.1.2 The generator

The generator is the agent that is used for producing fake examples of data. It maps the input of a latent variable (which is referred as $z$) to a data point in the learned approximate data distribution of the original data set. Latent variables are available in hidden layers of the network. In the case of GANs we use a "latent space" that we can sample from. We continuously stride this latent space which, when you have a trained GAN, will have substantial and understandable effects on the output. If the latent variable is denoted with $z$ and the target variable is denoted with $x$, the generator is trained to learn a function that maps from $z$ (the latent space) to $x$ (the approximated data distribution).

### 4.4.1.3 The discriminator

The role of the discriminator is to discriminate. It is used to guide the generator toward the goal of generating a better sample. The output of the discriminator will be a higher probability if the network learns a sample to be real.

### 4.4.1.4 The adversarial competition

The generator and discriminator are modeled in a dependent framework to learn from each other. They try to maximize opposite objectives: a generator to synthesize samples close to real data distribution and a discriminator to detect such synthesized samples. The name adversarial is the result of such opposing objectives of the components of a GAN.

### 4.4.1.5 The math

The training of the generator and the discriminator is carried out to minimize the loss function as defined below:

$$\min_{tt}\max_D L(G, D) = E(x - P_{\text{data}}(x))[\log(D(x))] + E(z - P_{\text{latent}}(z))[\log(1 - D(G(z)))]$$

To elaborate this equation, consider $D$, which tries to maximize this equation. $E[\log()]$ represents the log-likelihood of the sample. $D$ tries to identify the generated sample from the actual sample. Therefore the first term represents the expected log-likelihood of the discriminator. On the other hand, $G$ tries to minimize this equation. The second term in the equation represents the expected log-likelihood of $D$ given a sample generated by $G$. The $(1 - D(G(z)))$ represents the expectation of the generator

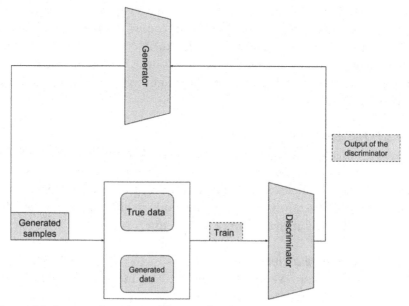

**Figure 4.2** A generative adversarial network.

that a sample generated by it fools the discriminator. Thus, GAN is setup as a min−max framework among the discriminator and the generator. A typical GAN architecture is shown in Fig. 4.2.

## 4.4.2 Using generative adversarial networks for generating synthetic images

Now we use a simple image data set and learn the implicit data distribution of these images. The generator learns to generate samples from this learnt distribution using the GAN architecture described.

The goal of such an implementation is to make the generator learn the distribution of the training data. Once the generator has successfully learnt the distribution, we can make the generator generate samples from this distribution that are very similar to the real data. Although the Modified National Institute of Standards and Technology (MNIST) data have a relatively small distribution, we can extend this approach to much more complicated data sets like animals, faces of celebrities, etc.

For the experiment, we will use the MNIST data set, which is a large database of handwritten numerics, commonly used as a benchmark for various image-processing tasks.

The MNIST database contains 70,000 images split into training and testing sets in the ration of 6:1. The data consist of 10 classes (0−9) of handwritten images normalized and scaled to 28 × 28 resolution. For the experiment, we only consider the training samples and ignore the training labels. The GAN is used to learn the function to generate images as close as possible to handwritten digits.

### 4.4.2.1 The experiment
Training a GAN is not an easy task. GANs are known to be very difficult to train and we must be very careful while training one. For the experiment, we have handpicked two architectures that have worked well with the MNIST data set, a simple neural network architecture and a complicated convolutional neural network architecture.

### 4.4.2.2 The simple architecture
As the name suggests, we used a neural network model with stacked hidden layers (with activations). As discussed above, a GAN contains two parts, the generator and the discriminator. Let us take a closer look at the simple architecture:
1. *Generator.* In short, the generator takes a 100 dimensional input and generates a 28 × 28 image. It consists of three hidden layers with a leaky rectified linear unit (ReLU) activation and the output layer has a tanh activation. The output of the last layer is reshaped to form a 28 × 28 image, which resembles a MNIST image.
2. *Discriminator.* In short, the discriminator takes a 28 × 28 dimensional image and predicts the probability of the image being real. The discriminator is made up of two hidden layers with a leaky ReLU activation and an output layer with a sigmoid activation.

### 4.4.2.3 The convolutional neural network architecture
CNNs have been proven time and again to work very well with images. For the purpose of building a GAN however, there is a slight difference in the CNN architecture. Let us take a deeper look to get a better understanding.
1. *Generator.* Just like the previous architecture, the generator in the CNN architecture also takes a 100 dimensional input and gives a 28 × 28 dimensional output. The first hidden layer contains 12,544 dense hidden units with a leaky ReLU activation. The output of this layer is reshaped to a shape of (7, 7, 256). This reshaped image is then passed through a 2D convolution transpose layer with 128 filters and a

kernel size of 5, with the same padding (pad with 0 equally on both ends of the image). This is where it becomes different from the regular convolutional layers we see. A convolution transpose layer is basically a convolutional layer, but it learns to up-sample the input for a higher dimensional output. We apply a batch normalization activation followed by a leaky ReLU to this layer. The output shape of this layer would be a shape of (14, 14, 128). This is fed into another series of up-sampling, convolutional transpose with 64 filters and a kernel size of 5 with the same padding, batch normalization, and leaky ReLU activation. The output of this layer is of the shape (28, 28, 64). This output is fed into another layer of up-sampling, convolutional transpose with 32 filters, and a kernel size of 5 with same padding, batch normalization, and leaky ReLU activation which gives an output of shape (28, 28, 32). The last layer of the generator is a convolution transpose layer with a single filter and a kernel size of 5 with the same padding and an activation of tanh. The output of this is a (28, 28, 1) image, which is the same shape as an actual MNIST image.

2. *Discriminator:* The input layer in the discriminator accepts an image of the shape (28, 28, 1) and passes it to the first hidden layer which is a convolutional layer with a kernel size of 5, 64 filters, and a stride of 2, with the same padding. We apply leaky ReLU activation and dropout. The output of the layer is of the shape (14, 14, 64). The next three layers are very similar to the previous layer but with kernel sizes of 128, 256, and 512, respectively. The output of this is an image of shape (4, 4, 512), which is flattened and fed into a dense layer of one unit, which has a softmax activation to predict the validity of the image.

### 4.4.2.4 The training

Now that we have defined the model architecture, how do we go about the training? The answer is simple. We perform the training in two steps. First, we logically connect the generator (learner) and the discriminator (teacher) models such that the output of the learner is fed as input to the discriminator, making it one big network which takes a 100 dimensional noise vector and outputs a probability. While training this big network, we make sure that we only explicitly weight the learner, and not the teacher. While training, we supply the ground truth (labels) of the images as 1, indicating that it is a real image. You may be wondering why we set the ground truth of the images as real even though the image is fake. This is because the aim of the learner is to "deceive" the teacher. Setting the image label as 1 instead of 0 would mean that the loss function will be low if the discriminator predicted the output as 1, and high if the discriminator predicted the output as 0. What this means is that if the discriminator predicted the output as 0, then the generator failed to "fool" the discriminator. This loss will be back-propagated to adjust the weights of the generator so that it will be better suited to generate content that might fool the discriminator, effectively forcing the loss to a minimum. In the second step, we use the images generated from the generator and the real images from the MNIST data set and label them as 0 and 1, respectively. We train the discriminator with this setting, effectively making the discriminator "fool proof."

We train the GAN by running the two steps mentioned above multiple times. The generator will learn to generate better images and the discriminator will learn to differentiate between the real images and the images generated from the generator. At convergence, the generator is supposed to generate images which are indistinguishable from the real images and the discriminator will predict a probability of .5 for every image (because they are actually indistinguishable).

The training was for 50,000 epochs with the ADAM optimizer [30] with a learning rate of 0.0002. The results are discussed below.

### 4.4.2.5 Results

The results of the architectures are show in Figs. 4.3−4.6. As we can see in the images generated by the generators in the two different

**Figure 4.3** Output of simple architecture after the first epoch.

**Figure 4.4** Output of simple architecture after 50,000 epochs.

**Figure 4.5** Output of convolutional neural network architecture after the first epoch.

**Figure 4.6** Output of convolutional neural network architecture after 50,000 epochs.

architectures, the CNN architecture gave much better results than the simple neural network.

### 4.4.3 Implications of results for fake news detection

GANs have the capability of learning the distribution of the data effectively enough to create believable fake content. One of the major hurdles of a deep neural network is the scarcity of data available to train the model, which makes us restrict the size of the network or risk overfitting the data. With GANs, we have access to lots of machine-generated data that can be used to train deeper networks and build a robust system to detect the fake examples from the real ones. Current systems use GANs to detect fake paintings effectively. A similar idea can be transferred to the domain of fake news detection. Using a GAN that can effectively generate text similar to the real text, we can build robust systems that are capable of detecting machine-generated news effectively.

### 4.4.4 Problems with generative adversarial networks for text data

Now that we have seen the effectiveness of GANs for generative modeling, let us look into why we need new approaches to train GANs for text data. GANs update the generator model based on the gradient update received from the discriminator. For example, in the case of images, the generator trains to generate the pixel value. Consider a pixel value generated as 0.57. The generator weights can be updated to generate a pixel value of 0.58 according to the output of the discriminator. This makes sense in the case that the data have continuous data distribution. But, in the case of text, the data distribution is discrete. In that case, GANs cannot be updated in the same way that they are updated in the case of continuously distributed data.

For example, consider an instance where the GAN produces an output "the girl is handsome". The token "handsome" cannot be updated to "handsome + 0.01." It should be updated from "handsome" to "beautiful" all the way. In such cases, the traditional GANs cannot be used for training. The inventor of GANs, Ian Goodfellow has quoted [31] this by stressing the fact that the working principle of GANs is based on learning the gradient of the discriminator network's output with reference to the generated data sample and updating the network weights to improve the generated data to make them more realistic. These updates are only possible within continuously spaced data. If the data are based on discrete numbers, making slight updates would be impossible. In the case of NLP, the data are represented in a discrete space with words or characters as tokens. This results in inapplicability of GANs to NLP data.

In order to overcome this drawback, a recent advancement called "SeqGAN" has been employed to use GANs for NLP tasks. This works on the principles of reinforcement learning (RL) and is discussed in detail below.

## 4.4.5 Introduction to SeqGAN, a generative adversarial network architecture for text data

SeqGAN stands for sequence GAN, which was introduced in 2017 [32] as an attempt to use GAN for text generation tasks. In order to overcome the problems discussed earlier, SeqGAN uses RL to train the generator. In a SeqGAN, the process of text generation is considered as a sequential process that is performed by a decision model. The generator is set up as an RL agent whose action is to predict the next word given a sequence of words or tokens. The RL agent (generator)'s state is defined as the set of tokens generated till the current time step and the action is defined as the prediction of a token given the current state, that is, the set of tokens generated till now. In order to avoid the problem with gradient propagation to generator in the case of discrete output, the generator is trained with a stochastic parameterized policy. In SeqGAN, for policy gradient, Monte Carlo search [33] is employed to arrive at the approximation of action-state values. Using this, the generator is trained directly using policy gradient update, which completely avoids the difficulty of differentiation with discrete outputs in the case of a standard GAN architecture.

Policy gradient methods [34] are most frequently used in RL. The principle of policy gradient is that the action that is taken by the agent is based directly on the observations that the model experiences on choosing the corresponding actions. That is "it observes and it acts." In brief, agent learns through experience. In specific to Monte Carlo methods, to update the policy gradients works in a rollout fashion where entire episodes of actions are rolled out to train and approximate the policy gradient. In a SeqGAN, the generator uses the REINFORCE algorithm to update its weights based on the prediction of the teacher (discriminator) network. In the REINFORCE algorithm, an episode of actions is sampled from the policy and the total rewards for the particular episode is calculated to update the policy using gradient. The total reward is calculated using the

Bellman equation. Since it is a stochastic model, only a few sampled episodes based on the policy are used to approximate the policy gradient.

In SeqGAN, the output of the discriminator is provided as the reward to the generating agent. The issue with this is that the discriminator provides the reward only at the end of the sequence. Since we need to optimize the long-term reward of the token generation, we should not only take the seen tokens into account but also the predicted unseen outcomes. This is similar to strategic players of Go or chess, where immediate rewards are sacrificed for long-term returns [35]. Thus, to evaluate the action-value of the immediate state, we employ the Monte Carlo search on a roll-out policy to sample the remaining unseen tokens of the sequence. In SeqGAN, this roll-out policy is the same as the generator policy. Therefore by learning the action-value of the states, we in turn train the generator. The top-level architecture of SeqGAN is as shown in Fig. 4.7.

In a practical context, we run the roll-out policy for $N$ number of times to get a batch of $N$ sample sequences. These sequences are provided as negative samples for the discriminator. The positive examples are randomly sampled from the real data. These negative and positive samples are used to train the discriminator. A benefit of using the discriminator as the reward function is that it can be updated on the go, to improve the

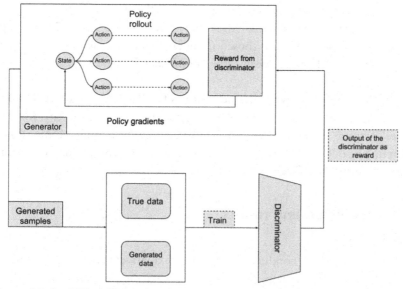

**Figure 4.7** SeqGAN architecture.

generator further in an iterative fashion. Therefore once the generator provides more realistic generated samples in the next run, we can update the discriminator to detect these samples. Similarly, each time a new discriminator model is available, we can use it to update the generator, thus placing them effectively in a zero-sum game. The following steps are followed in training a SeqGAN model:

1. Initially choose "$g$" and "$d$" as the number of steps the generator and discriminator are trained in, respectively, before arriving at a new model.
2. Pretrain the generator $G$ using maximum-likelihood estimation based on the real samples.
3. Generate a set of samples $S$ using $G$ to train the discriminator $D$.
4. Train $D$ using $S$ by minimizing the cross-entropy (using valid samples along with $S$).
5. Once pretraining is done, generate a batch of samples using $G$ and to compute the action-value of the current state for each token in the generated sequence. Then update the generator parameters using policy gradients. Repeat this $g$ times.
6. Once the generator is updated, use the current generator to generate a batch of negative examples $S$ and combine them with a sample of real samples to get the training batch.

    $T$. Using $T$, train the discriminator for the preferred number of epochs $k$. Repeat this step $d$ times.
7. Steps 5 and 6 are considered as one epoch of the SeqGAN training. Repeat these steps for a chosen number of times known as the number of epochs. This is ideally the number of steps required by the SeqGAN to converge.

In this way, SeqGAN is trained. In brief, a SeqGAN is a GAN architecture that overcomes the problem of gradient descent in GANs for discrete outputs by employing an RL-based approach and Monte Carlo search. Thus, it can be used to train text generators with an ideology similar to traditional GANs.

## 4.5 Experiment and results

### 4.5.1 Setup

This experiment is conducted using the extensive hardware capabilities made available by Amazon Web Services. A *p2.xlarge* instance was used to train the models. The instance uses a NVIDIA K80 graphics accelerator with 61 GB of RAM. The NVIDIA K80 graphics processor comes with 24 GB of video memory, which can be used to accelerate the deep learning workloads.

## 4.5.2 Process

The classifier is the agent responsible for identifying the data as fake or real. Unlike the discriminator, the classifier is built with a much larger model capacity. This allows the classifier to learn complex functions that results in much higher accuracy. The classifier is based on Google's BERT model [36]. The classifier is trained to distinguish the fake articles generated from the generator and the real articles from the data set. Once the desired accuracy is obtained, the model is used for prediction. The classification model is trained using the GAN technique. Using the technique, we do not need examples for both classes. Instead, using just the positive examples, we train a model that is capable of classifying the input into two classes. For the machine-generated content detection framework, we provide examples of real news articles to the GAN. The GAN then internally trains a fake content generator along with a classifier. The classifier is then trained to identify the real examples from the examples generated by the generator.

## 4.5.3 Results

The data set used for the training of the classification model consisted of 105,104 news headlines. This data set was randomly shuffled and split into training, validation, and testing sets with 40% of the headlines for training, 35% for validation, and 25% for testing, resulting in 40,990 headlines for training, 27,327 headlines for validation, and 36,788 headlines for testing. The training set is fed into the classifier, and the classifier is then tested on the testing set. The validation accuracy obtained was approximately equal to 95.3%. On testing, a testing accuracy of 94.8% was achieved.

The confusion matrix for the testing set is shown in Table 4.1.

**Table 4.1** Confusion matrix.

| Predicted | Generated | Real |
| --- | --- | --- |
| Actual | | |
| Generated | 15,759 | 1600 |
| Real | 307 | 19,121 |

## 4.6 Summary

In this chapter, we have presented the adverse affects of fake news on society, especially due to the increase in social media consumption. GANs have proven to be one of the most vital theoretical advances in deep learning in recent times. They have been shown to be exceptionally well suited for the tasks of learning data distribution. The effectiveness of GANs on image data has been presented along with the implications of such results for the domain of fake news. A variation of GAN called SeqGAN is presented as the initial steps toward applying GANs to NLP. A possible solution to fake news detection using SeqGAN is outlined and discussed in brief.

## References

[1] J. Bapu Ahire, Fake news detector AI, 2018. Retrieved from: <https://medium.com/@jayeshbahire/fake-news-detector-ai-991af18c2eb5>.

[2] C. Emma, Fake news: what it is, and how to spot it, 2019. Retrieved from: <https://www.weforum.org/agenda/2019/03/fake-news-what-it-is-and-how-to-spot-it/>.

[3] S. Ruder, An overview of gradient descent optimization algorithms, 2016. arXiv preprint arXiv:1609.04747.

[4] D.P. Mandic, J. Chambers, Recurrent Neural Networks for Prediction: Learning Algorithms, Architectures and Stability, John Wiley & Sons, Inc, 2001.

[5] S. Hochreiter, J. Schmidhuber, Long short-term memory, Neural Comput. 9 (8) (1997) 1735–1780.

[6] K. Cho, B. Van Merriënboer, C. Gulcehre, D. Bahdanau, F. Bougares, H. Schwenk, et al., Learning phrase representations using RNN encoder-decoder for statistical machine translation, 2014. arXiv preprint arXiv:1406.1078.

[7] S. Haykin, Neural Networks, vol. 2, Prentice Hall, New York, 1994.

[8] Y. LeCun, L. Bottou, Y. Bengio, P. Haffner, Gradient-based learning applied to document recognition, Proc. IEEE 86 (11) (1998) 2278–2324.

[9] A. Karpathy, G. Toderici, S. Shetty, T. Leung, R. Sukthankar, L. Fei-Fei, Large-scale video classification with convolutional neural networks, in: Proceedings of the IEEE Conference on Computer Vision and Pattern Recognition, IEEE, 2014, pp. 1725–1732.

[10] D. Britz, Understanding convolutional neural networks for NLP, 2015, <http://www.wildml.com/2015/11/understanding-convolutional-neuralnetworks-for-nlp/> (accessed 11.07.15).

[11] Q. You, H. Jin, Z. Wang, C. Fang, J. Luo, Image captioning with semantic attention, in: Proceedings of the IEEE Conference on Computer Vision and Pattern Recognition, 2016, pp. 4651–4659.

[12] C. Wang, H. Yang, C. Bartz, C. Meinel, Image captioning with deep bidirectional LSTMs, in: Proceedings of the 24th ACM International Conference on Multimedia, ACM, October 2016, pp. 988–997.

[13] G.E. Hinton, Deep belief networks, Scholarpedia 4 (5) (2009) 5947.

[14] L. Deng, X. He, J. Gao, Deep stacking networks for information retrieval, in: 2013 IEEE International Conference on Acoustics, Speech and Signal Processing, IEEE, May 2013, pp. 3153–3157.

[15] R. Dahl, M. Norouzi, J. Shlens, Pixel recursive super resolution, in: Proceedings of the IEEE International Conference on Computer Vision, IEEE, 2017, pp. 5439–5448.

[16] C.Y. Lee, S. Osindero, Recursive recurrent nets with attention modeling for ocr in the wild, in: Proceedings of the IEEE Conference on Computer Vision and Pattern Recognition, IEEE, 2016, pp. 2231–2239.

[17] C. Bartz, H. Yang, C. Meinel, STN-OCR: a single neural network for text detection and text recognition, 2017. arXiv preprint arXiv:1707.08831.

[18] J. Shen, R. Pang, R.J. Weiss, M. Schuster, N. Jaitly, Z. Yang, et al., Natural tts synthesis by conditioning wavenet on mel spectrogram predictions, in: 2018 IEEE International Conference on Acoustics, Speech and Signal Processing (ICASSP), IEEE, April 2018, pp. 4779–4783.

[19] B. Pang, L. Lee, Opinion mining and sentiment analysis, Found. Trends Inform. Retriev. 2 (1–2) (2008) 1–135.

[20] Y. Wu, M. Schuster, Z. Chen, Q.V. Le, M. Norouzi, W. Macherey, et al., Google's neural machine translation system: bridging the gap between human and machine translation, 2016. arXiv preprint arXiv:1609.08144.

[21] I. Goodfellow, J. Pouget-Abadie, M. Mirza, B. Xu, D. Warde-Farley, S. Ozair, et al., Generative adversarial nets, in: Advances in Neural Information Processing Systems, 2014, pp. 2672–2680.

[22] W. Li, M. Gauci, R. Gross, Turing learning: a metric-free approach to inferring behavior and its application to swarms, Swarm Intell. 10 (3) (2016) 211–243.

[23] A.M. Turing, Computing machinery and intelligence, Parsing the Turing Test, Springer, Dordrecht, 2009, pp. 23–65.

[24] J. Schmidhuber, Learning factorial codes by predictability minimization, Neural Comput. 4 (6) (1992) 863–879.

[25] S. Zhu, R. Urtasun, S. Fidler, D. Lin, C. Change Loy, Be your own prada: fashion synthesis with structural coherence, in: Proceedings of the IEEE International Conference on Computer Vision, IEEE, 2017, pp. 1680–1688.

[26] J. Merel, Y. Tassa, S. Srinivasan, J. Lemmon, Z. Wang, G. Wayne, et al., Learning human behaviors from motion capture by adversarial imitation, 2017. arXiv preprint arXiv:1707.02201.

[27] J. Wu, C. Zhang, T. Xue, B. Freeman, J. Tenenbaum, Learning a probabilistic latent space of object shapes via 3D generative-adversarial modeling, in: Advances in Neural Information Processing Systems, 2016, pp. 82–90.

[28] C. Ledig, L. Theis, F. Huszár, J. Caballero, A. Cunningham, A. Acosta, et al., Photo-realistic single image super-resolution using a generative adversarial network, in: Proceedings of the IEEE Conference on Computer Vision and Pattern Recognition, 2017, pp. 4681–4690.

[29] J.R. Hershey, P.A. Olsen, Approximating the Kullback Leibler divergence between Gaussian mixture models, in: 2007 IEEE International Conference on Acoustics, Speech and Signal Processing-ICASSP'07, vol. 4, IEEE, April 2007, pp. IV–317.

[30] D.P. Kingma, J. Ba, Adam: a method for stochastic optimization, 2014. arXiv preprint arXiv:1412.6980.

[31] W. William, Generative Adversarial Networks for Text, Reddit. Reddit, Inc. Web. January 12, 2016.

[32] L. Yu, W. Zhang, J. Wang, Y. Yu, Seqgan: sequence generative adversarial nets with policy gradient, in: Thirty-First AAAI Conference on Artificial Intelligence, February 2017.

[33] C.B. Browne, E. Powley, D. Whitehouse, S.M. Lucas, P.I. Cowling, P. Rohlfshagen, et al., A survey of monte carlo tree search methods, in: IEEE Transactions on Computational Intelligence and AI in Games, vol. 4(1), 2012, pp. 1−43.

[34] R.S. Sutton, D.A. McAllester, S.P. Singh, Y. Mansour, Policy gradient methods for reinforcement learning with function approximation, in: Advances in Neural Information Processing Systems, 2000, pp. 1057−1063.

[35] D. Silver, A. Huang, C.J. Maddison, A. Guez, L. Sifre, G. Van Den Driessche, et al., Mastering the game of Go with deep neural networks and tree search, Nature 529 (7587) (2016) 484.

[36] J. Devlin, et al., Bert: pre-training of deep bidirectional transformers for language understanding, 2018, arXiv preprint arXiv:1810.04805.

## Further reading

L. Deng, The MNIST database of handwritten digit images for machine learning research [best of the web], IEEE Signal Process. Mag. 29 (6) (2012) 141−142.

# CHAPTER 5

# Hybrid computational intelligence for healthcare and disease diagnosis

**R. Manikandan[1], Ambeshwar Kumar[1] and Deepak Gupta[2]**
[1]School of Computing SASTRA Deemed University, Thanjavur, India
[2]Department of Computer Science and Engineering, Maharaja Agrasen Institute of Technology, Guru Gobind Singh Indraprastha University, Delhi, India

## 5.1 Introduction

One of the innovative environments for building hybrid intelligent systems is computational intelligence. With the aid of computational intelligence that employs an innovative framework, intelligent hybrid environments, namely neural networks, fuzzy inference systems (FISs), evolutionary computation, and swarm intelligence have been modeled. The majority of these hybridization methods however, apply an ad hoc design, rationalized by definite application domains. Deep learning techniques, such as convolutional neural networks and recurrent neural networks (RNNs) are helping to achieve high performance rates for segmenting of images. In image segmentation the given image is split into segments that are analogous with each other in one or more characteristics under certain conditions, and medical image classification is used to classify the medical images into several elements to assist medical practitioners or physicists in diagnosing disease with high accuracy and in the minimum time.

Due to the absence of a customary environment, it frequently remains cumbersome to differentiate the several hybrid systems theoretically and to assess their execution analogously. Different adaptive hybrid computational intelligence environments have been designed and structured. Many of these materials and methods utilize a synthesis of several knowledge representation strategies, decision-making methods, and learning techniques to solve computational tasks. This combination focuses on controlling the disadvantages of individual materials and methods via hybridization of several techniques.

*Hybrid Computational Intelligence*
DOI: https://doi.org/10.1016/B978-0-12-818699-2.00006-8

The remainder of this chapter is formulated as follows. In Section 5.1.1, a brief description of hybrid intelligence is presented. Section 5.2 describes medical image segmentation and classification. Section 5.3 describes the disease and diagnosis approach; Section 5.4 describes the identification of brain activity using a state classifier, while Section 5.5 discusses genomics. Section 5.6 discusses health bioinformatics, and Section 5.7 presents the discussion section for the chapter. Section 5.8 contains the conclusion of the chapter.

## 5.1.1 A brief description of hybrid intelligence

Each technology possesses advantages and disadvantages. In many real-world scenarios, it is necessary to integrate several intelligent technologies. Each technology indemnifies for the weak areas of the other technology. A hybrid intelligent system is one that integrates two intelligent technologies. For example, integrating a neural network with a fuzzy technique results in a hybrid neuro fuzzy technique. The integration of probabilities reasoning and neural networks hence forms the fundamentals or essentials of soft computing. This soft computing is considered as an unfolding perspective to construct hybrid intelligent systems competent of reasoning and learning in an unresolved and vague framework.

### 5.1.1.1 Example hybrid intelligence: hybrid neuro-expert system

Fig. 5.1 shows the combination of a neural network with an expert system resulting in a hybrid neuro-expert system.

As shown in Fig. 5.1, the test data form the input for both the neural network system and the expert system. The result therefore forms a trained neural network system and a trained expert system. The neural network units are comprised of several neurons, differentiated by weights via layers. As also illustrated in the figure, the first layer is comprised of two neurons, the second layer is comprised of three neurons and, finally, the third layer is comprised of two neurons. On the other hand, in the trained expert system, rules are extracted via the neural knowledge base resulting in the implicit rules. The reasoning prerequisites describe to the user how the neural expert system reaches a specific result when operating with new input data. The user interface forms the means of communicating between the user and the neural expert system. Finally, the inference engine manages the information passage in the system and commences reasoning over the neural knowledge base.

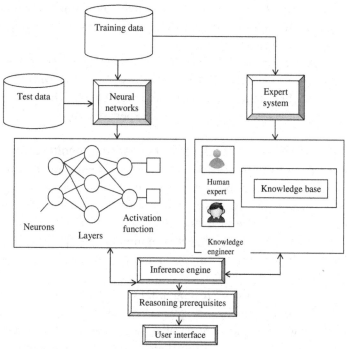

**Figure 5.1** Schematic view of a neuro-expert system.

## 5.1.1.2 Overview of a hybrid intelligent system: neural expert system

- Expert systems depend on logical reasoning and decision trees in addition to concentration made by creating human reasoning. On the other hand, neural networks depend on processing the raw data in a parallel fashion and concentrate on modeling a human brain.
- The second main constituent of the expert systems is that the expert system serves the brain as a black box and neural network consider as its formation and consequences, specifically at its potentiality to master.
- The knowledge in the rule-based expert system is denoted by if—then conditional rules, whereas the knowledge in neural networks is cached as synaptic weights connecting neurons.
- In the case of expert systems, knowledge is said to be split into discrete rules and the user has the perspective to perceive and figure out the portion of knowledge applied by the system. In the case of neural networks, single synaptic weight is not said to be chosen by the user as a distinct section of knowledge. Hence, the knowledge here is

integrated into the entire network, where individual pieces are not said to be attained. Therefore changes in the synaptic weight may result in unforeseeable results.

- By integrating the merits of neural networks and expert systems, a more robust and efficient expert system is said to be organized.
- Hence, a hybrid framework that integrates a neural network and an expert system is referred to as a neural expert system.

### 5.1.1.3 Evolution of computational intelligence in health care

The emergence of the Information Age, also frequently referred to as the Digital Age, has had an overwhelming impact on the health sciences. Enormous amounts of data sets now pass through several areas of healthcare organizations. Hence, it is essential to extract knowledge and utilize it effectively in all aspects. Intelligent computer systems [1] bestow a foundation to health professionals involved both in medical and managerial areas.

Among these systems, increasing popularity has been gained in the area of computational intelligence given their potentiality to manage large amounts of raw data and inconclusive information. This involves the comprehensive investigation of the sketch of intelligent agents. In addition, an intelligent agent is also referred to as a system that acts in an intelligent manner, where it initially identifies the situation and its objective, and performs the task accordingly, with the involvement of flexibility to uncertain environments and dynamic objectives, analyzing from its experience and taking suitable alternatives according to the noncognitive disadvantages and restricted calculations.

Computational intelligence forms the origin of the basis of computational materials and methods according to biological concepts. The crucial pillars that formulate this field are neural networks, expert systems, genetic algorithms, and fuzzy systems. Computational intelligence methods have been profitably utilized in several real-world applications with heterogeneity of engineering problems. Computational intelligence also is found to be highly useful in the medical research area.

In addition, computational intelligence provides a sizeable guarantee for strengthening several characteristics of healthcare practice, consisting of management of disease in a clinical manner, such as avoidance, detection, therapy, and follow-up. Apart from the above characteristics, managerial aspects of patients, such as patient information and healthcare delivery, are also maintained. Intelligent computing in medical imaging describes technologically advanced method to receive the response from an real time environment [2]. The recent advancement of intelligent computing techniques for analysis of biomedical applications can be summarized as the use of specialized statistical, machine learning, pattern recognition, data abstraction, and visualization of tools for processing data and for discovery of the mechanisms that produced the data.

### 5.1.1.4 Healthcare safety issues

As far as health care is concerned, one of the most serious issues of real concern is patient safety. Hence, it is called health "care." Over the past few years, the level of scrutiny has been increased in regard to clinical organizations with respect to the safety aspects of patients and improvements occurring from demand through public voices. In addition to the cost, effectiveness, and the method of processing, concern toward patient safety has become one of the most critical issues covering health care today. In a broad way, the healthcare domain has been categorized into four analytical parts: descriptive, diagnostic, predictive, and prescriptive analytics.

Descriptive analytics consists of elaborating current situations and reporting on them. Many techniques are employed to perform this level of analytics. It aims to enlighten why certain proceedings have occurred and what the factors are that triggered them. For example, diagnostic analysis attempts to understand the reasons behind the normal readmission of some patients using numerous methods such as decision trees, clustering, and naïve Bayes classifiers. Predictive analytics reflects the capacity to predict future events; it also helps in recognizing the trends and formative probabilities of uncertain outcomes. A description of its roles and responsibilities is to predict whether a patient will suffer from a certain disease in the future or not. Predictive models are habitually built using machine learning techniques. The goal of prescriptive analytics is to propose appropriate actions to enable optimal decision-making. As an illustration, prescriptive analysis may suggest rejecting a given treatment in the case of a harmful side effect with high probability. To perform prescriptive analytics, decision trees and Monte Carlo simulations may be applied.

As far as healthcare safety issues are concerned, there is a rising gap in its culture and the way that healthcare systems use the data to possess knowledge about the hazards to a patient and how to solve these hazards in a safe manner for patients. The data collection involved in the healthcare sector is generally manual, and therefore not homogeneous from a

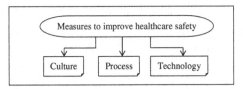

**Figure 5.2** Healthcare safety measures.

financial or operational aspect. Therefore this results in a scattered approach that is not predictive in nature. Although several metrics and attributes regarding patients are recorded, the real work to make patients safer is found to be highly incomplete. Some of the measures to improve healthcare safety rely on three factors: culture, process, and technology.

As shown in Fig. 5.2, the healthcare safety measures center on three different actions: estimate, interfere, and stop. To start with, first, the healthcare system identifies and estimates a safety aspect, acts to assist the patient (i.e., interferes), and then stops similar incidents in the near future, therefore forming a combination of culture, process, and technology. As illustrated in the figure, this culture is comprised of care based on patient and family centeredness and teamwork, so that the hospital and patient work cooperatively to accomplish the task of patient monitoring. Next, the process is comprised of organizational integrity, authenticity, and process enhancement. Finally, the technology consists of data analytics and decision support for the healthcare system.

## 5.2 Medical image segmentation and classification

In medical diagnosis and therapy, medical images have become vital. These medical images play an essential role in medical applications. This is due to the fact that medical practitioners and physicians have an interest in viewing the internal anatomy. To meet these requirements, several imaging techniques are used with specific operations. Medical imaging advances visual characterizations of the inside view of a body clinical examination, providing vital information hidden by skin and bones. In addition, the medical image processing basically generates a database for standard anatomy and physiology. Due to these different types of views, the presence of abnormalities is identified employing both grayscale and color images.

Several methods have been designed on the basis of X-ray and cross-sectional images, or other tomographic modalities. Over the years,

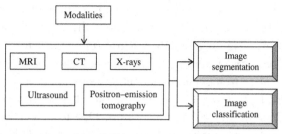

**Figure 5.3** Schematic view of medical image processes.

medical image processing has bestowed many improvements on medical applications and investigations. For example, the use of segmentation of image, registration of image, and image-guided surgery has found its place in medical surgery. One of the most important imaging techniques providing an enormous arrangement of information about internal organs is magnetic resonance imaging (MRI). MRI possesses several advantages when compared to other imaging techniques, hence it is frequently used in several applications. Fig. 5.3 shows a schematic view of medical image processes.

As shown in the figure, two important constituents of images, namely, image segmentation and image classification, using hybrid approaches are concentrated on in this chapter. To start with, there are different modalities for extracting the images. These modalities range from MRI [3], to computed tomography (CT) scans, to X-rays, ultrasound, and positron-emission tomography (PET). With any of these images acquired as input, the process of either image segmentation or classification is said to be performed using a hybrid approach. Therefore this chapter starts with discussions of medical image segmentation and medical image classification.

## 5.2.1 Medical image segmentation

For medical imaging applications, image segmentation plays a key role in extracting useful information and attributes from images. Image segmentation is considered to be one of the most elementary steps resulting in understanding of images, analysis of images, and interpreting the same in a more meaningful manner. The main purpose of image segmentation is to split the given image into segments that are analogous with each other in one or more characteristics under certain conditions. This physical analysis behavior is time consuming and prone to errors due to its various inter- or intraoperator inconsistency studies. These difficulties in brain MRI image data analysis require inventions in computerized methods to improve the disease diagnosis rate and reduce the diagnosis time and testing. In addition, image segmentation is not only salient for extracting the required and essential features and visualization, but is also excellent for measuring images. It has established ubiquitous applications in locating tumors, surgical planning, image registration, classification of several tissues, and estimating the volume of tumors. Due to certain issues, such as substandard spatial resolution, indistinct boundaries, and the presence of noise, image segmentation remains a laborious task. Despite these issues faced in the area of image segmentation [4], there have been certain notable advances in this domain, specifically due to persisting advancements in instrumentation. According to the above definitions, there are four types of image segmentation techniques and computer technology:

- thresholding,
- edge-based segmentation,
- region-based segmentation, and
- pixel classification.

### 5.2.1.1 Thresholding
In thresholding, a predefined value or threshold is chosen and the input image is split into different types of classes of pixels possessing values superior to or identical with the threshold and groups of pixels with a lower value than the threshold.

### 5.2.1.2 Edge-based segmentation
As the name implies, segmentation here is performed with the edge being the primary factor for positioning.

### 5.2.1.3 Region-based segmentation
Region-based segmentation identifies the pixels present in an image with which it forms disjointed regions by combining the neighboring pixels with homogeneous properties on the basis of a predefined similarity criterion.

### 5.2.1.4 Pixel classification
Pixel classification uses histogram measures to define single or multiple thresholds.

## 5.2.2 Medical image classification

One of the most imperative problems faced in the domain area of image recognition is the classification of medical images. The major intention of medical image classification is to classify medical images into several elements to assist medical practitioners or physicists in diagnosing disease. Hence, medical image classification is split into two steps. The first and foremost step of medical image classification is to extract the essential features from the acquired input image. The second step in medical image classification is utilizing the features to construct models that classify the image data set. In the recent past, medical practitioners customarily utilized their specialized experience to extract features so that classification of medical images could be performed into several classes. However, this manual medical image classification was found to be highly cumbersome and time consuming.

Medical image classification [5] involves the process of segregating medical-related information into a useful form. Classification of medical images is based on placing image pixels with similar values into groups. With the placement of similar values into groups, common pixels are identified and are denoted by these pixels. Hence, a correctly classified image usually denotes the areas on the ground that share specific features as specified in the classification scheme. From the above specification, images are classified into two types:
1. supervised classification and
2. unsupervised classification

### 5.2.2.1 Supervised classification
Supervised classification utilizes the spectral signatures acquired from training samples with the purpose of classifying a given input image.

### 5.2.2.2 Unsupervised classification
In contrast, an unsupervised classification identifies spectral classes present in a multiband image with the human interference.

## 5.2.3 Medical image classification based on a hybrid approach

Millions of images pertaining to medical data are produced by healthcare centers. One of the most favored diagnostic tools preferred by several medical practitioners is imaging. This necessitates methods for effective mining in databases of images, which are more cumbersome than mining in completely numerical databases. In addition, imaging techniques available in the medical industry, including MRI, PET, and ECG signals, produce gigabytes of information daily. This therefore necessitates storage devices with higher capacity and innovative machines to examine such information. On the other hand, the hybrid segmentation technique that follows the integration of two or more techniques efficiently produces better results than those produced by segmentation techniques working alone. This is achieved in the area of image processing, specifically in the area of medical image segmentation. Some medical image classifications based on hybrid approaches are described in the following subsections.

### 5.2.3.1 Neuro fuzzy system

An integration of fuzzy inference with artificial neural network (ANN) systems is referred to as the neuro fuzzy system. In recent years, combinations of neural networks and fuzzy systems have gained attention from different research groups in a variety of scientific and engineering applications due to the increasing requirement for a feedforward neural network that can estimate any fuzzy-rule-based [6] system and any feedforward neural network may be approximated by the rule-based FIS.

A combination of ANNs and FISs has gain attention among scientists and researchers in various scientific and engineering areas due to the increasing requirement for adaptive intelligent systems. The features and characteristics of an integration of neural networks and fuzzy systems are discernible. Fig. 5.4 shows a schematic representation of a rule-based FIS.

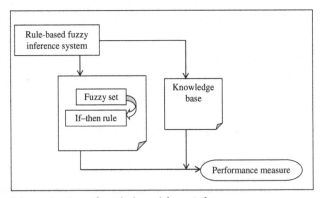

**Figure 5.4** Schematic view of a rule-based fuzzy inference system.

An in-depth investigation discloses that the disadvantages to these methods appear interdependent and, hence, a review constructing an integrated approach is needed. While the learning potentiality is taken from the perspective of a fuzzy system, the instinctive emergence of a linguistic rule base is taken from the perspective of neural networks.

### 5.2.3.2 Neural expert systems

In certain cases, neural networking systems are restoring expert systems and other artificial intelligence (AI) techniques. In certain other applications, a neural network presents a feature not possible with conventional AI systems and may bestow perspectives of intelligent behavior that have thus far eluded AI. Fig. 5.5 shows a schematic view of a neural expert system.

Embedding a neural network within an expert system seems to be an efficient framework for medical image diagnosis. Much of the information required by the medical diagnostic system appears to be numeric in nature (process sensor readings related to temperature, pressure, sugar monitoring, and so on), which is precisely and effortlessly grasped by the neural networks. The expert system, on the other hand, initiates the neural diagnosis to produce the possible faulty images being diagnosed.

It then examines the outputs produced by the neural network and indicates the presence or absence of disease. The expert system considers the information pertaining to symbolic value that is not precisely handled by neural networks. The expert system is concerned with AI applications that utilize the knowledge base of human competence for solving problems. When concerned with the neural network expert system,

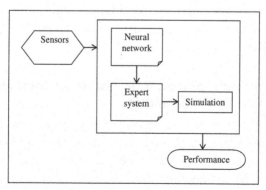

**Figure 5.5** Schematic view of a neural expert systems.

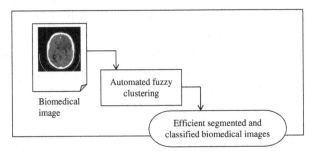

**Figure 5.6** Block diagram of automated fuzzy clustering.

the knowledge is encoded in the form of weight, with which the ANN produces rules based on the inferences.

## 5.2.4 Automated fuzzy clustering for biomedical images

One of the most important factors with regards to segmentation and classification in real-world applications is fuzziness. The automated fuzzy clustering algorithm is considered as the optimization problem where the variables are decided the user in an automatic manner. That is one of the major objectives behind the automated form and hence it is used in several fields of applications, including image diagnosis for health care. Fig. 5.6 shows a block diagram of automated fuzzy clustering applied in the area of healthcare biomedical imaging for disease diagnosis.

Automated fuzzy clustering is a method of clustering that provides one element of data or image belonging to two or more clusters. The method works by allocating membership values to each image point correlated to each cluster center based on the distance between the cluster center and the image point. The closer the image is to the cluster center the higher its membership value is said to be toward the specific cluster center. Upon completion of each iteration, values pertaining to membership and cluster centers are updated.

## 5.2.5 Segmentation of magnetic resonance imaging images using neural network techniques

MRI is an accepted diagnostic instrument for several diseases and disorders. Therefore it plays a pivotal element in clinical image diagnosis. Utilizing this method with automated classification and segmentation instruments is done to minimize the errors and time consumed to produce a decisive result. One of the most widely used methods for scanning medical images is MRI. The purpose of using MRI in healthcare applications is because the quality of the images is very high. This is because MRI provides an exceptional angle inside the human body and it also shows a comprehensive view as compared with other scanning instruments, such as X-rays and CT scans.

Image segmentation refers to the procedure of dividing a raw input image into multiple homogeneous parts, with the objective of localizing and identifying the objects and edges present in the image. Some of the real-time applications of image segmentation range from removing noise from images, locating tumors, surgery aided by computer-guided surgery, diagnosis, treatment planning, iris recognition, fingerprint recognition, etc.

Machine learning has gained a massive amount of awareness over the last few years. The current situation was initiated in 2009 when deep ANNs were shown to outperform other methods. In the current scenario, deep neural networks are now the state-of-the-art machine learning methods applied over a wide area of domains, starting from image analysis for disease diagnosis to evaluating natural language processing, and they are extensively applied in the fields of education and industry. The unanticipated advancement and comprehensive extent of deep learning, and the emerging outpouring of awareness and increased investment, have resulted in an exemplary cycle of advancements in the entire field of machine learning. Healthcare providers produce and acquire huge data containing a greater amount of beneficial signals and information, therefore acting as a means to swiftly integrate, analyze, and make predictions based on heterogeneous data sets pertaining to health informatics. An extensive variety of such biomedical signals is commonly encountered in the clinic, research laboratory, and occasionally even at home. Examples include electrical activity from the heart; speech signals voice recognition or electrical activity from the brain or electrical responses of the brain to explicit peripheral stimulation; the electroneurogram, or field potentials from local regions in the brain; action potential signals which are sent from individual neurons or heart cells to identify the behavior or electrical activity from the muscle to the brain to undertake a quick action; the electroretinogram from the eye passes a signal to the brain; and so on. Clinically, biomedical signals are mainly acquired for monitoring, detecting, and recognizing the specific physiological states for the purposes of disease diagnosis and evaluating therapy. In various critical researches, they were also used for decoding and eventual modeling of specific biological systems. Furthermore, recent technology allows the acquisition of data from multiple channels of these signals.

Big medical data play a major role in finding disease diagnosis information. Healthcare data analytics applications play an important role in detecting disease and diagnosis within a limited period of time. It enables the facilitation of a "prevention is better than cure" ethos by providing a comprehensive image of patient data which helps to provide a tailored treatment package. The industrial organization also involves to gather the patient's data from hospital or clinics for providing better technology to establish the proper communication between doctor and patients. This is the reason for healthcare data analytics: using data to predict and resolve a disease before diagnosis is too late, and also for assessing numerous methods and treatments to act quicker, to keep a better track of inventory, and more patient involvement and empowerment.

Parameter optimization for local polynomial approximation (LPA) is based on the intersection confidence interval (ICI) filter using a genetic algorithm: an application for denoising or reducing the noise from the brain MRI image [7]. LPA-based ICI filter is one type of flourishing denoising filter which also requires an adjustment of the ICI parameters for proficient window size selection. From the extensive range of ICI parametric values, searching out the best set of values is itself an optimization problem. However, noise reduction performance is not efficient.

Contrast-enhanced medical MRI image estimation using Tsallis entropy and region-based growing (RBG) segmentation [8] considers the incorporation of a Bat algorithm and Tsallis-based thresholding in addition to RBG segmentation. The proposed approach is carried out on region based growing (RGB)/grayscale brain MRI images and breast MRI images recorded using a contrast agent. After withdrawal from the infected region, its texture features are extracted using a Haralick function process to assess the surface details of the abnormal section. The clinical significance of the proposed technique is also validated using brain MRI images of BRATS as recorded using T1C modality. However, contrast image enhancement is insufficient.

Meta heuristic algorithm like Genetic Algorithm and particle swarm optimization is an effective algorithm in the domain of medical image segmentation to classify and recognize the disease [9]. It is based on the principle of stochastic exploration of a combined ant colony with the theory of Markov fields for modeling the field labels and observations. However, it is disposed to human bias/error as well as being a tedious process.

## 5.3  Disease and diagnosis approach

Medical diagnosis refers to the procedure of determining the disease pertaining to a patient according to their symptoms and signs. The required data or information from the patient are collected for disease diagnosis based on diagnostic tests. The process of diagnosis is considered to be the most challenging process due to the fact that several symptoms are nonspecific. Hence, different diagnosis tests have to be performed with the possibility of the presence of several diseases, particularly in the early stages. This therefore involves correlation of information. In addition, valuable information, recognition of patterns, and differentiation between patterns has to be made in a timely manner.

### 5.3.1  Hybrid computational intelligence for the prediction of breast cancer

One of the foremost causes of death in females is breast cancer. Though the major causes of death due to breast cancer are not yet known, early breast cancer detection would result in better treatment and therefore enhanced recovery. The areas of occurrence of breast cancer initiate from various areas, such as the ducts, the lobules, and the tissue in between. Hence, the etiologies of breast cancer are found to be unclear, with no single major cause identified, and with early detection being the only solution.

One of the most extensively used methods for medical image diagnosis is the ANN. Different ANN methods, such as multilayer perceptron neural networks, radial basis function networks, learning vector quantization networks, probabilistic neural networks (PNNs), and RNNs have been used in the past few years for diagnosing breast cancer.

The application of the above methods has enhanced efficient breast cancer detection, but their limitations result in suboptimality that requires to be addressed. The problems specifically become predominant when the training data are very complex. In most of these methods, for various disease diagnoses, the disadvantages of these systems is said to increase and hence the issue (i.e., breast cancer detection) is not solved in an optimal manner with the aid of a single system alone. Therefore there arises a requirement for a combination of systems with the objective of integrating the positive features of the individual systems and discarding their negative features. In other words, the negative features of the system are eliminated by the positive features of another system. Hence, hybrid methods currently form a very promising area of research. In these hybrid systems several methods are combined, for example, neural networks are combined with evolutionary algorithms to make a much more efficient system.

### 5.3.1.1 Breast cancer detection and artificial neural networks

Breast cancer detection using ANNs has taken place for over 20 years. At the same time, for purposes involving medical analysis, several AI methods have been utilized to increase these diagnosis methods and to assist the efforts of medical practitioner. As of now many techniques have been developed to detect and recognize the cancer for achieving higher accuracy to help the cancer specialist.

A classification approach for breast cancer detection using a backpropagation algorithm was used in a case study [10], in this paper the author proposed to examine the WBCD in which it compares the 683 patients data. The implementation based on chosen feature is to train the data from the back propagation algorithm. The performance of the proposed method was analyzed on the basis of classification techniques, accuracy, specificity, optimistic and pessimistic predictor values, and a confusion matrix. A total of six features were used to classify the breast cancer, with an accuracy of 98.27%. However, the processing time of the disease diagnosis was long.

Principal component analysis (PCA)-PNN and PCA-SVM (support vector machine) based CAD proposed systems for breast density classification were explained in a paper [11]. The SVM and PNN classifiers were used for classifying the task. It was observed that the highest classification accuracy of 92.5% was achieved with the first four principal components derived from texture features computed with Laws' masks of length 7 using a PNN classifier and the highest classification accuracy of 94.4% was achieved with the first four principal components derived from texture features computed with Laws' masks of length 5 using an SVM classifier. However, minimizing the feature space dimensionality was not sufficient. An adaptive semisupervised SVM was used with features cooperation for breast cancer classification [12]; it was appropriate for applications requiring high-accuracy classification. For breast cancer classification semi supervised learning S3VM has been adapt with feature cooperation [13], a computer-assisted recognition system for the diagnosis of disease based on a meticulous method on the use of the semisupervised learning technique using S3VM with these different kernel functions. However, it was not easy to gather the labeled patient important records using these two methods.

### 5.3.1.2 Intelligent techniques and breast cancer detection

In the domain of medical technology, intelligent techniques are supposed to be an inductive engine that measures the decision features of the diseases (e.g., breast cancer) and are then utilized to diagnose future patients with uncertain disease states. Hence, it has found a place for medical practitioners in medical diagnostic support systems for effective diagnosis of disease at an early stage. Several intelligent techniques were utilized for the construction of image classification, such as hard C-means, feature selection and clustering, nearest neighbor classification, neuro fuzzy classification, and machine learning. Different data mining models along with ANN were also applied, such as linear discriminatory analysis, nonlinear discriminatory analysis, PCA, and SVM for image classification for breast cancer detection.

## 5.3.2 Genetic algorithms and partial swarm optimization

As described in the above section, using different intelligent techniques, breast cancer detection is performed in an efficient manner. In this section, genetic algorithm and partial swarm optimization are applied to input breast images for breast cancer detection at an early stage.

### 5.3.2.1 Genetic algorithms

GAs were developed in recent years to obtain a thorough understanding of natural processing systems. Followed by natural processing systems, GAs were then utilized for optimization and machine learning. In GA, a crossover operator was applied by mating the parents (individual breast images). After applying the crossover operator, the mutation operator was applied in a random manner to produce diversity to produce a new offspring. In addition, a replacement operation is selected where the parents are replaced systematically by the offspring. On the basis of n-point a crossover operator is used, and on the basis of bit flipping a uniform crossover operation is used.

### 5.3.2.2 Particle swarm optimization

One of the population-based methods used for disease diagnosis and prediction is PSO. The design of PSO is inspired from the behavior of birds. Here, the swarm (i.e., breast images) in the search space (i.e., the overall image)

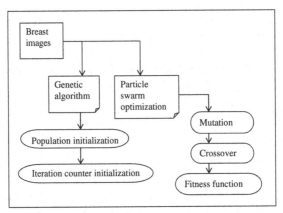

**Figure 5.7** Block diagram of genetic algorithm and partial swarm optimization.

represents the population. The individuals (i.e., portions of breast) are called particles. In the search space, every particle moves with a certain velocity. The particle uses this velocity due to swapping of information between the neighbors. During every iteration the particles consume a portion of memory to save their best position along with the overall best particle positions. The best particle position is saved as the best local position, whereas the best overall particle position is saved as the best global position. Fig. 5.7 shows a block diagram of genetic algorithm and partial swarm optimization.

As illustrated in this figure, using GA, initialization of the population and iteration counter is performed. Followed by initialization, new solutions are generated by applying PSO. Here, to start with, an intermediate population is selected. Following which, the current population is split into a new population to which the crossover and mutation operator is applied. Finally, the solutions are evaluated by applying a fitness function.

## 5.4 Identifying brain activity using a state classifier

One of the upcoming research areas increasing rapidly is human brain activities. This rapid growth has been specifically due to MRI. The main issue in identifying brain activity is identifying the mental faculties of several tasks and measuring how these mental states are transformed into neural brain activity [14]. In simple terms, brain mapping is referred to as the correlation of cognitive states that are intuitive with patterns of brain activity. MRI is meticulously utilized in testing the theory of activation

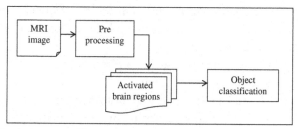

**Figure 5.8** Block diagram of brain activity using a state classifier.

locations of various brain activities, resulting in three-dimensional images corresponding to human brains.

As shown in Fig. 5.8, using the multivariate analysis methods, various classifiers, such as SVMs, Bayes classifiers were utilized to decode the mental processes of neural activity patterns of the human brain. Statistical learning models are also utilized to analyze the functional brain imaging data via MRI images. Upon successful collection of data for the purpose of detecting cognitive states, machine learning classifier methods are trained to decode the states of human activities. In addition, an integrated approach like EEG and MRI image features is also utilized to classify brain activities with the aid of SVM classification.

### 5.4.1 Modeling the data science for a diagnosis technique

Data science is regarded as a multidisciplinary area that utilizes several scientific materials and methods, in-depth processes, algorithms to acquire knowledge, and through it gain insights from data in several forms, corresponding to both structured and unstructured forms of image data. Data science is also used for the diagnosis of diseases, including detection of tumors, breast cancer, and lung cancer. Though the occurrence of cancers differs in different regions, using data science diagnosis techniques can be modeled.

### 5.5 Genomics

One of the interdisciplinary fields of biology with the main focus on function, evolution, mapping, and editing is referred to as genomics. A genome includes an organism's complete set of DNA, consisting of all of its genes. Genetics refers to the study of individual genes and their roles in inheritance. Genomics also performs the task of collective characterization and gene quantification, which in turn directs the production of proteins via enzymes and messenger molecules. Finally, the proteins constitute the entire body structures, where the organs and tissues control chemical reactions that also carry signals between cells.

Pattern analysis of genetics and genomics is a survey of the state-of-the-art as discussed in Ref. [15], where the region of pattern analysis, which is used to build up computer algorithms that extend knowledge, embraces the capacity to make powerful computers that support the analysis of complex problems, including large genetic and genomic data sets. Here, an overview of pattern analysis techniques for the study of genome sequencing data sets, as well as the proteomics, epigenetic, and metabolomic data is delivered. These techniques employ data preprocessing techniques to smoothen the data, feature extraction and selection for the region of interest, and classification and clustering in order to organize homogeneous data from the same region. However, it is unsuccessful in terms of accuracy. The $k$-mer role in composition vector method for comparing genome sequences [16]. Generally, composition vector methods using $k$-mer are applied under choice of different value of $k$ to compare genome sequences. For some values of $k$, the results are satisfactory, but for other values of $k$, the results are unsatisfactory. To resolve the issues of accuracy, a standard composition vector method is carried out in the proposed work using 3-mer string length. In addition, a special type of information-based similarity index is used as a distance measure. This establishes the use of 3-mer and information-based similarity index and provides satisfactory results, especially for comparison of whole-genome sequences in all cases. However, predicting the accuracy is not efficient.

## 5.5.1 Method for gene functional enrichments

Gene set functional enrichment is a method to identify classes of genes that are denoted in the form of large sets of genes and that possess correlation with disease phenotypes. The gene set functional enrichment method utilizes statistical models to identify extensive or depleted gene patterns. In order to seek out genes correlated with certain diseases, researchers used DNA microarrays [17] that measured the number of gene expressions present in several cells. They utilized these microarrays on several thousand to millions of genes, and analyzed the resultant value of two different cells to arrive at whether they were normal or cancerous cells. However, this method of comparison was not found to be sensitive enough to identify the disparity between individual gene expressions.

This is because diseases involved entire gene groups. On the other hand, gene functional enrichment utilizes a priori genes that have been clustered by their involvement in a similar biological pathway. Three steps are said to be involved in the process of gene functional enrichment:

- gene enrichment score,
- statistical estimation of gene enrichment score, and
- multiple hypothesis testing.

### 5.5.1.1 Gene enrichment score

The gene enrichment score that denotes the amount to which the genes in the overall set are denoted is evaluated, and placed at either the top or bottom of the list. This score is referred to as the Kolmogorov–Smirnov-like statistic.

### 5.5.1.2 Statistical estimation of gene enrichment score

The statistical importance of the estimation score is evaluated. This calculation is performed using a phenotypic-based permutation test. The permutation test is performed in such a manner that a null distribution for the corresponding estimation score is produced.

### 5.5.1.3 Multiple hypothesis testing

Finally, an adjustment for multiple hypothesis testing is performed. This is performed when greater gene sets are being measured at a single round. At this stage, an enrichment score is normalized for each set with which the possibility of any false discovery rate is measured.

## 5.5.2 Modern artificial file

With a measure to eradicate the disadvantages found in traditional computer-aided disease diagnosis, researchers have designed programs in such a manner that they perform simulation by expert human reasoning. However, efforts made using computer-aided disease diagnosis by expert human reasoning have not been clinically fulfilled, and several issues remain to be solved. Methods have been designed to limit the frequency of hypotheses that a program must take into consideration and to formulate pathophysiologic reasoning. With this innovation, a program is said to be analyzed with which one disorder has a higher influential rate on the other.

## 5.6 Health bioinformatics

The term health bioinformatics [18] refers to obtaining, storing, retrieving, and utilizing the information pertaining to healthcare data to provide a better understanding of a patient's various healthcare providers. Health bioinformatics plays a major role in healthcare reform. Health bioinformatics refers to an evolving specialization technique that links several technologies such as information technology, data communications, and health care with the objective of improving the quality of life and at the same time ensuring the safety of patient care.

Health bioinformatics [19] with the aid of information technology initially organizes and then analyzes the records pertaining to patients with the objective of improving healthcare outcomes. Health bioinformatics not only deals with the resources, instruments, materials, and methods, but also uses the acquisition of medical data, storage retrieval, and medical data, in addition to the use of information in the fields of health care and medicine. The advantage of using healthcare bioinformatics is that it provides access to medical records in an electronic form that are useful for not only the patients, but also for the medical practitioners, physicians, hospital management, insurance companies, etc.

A review of data mining and deep learning in bioinformatics [20] and data mining with core techniques of machine learning algorithms is an extensively promising approach to achieve such goals in both explicit and implicit IT ways. However, some issues such as shallow, static, batch-oriented, and nongeneralized performance have emerged, causing troublesome bottlenecks. However, the performance of deep learning is not efficient. A map reduction approach was used to diminish the imbalance parameters for a large deoxyribonucleic acid data set [21], and in this analysis, a contemporary distributed clustering methodology for misbalancing the data reduction using the $k$-nearest neighbor ($k$-NN) classification approach has been introduced. The pivotal objective of this work is to illustrate real training data sets with reduced amounts of elements or instances. These reduced amounts of data sets will ensure faster data classification and standard storage management with less sensitivity. However, general data reduction methods cannot manage very large data sets.

### 5.6.1 Multimodal medical image fusion

Over the past few years, with the availability of modern diagnostic methods in the field of health care, medical image processing has received much attraction. The main idea behind medical image fusion is to fuse all types of information from multimodal medical images with the purpose of obtaining high-quality images. Hence, multimodal medical image fusion [22] has found a significant area in biomedical research and is used for clinical diagnosis. Medical images have different types of species with applications in different areas, including CT, MRI, and PET images.

CT images provide anatomical information, whereas PET images deliver functional information, and MRI images are found to be highly superior for differentiating between normal and pathological soft tissue. With the different types of information available through CT and MRI images, edge preservation and edge detection are obtained by fusing CT and MRI images. This in turn provides the doctor with a high-quality fused image that serves as a means for precise and accurate diagnosis. Hence, the area of fusion of multimodal medical images has drawn attention from several experts and researchers around the globe.

For example, the fusion of CT and PET images assists oncologists to supervise and have continuous monitoring of cancer treatment and also assists cardiologists to measure for the presence or absence of affected portions with an additional extent of coronary artery disease. The fusion of SPECT (single-photon emission computed tomography) and CT images provides means for localization and identification of the stage of neuroendocrine tumors. In addition, the fusion of CT images and MRI images is utilized for neuro-navigation for surgery oriented toward the skull. In addition, fusion of PET and MRI images is also widely used in the detection of diseases from disorders related to neurodegenerative to cardiovascular diseases.

The Discrete wavelet transform (DWT)−PCA image combination technique was used to develop the segmentation accuracy in brain tumor analysis [23], this approach was experimentally assessed with the MICCAI brain cancer segmentation (BRATS 2013) challenge database. Because of its high clinical significance and varied modalities, MRI procedures are widely adopted in medical disciplines to trace the abnormalities arising in a variety of internal organs of the human body. However, the prediction time of the disease diagnosis is high and analysis process is not sufficient. However, the brain MR image analysis process is not sufficient. DWT and a multiscale pixel conversion fusion were operating using a parameter estimation optimized Gaussian mixture model [24]. The output image was used in a fuzzy weighted evaluation system that included the following evaluation indices: mean, standard deviation, entropy, average gradient, and spatial frequency; the difference with the reference image, including the root mean square error, signal-to-noise ratio (SNR), and the peak SNR; and the difference with the source image including the cross entropy, joint entropy, mutual information, deviation index, correlation coefficient, and the degree of distortion. However, the performance of disease prediction was not sufficient.

## 5.6.2 Recognition critical genes in Austin syndrome

Fusion of images helps in diagnosing and detecting this syndrome at an early stage, so that accurate and precise treatment can be done. The presence of genes and the detection of genes in the most sensitive and delicate portions are said to be highly possible with the fusion of images. This is because each image obtained through various formats possesses both advantages and disadvantages. Therefore by means of fusion, the advantages of two different types of images are used with the objective of analyzing the critical gene. In this way, via fusion, critical gene recognition in Austin syndrome can be performed.

## 5.7 Discussion

In biomedical imaging and health care, several techniques are used to identify diseases based on CT and MRI images. Existing heartbeat time series classification with SVM is designed for classification of signals presenting very low SNRs. This achieves a very accurate classification of subjects, contrary to the most common heart rate variability (HRV) analysis methods that failed to categorize the same signals accurately. However, it failed in the feature selection process. Next, fuzzy c-means clustering and gradient vector flow snake algorithm for lesion contour segmentation on breast magnetic resonance imaging (BMRI) was used. This technique also quantified morphological and texture features and improved the objectivity and efficiency of BMRI interpretation with a certain clinical value. This method failed in authentication and assessment on a larger independent database. After that, an ischemic stroke detection system with computer-aided diagnostic ability using a four-step unsupervised feature perception enhancement method was used for effectively diagnosing stroke areas in a short time, while also reducing error rates. However, the false acceptance rate (FAR) value is too high. In order to overcome these limitations, hybrid computational intelligence has been introduces in biomedical imaging and healthcare systems. This method enhances performance in terms of the proposed prediction accuracy, detection rate, false alarm rate, correction classification rate, and also reduces the prediction time.

## 5.8 Conclusion

In this chapter, hybrid computational intelligence has been proposed for medical image diagnosis. Hybrid computational intelligence is a combination of at least two methods. In this method, classification and segmentation instruments are used to minimize the errors and time consumed to produce a decisive detection. This method increases the disease diagnostic accuracy with minimum time compared to existing methods. In future work, ensemble clustering is considered in disease diagnosis for greater accuracy in large data sets.

## References

[1] A. Kampouraki, G. Manis, C. Nikou, Member, IEEE, heartbeat time series classification with support vector machines, IEEE Trans. Inf. Technol. Biomed. 13 (4) (2009) 512–518.
[2] S. Chakraborty, et al., Intelligent computing in medical imaging: a study, Advancements in Applied Metaheuristic Computing, IGI Global, 2018, pp. 143–163.
[3] Y. Pang, W. Hu, Y. Peng, L. Liu, Y. Shao, Computerized segmentation and characterization of breast lesions in dynamic contrast-enhanced MR images using fuzzy c-means clustering and snake algorithm, Hindawi Publ. Corp. Comput. Math. Methods Med. 2012 (2012).
[4] Y.-S. Tyan, M.-C. Wu, C.-L. Chin, Y.-L. Kuo, M.-S. Lee, H.-Y. Chang, Ischemic stroke detection system with a computer-aided diagnostic ability using an unsupervised feature perception enhancement method, Hindawi Publ. Corp. Int. J. Biomed. Imaging 2014 (2014) 12.
[5] R. Kumar, R. Srivastava, S. Srivastava, Detection and classification of cancer from microscopic biopsy images using clinically significant and biologically interpretable features, Hindawi Publ. Corp. J. Med. Eng. 2015 (2015).
[6] A. Fernández, S.D. Río, A. Bawakid, F. Herrera, Fuzzy rule based classification systems for big data with MapReduce: granularity analysis, Adv. Data Anal. Classif. 11 (4) (2017) 711–730. Springer.
[7] N. Dey, A. Ashour, S. Beagum, D. Pistola, M. Gospodinov, E Gospodinova, et al., Parameter optimization for local polynomial approximation based intersection confidence interval filter using genetic algorithm: an application for brain MRI image denoising, J. Imaging 1 (1) (2015) 60–84.
[8] N. Sri Madhava Raja, S.L. Fernandes, N. Dey, S.C. Satapathy, V. Rajinikanth, Contrast enhanced medical MRI evaluation using Tsallis entropy and region growing segmentation, J. Ambient. Intell. Humanized Comput. (2018) 1–12.
[9] S. Riahi, A. Riahi, GA, PSO: Meta-heuristic algorithms in medical image segmentation: a review, Int. J. Comput. Trends Technol. (IJCTT) 54 (2017) 1–16.

[10] A. Bhattacherjee, S. Roy, S. Paul, P. Roy, N. Kausar, N. Dey, Classification approach for breast cancer detection using back propagation neural network: a study. In: Deep Learning and Neural Networks: Concepts, Methodologies, Tools, and Applications. (2020) (pp. 1410−1421).
[11] Kriti, J. Virmani, N. Dey, V. Kumar, PCA−PNN and PCA−SVM based CAD systems for breast density classification, Appl. Intell. Optim. Biol. Med. (2015) 159−180.
[12] N. Zemmal, N. Azizi, N. Dey, M. Sellami, Adaptive semi supervised support vector machine semi supervised learning with features cooperation for breast cancer classification, J. Med. Imaging Health Inform. 6 (1) (2016) 53−62.
[13] N. Zemmal, N. Azizi, M. Sellami, Adaptative S3VM semi supervised learning with features cooperation for breast cancer classification, J. Med. Imaging Health Inform. 6 (4) (2016) 957−967.
[14] B. Rakesh, T. Kavitha, K. Lalitha, K. Thejaswi, N.B. Muppalaneni, Cognitive state classifiers for identifying brain activities, Computational Intelligence and Big Data Analytics, Springer, 2019, pp. 15−20.
[15] J. Chaki, N. Dey, Pattern analysis of genetics and genomics: a survey of the state-of-art, Multimed. Tools Appl. (2019).
[16] S. Das, T. Deb, N. Dey, A.S. Ashour, D.K. Bhattacharya, D.N. Tibarewala, Optimal choice of $k$-mer in composition vector method for genome sequence comparison, Genomics 110 (5) (2018) 263−273.
[17] M. Herland, T.M. Khoshgoftaar, R. Wald, A review of data mining using big data in health informatics, J. Big Data 5 (3) (2015) 1−7. Springer.
[18] T. Nguyen, A. Khosravi, D. Creighton, S. Nahavandi, Classification of healthcare data using genetic fuzzy logic system and wavelets, Expert Syst. Appl. 42 (4) (2015) 2184−2197. Elsevier.
[19] Z. Liu, H. Yin, Y. Chai, S.X. Yang, A novel approach for multimodal medical image fusion, Expert Syst. Appl. 41 (16) (2014) 7425−7435. Elsevier.
[20] K. Lan, D. Wang, S. Fong, L. Liu, K.K.L. Wong, N. Dey, A survey of data mining and deep learning in bioinformatics, J. Med. Syst. 42 (8) (2018) 1−20.
[21] S. Kamal, S.H. Ripon, N. Dey, A.S. Ashour, V. Santhi, A map reduce approach to diminish imbalance parameters for big deoxyribonucleic acid dataset, Comput. Methods Prog. Biomed. 131 (2016) 191−206.
[22] M. Manchanda, R. Sharma, An improved multimodal medical image fusion algorithm based on fuzzy transform, J. Vis. Commun. Image Represent. 51 (2018) 76−94. Elsevier.
[23] V. Rajinikanth, S.C. Satapathy, N. Dey, R. Vijayarajan, DWT-PCA image fusion technique to improve segmentation accuracy in brain tumor analysis, in: Microelectronics, Electromagnetics and Telecommunication, 2018, pp. 453-462.
[24] D. Wang, Z. Li, L. Cao, V.E. Balas, N. Dey, A.S. Ashour, et al., Image fusion incorporating parameter estimation optimized Gaussian mixture model and fuzzy weighted evaluation system: a case study in time-series plantar pressure data set, IEEE Sens. J. 17 (5) (2017) 1407−1420.

## CHAPTER 6

# Application of hybrid computational intelligence in health care

**Moolchand Sharma[1], Suyash Agrawal[1] and Suman Deswal[2]**
[1]Maharaja Agrasen Institute of Technology, Delhi, India
[2]Deenbandhu Chhotu Ram University of Science and Technology, Sonepat, India

## 6.1 Introduction

The first question which comes to mind when one reads the name of this chapter is why a hybrid computational intelligent system should be chosen over a more conventional computational intelligent system. The main reason for this is the extensive experimentation done on various application domains where a standard computational approach has played a great role.

The decision to choose an accurate hybrid intelligent system should be made after consideration of various parameters, such as performance, approach, accuracy, increase in production, the future scope, effectiveness, and recent real-world work done with them. In addition, the various advantages and disadvantages of using that hybrid model should be considered.

The importance of computation came into the limelight when data-mining techniques were unable to be applied directly to the healthcare sector due to the cutoff between the medical communities and information and communication engineering [1]. One cannot expect physicians to be working on the software and the respective training to be provided to them or also, one cannot place a computer system in such a sterile environment, as both situations lead to many practical issues which on paper may not seem to be of much consideration.

To tackle such problems, the most complex algorithms of computational intelligence are being applied to the medical data sets so as to achieve the highest accuracy attainable. The system already in use, that is, the clinical decision support (CDS) system, is in wide use but the

123

professionals associated with health care are unable to take full use of it because of the difficulties faced by them in keeping an electronic record of each and every entry. They need something much simpler and more understandable. Despite all these issues, professionals are still relying more and more on the data.

The healthcare system database contains lifesaving data related to different fields, such as the patient's records, monitoring information, and the physician's diagnosis. The functionality for the interpretation of the meaning of analyzed data has been frequently enhanced by the use of a data analysis system. The use of cognitive data interpretation formulas, including analysis, semantic reasoning, and linguistic descriptions, make such analysis possible. The cognitive data analysis systems have gradually replaced the traditional information system which was used for the data analysis.

When we look into the field of community medicine and telemedicine, we find that a vital role is played by the extraction of knowledge for diagnosing the problem and providing the respective medical treatment. The medical data have various applications including different machine learning (ML) algorithms such as genetic algorithms (GAs), the artificial neural network, the roughest, the decision tree, and the support vector machine (SVM). There is also a much greater scope for the feature's selection in addition to various other ML techniques. From previous researches, one can conclude that the support vector machine is the most commonly used and powerful ML algorithm, which has been developed with those very principles and also it has achieved some very breakthrough achievements in the area of medical health care.

The principal logic behind all of this is to build such a model which has great accuracy and that can give accurate results using only the knowledge of the number and details of the best attributes selected from the data set. Therefore, as it is the preprocessing methodology, the selection of features is basically used to obtain the best attributes from all data. Also, the impact can easily be understood with the use of a feature selection algorithm. The process in its various step gives us a correlation of one feature with all other features present in the class and with the class itself, and this action leads us to selection of a particular subset which has a unique structure from others, by developing a varied number of feature selection techniques.

In the process of selection of the subset, all the information which are redundant and irrelevant are identified and removed subsequently.

Generally, we classify the feature selection technique into two different approaches, that is, the feature ranking method and the optimal feature selection method. The number of currently used data analytical systems is increasing and they are also enhanced by the addition of those functionalities which are used for the interpretation of the analyzed data's meaning. The practice of using cognitive data interpreting formulas makes possible all the analyses. The methods used are:

- Analyses
- Linguistic description
- Semantic reasoning

The cognitive data analytical system has been steadily replaced by a traditional system for information sharing which has been in use for the analysis of data. The formalism of the meaning-based data interpretation is the basis of the basic cognitive analysis of data, of which the foundation can be founded in the basics of psychology and philosophy. The decision-making process in which the main importance is the acquisition of the information, storage and transmission of the acquired information, and human cognition is very similar to the meaning-based information acquisition and its interpretation, followed by the understanding and analysis of the information.

One of the most rapidly developing fields of science is the medical domain. New machines and techniques are invented and developed in the fields of medicine and health care emerge on an almost daily basis. Related branches and fields also benefit from the developments made in health care and medicine. The number of research and related studies has increased with the inflow of funds and researchers devoting their time and resources to this particular field. The number of published works has also seen a great rise in the medical healthcare. This is creating a base and a platform for future work in this field. Not only will health care benefit, but related fields will also obtain advantages in their researches.

Medical health care is a field in which the future cannot be fully foreseen beforehand. Fuzzy logic is a direction and path which will define the future in the medical healthcare field. New techniques and mechanisms will lead to the extinction of many pre-existing applications. Medical imaging based on the concept of image processing is a definite area in which advancements are being made and will be made in the future. Developments in this field including techniques and equipment are made regularly. Soft computing methodology has a great role to play in the field of medical image processing. Fuzzy imaging is also a developing technique for the future. The database also plays a vital role in the medical field.

Fuzzy database management is one of the major contributors to competence in this field. The hybrid of soft computing along with a fuzzy database has a great role for the future. With the increase in such advancements, one can very easily expect more hybrid techniques and applications in the future.

## 6.1.1 Computational intelligence

Before discussing computation intelligence, we need to understand computational intelligence. Computational intelligence can be thought of as the gathering of two complementary views of artificial intelligence (AI), one being the engineering focused on the formation of machines that are intelligent and the other being the basic core science concentrated toward a computational model of an human intelligent system [2].

Natural systems, such as the immunity system, the nervous system, our society, and our ecology, along with artificial systems, such as artificial neural networks, AI systems, the distributed and parallel computing system, and evolutionary programs, are characterized by evident complex behavior that is the outcome of the nondirect spatial—transient cooperation among a shifted number of segment frameworks at the association's diverse dimension. As a result of research and study over time, scientists and researchers distinguished in their distinct fields, such as those of AI, computer science, cognitive science, neural networks, mathematics, computational economics, complexity theory, optimization, control system, neuroscience, biology, engineering, psychology, medicine, and health care, have started to address the theoretical and experimental research synthesis and the analysis of these systems through a combination of basic, as well as application, techniques. The above discussion suggests that AI devices mainly fall into two major categories. The first category includes ML techniques that analyze structured data, such as imaging, genetic, and EP data. In the medical applications, the ML procedures attempt to cluster patients' traits, or infer the probability of the disease outcomes. The second category includes natural language processing (NLP) methods that extract information from unstructured data, such as clinical notes and medical journals, to supplement and enrich structured medical data. The NLP procedures target turning texts into machine-readable structured data, which can then be analyzed by ML techniques. For a better understanding Fig. 6.1 shows AI in health care of the past, present, and future.

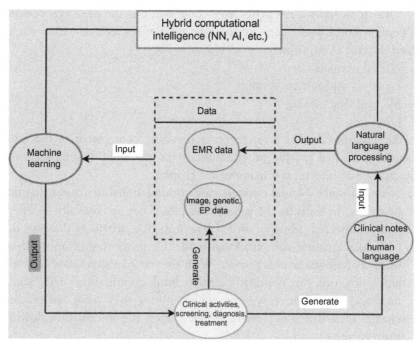

**Figure 6.1** Artificial intelligence in health care: past, present, and future. *NN*, Neural Network.

Intelligent frameworks are characterized as those frameworks which represent the properties of the adaptivity, self-upkeep, increment in multifaceted nature, and the data protection, however they utilize different methods to accomplish these destinations. Human healthcare services and their applications being truly reasonable by use of the calculation insight apparatuses and procedures. These strategies and apparatuses have pushed ahead from their thought of being only another creative and promising future methodology [3]. The aim has now changed to a strategy for decision for areas and issues having a particular arrangement of qualities, for example, the etymological portrayal of ideas or choice factors, a high level of multifaceted nature, absence of exact or complete informational indexes, a high level of vulnerability, and so on.

Computational intelligence ought to be used as a corresponding toolkit to the standard operational research strategies and procedures for critical thinking, improvement, and basic leadership, that is, reproduction, numerical programming, probabilistic thinking, etc. [4]. Due to the adequacy of computational knowledge in confronting real issues, a few areas of computational insight have turned out to be prominent after some time.

Over time, various researches have concluded that the main components of computational intelligence are the four areas of research that have dominated the area of AI, namely:

- Neural networks
- Fuzzy set and soft computing
- ML and data mining
- GAs

An attempt to make a reference to the basic component of the most popular and used intelligent components of the hybrid computational intelligence architectures is made in the chapter.

1. *Neural networks*: Neural networks are computational structures that can be trained to learn by the use of examples. They are basically an internally connected group of artificial neuron-like structures that use the basic mathematical computational model for processing of information using a computational approach. With the use of a supervised learning algorithm, one can perform excellent local optimization. The neural networks are adaptive systems, which means they learn, adapt, and change their structure over time based upon the information flowing through their system.

2. *Fuzzy set and soft computing*: Fuzzy language is the language using linguistic structure and neighborhood semantics, where one can engrave any subjective information about the task in hand. The main aspect of fuzzy logic is the agility of its interpolative reasoning mechanisms. Soft computing is basically the use of not the exact solution to compute such hard tasks for which there is no exact solution and for which no algorithm can compute an exact solution. Soft computing has space for imprecision, uncertainty, approximation, and near about answers.

3. *Machine learning and data mining*: ML is conceived mainly for the improvement of computational techniques that could help in actualizing different types of adapting, especially, those instruments capable of the induction of knowledge from the examples or the data sets. Data mining is the process for pattern discovery in a large set of data using methods combining statistics, ML, and database systems. It is the basic analytical step for the deep discovery of knowledge in a database. In data mining, the data are not extracted, but the pattern and knowledge from the large database are extracted.

4. *Genetic algorithms*: GAs provide a path for performing randomized global search in a solution space. Usually, a certain population of the candidate solution is assessed by the fitness function. The best

chromosomes are consolidated and reproduction is done for the subsequent generation [5]. Genetic programming, originally an extension of the GA, is composed by a variable length tree such as using candidate solutions. Each of these candidates has a functional node, which enables a solution to perform arbitrarily large actions.

Problems lacking algorithmic solutions, informally stated, or those that are ill-defined, appear to be particularly desirable for knowledge induction. Mostly, researches in the ML have been to develop such effective methods for building the learning systems that can acquire high-level concepts and can also help in problem-solving strategies in ways that are analogous to human learning. Many of the complex domain problems are either difficult to model, are ill-defined, or have a very large solution space. Hence, for such cases, the hybrid is equipped to portray the surmised thinking for these spaces. The crossover frameworks end up being better than each one of their hidden computational intelligent frameworks, consequently furnishing us with much better and propelled critical thinking apparatuses. A move toward a combination of intelligent systems and tools and techniques that can work in theories along with the practical work, such as adaptive and hybrid systems, have been used in current AI-oriented computer science.

## 6.1.2 Hybrid computational intelligence

Hybrid computational knowledge can be characterized as a successful blend of savvy systems that can perform predominantly or in an approach to basic standard computational astute procedures. Hybrid knowledge was essentially created as an augmentation to standard experimentation with a significant number of notable strategies in different application areas.

Intelligent hybrid systems are intended to be a combination of intelligent technologies such as genetic-machine algorithms, neuro-fuzzy approaches, and evolutionary optimized networks, but particularly those which prove to be obviously advantageous in their execution when connected to complex areas of use, with the focal points being either methods for exactness or the understandability of the obtained results [6]. With the advancement of installed hybrid insights, a requirement for setting up rules in regards to planning, evaluation, and testing, just as a requirement for improved comprehension of the key idea of designing frameworks, has been created.

Applications in the healthcare domain such as monitoring of an evolving situation, medical diagnosis from pictorial information or atypical attributes, basic leadership under vulnerability, identification of an abrupt difference in status of a living framework, and so on, is by all accounts included as a focal field of research for maintaining the adequacy and convenience of the application of hybrid computational intelligence architectures. The basic idea behind implementing a hybrid computational system of neural networks and evolutionary algorithms is for use of the evolutionary algorithm to decide the neural system's loads, design, or both [7]. The neural systems are either tuned or produced by an evolutionary algorithm or created and tuned simultaneously.

Fuzzy logic, along with neural networks, is one of the most successful hybrid computational intelligent combination techniques used around AI [8]. It is also known as neuro-fuzzy techniques and systems. The neuro-fuzzy system has always had a much higher success rate when implemented in the compound domain of applications, as compared to when either the neural network dominates the architecture of the system or when the heart of the system is dominated by the fuzzy set theory. The main central principle of this combination may be noted as the fusion of fuzzy functions in neural networks' nodes or as neural-like training for the member functions of the fuzzy system. According to some of the research, the neuro-fuzzy system is the most popular and commonly used hybrid intelligent system due to its efficiency, design, and implementation in health care. Neuro-fuzzy systems are better than simple neural networks, due to their ability to absorb the noise that a neural network suffers from. Also, a neuro-fuzzy system is better than a simple fuzzy system, as it is a rule-based system does not require to tune itself.

The difference between computational intelligence and hybrid computational intelligence with AI is shown below in tabular form. From Table 6.1 it can be seen that hybrid computational intelligence is better in health care as well as in other applications as it is a combination of two or more computational techniques.

## 6.1.3 Health care

Health care can be defined as the improvement and maintenance of health with regular diagnoses, prevention, and treatment of diseases, injuries, and illnesses. Health professionals, include, physicians, and those involved in medicines, dentistry, nursing, pharmacy, etc. Health care has

Table 6.1 The differences between artificial intelligence (AI), computational
intelligence (CI), and hybrid computational intelligence (HCI).

| AI | CI | HCI |
|---|---|---|
| AI is a field of study of the design of intelligent agents to create a machine that can exhibit intelligence | CI is like traditional/ old-fashioned AI which uses methods inspired by nature to solve problems | The development of software systems which employ, in parallel, a combination of methods and techniques |
| Requires programs to be written | Can evolve its own programs | Can evolve its own programs using two or more models, such as ANN, FL, SVM, etc. |
| Deterministic in nature | Stochastic in nature | Stochastic in nature |
| Requires exact input | Can deal with ambiguous and noisy data | Can deal with ambiguous and noisy data |
| Produces precise answers | Produces approximate answers | Produces approximate answers |

*ANN*, Artificial neural network; *FL, fuzzy logic*; *SVM*, support vector machine.

always been a major topic of discussion. Every healthcare system has its advantages and disadvantages, due to the fact that health care in itself will never be perfect. Even in developed countries, although their healthcare systems may arguably be better than that in the United States, they remain a work in progress.

The body system requires proper functioning in order to perform its daily activities. Unfortunately, there have been many health-related issues that are serious problems for humankind. Diseases such as HIV, cancer, unpredicted accidents, and chronic illnesses have been unavoidable for many people. Each ethnic group also has genetically caused illnesses. Lack of education and poverty play a major role in these health issues. Often, when people are unable to obtain good health insurance, they are left to suffer in miserable conditions. Health care is not a liability but a basic amenity which must be given to each and every citizen of all countries.

Healthcare systems are designed to treat sick people with the least available amount of resources. Primarily, a healthcare system needs qualified healthcare providers, patients, clean facilities, and much needed financial support. To meet the demands of a healthcare system while still providing quality care can be a difficult task as the need for healthcare services cannot be predicted. Neither patients nor healthcare providers can predict with certainty when health care will become a life-sustaining event. When the need arises, trained professionals and healthcare facilities are critical to a successful healthcare outcome. Infrastructure and funding are at the foremost of all healthcare needs. Consequently, a healthcare system needs to be prepared to provide a proactive approach to healthcare versus a reactive one. Models of healthcare systems vary from country to country.

Currently, healthcare is one of the most knowledge and information intensive areas globally, where, for the future, the focus of all healthcare professionals is on the use of information technology for the purposes of the acquisition, management, analysis, and dissemination of knowledge and information pertaining to health care. The major flaws and deficiencies prevalent within healthcare systems currently are:

- Inadequate care provided
- Super-flawed and incorrect health care
- Immensely high inefficiencies
- High cost
- Inequality in accessing care

As a result of the aforesaid problems, federal policymakers have diverted their complete focus on creating and interchanging electronic healthcare information and on the intensive use of information technology as a critical and a must-have infrastructure improvement, after whose deployment there will be a great help in addressing some of the deficiencies mentioned above [9]. The continuous effort which has been made to change healthcare and medical care information and its management model from the old and traditional one which was paper-based to the new and trending format, which is based on information technology, must address and pass two basic challenges:

1. To use the best technology and technical advancements which are available today for building and deployment of the system in such a short timescale.
2. To identify the gap which exists between today's best technology and the eventual needs for the improvement of health care.

The first challenge gives us a rapid improvement which can be made, while the second challenge gives us the information for the basic research needed and the design for future systems. A great number of studies are needed for the purpose of elucidating how research based on computer science could help a community in meeting both of the above-mentioned challenges. Researchers are now well versed with the latest and trending ideas being implemented in the field of computer science, and are hence are able to provide an insight as to how these ideas can be implemented for the betterment of health care and its problems today. Not only this, but it will also help in identifying opportunities there for new advancements.

Presently, works are being done by the combined efforts of experts from the fields of both health care and biomedicine, along with people from computer science, which include experts in the fields of networking, security, database, large-scale deployment of systems, and the interaction between humans and computers. The main purpose for this is to provide a suitable ground for considering and looking into the realities and thinking of these disciplines. After intensive research, a conclusion has been reached which presents a suggestion that the present techniques will not be self-sufficient to deploy the health care in conjunction with information technology on a national scale, creating a great setback.

A great emphasis needs to be made on providing cognitive support for patients, their families, caretakers, and healthcare providers. These cognitive supports, which mainly comprise of tools which are computer-based, along with the system offering both patients and clinical staff with the assistance to think about problems and to gain the ability to solve them related to some particular cases of health care, needs to be provided by the respective healthcare organizations, vendors, and mainly government. With the advancements which we are making in the field of computational intelligence and hybrid computational intelligence, there is great potential to revolutionize healthcare practices.

As these advances are being made, data are collected, and these massive amounts of data from the healthcare sector mostly contain information about patients. However, these huge amounts of data are not analyzable by humans because of their bulkiness. Therefore, in those cases we need to implement ML as it provides us with a way of automatically finding patterns in and about the data and it also allows healthcare professionals to move to more personalized care of each and every patient, which is known as precision medicine. The possibilities of using ML in the field of health care are great and each is dependent upon the availability of sufficient data and the respective permission needed to access and use them.

To understand the impact and influence of ML in the field of health care, we can look upon an example, such as taking an anonymous record of the patients from a hospital along with the area that it serves.

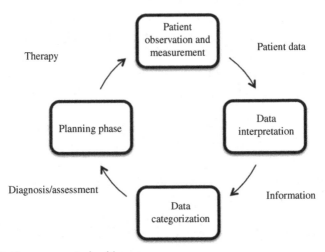

**Figure 6.2** Flow process in health care.

Now, healthcare providers can use it to their advantage by using ML to predict the hospital's readmission rates for regularly ill patients. The flow process in health care is shown in Fig. 6.2. Therefore those patients identified as most regular, need to be provided with more after-discharge services and support, so as to lower their readmission rate. The basic advantage which one will get by getting a lower readmission rate is that it will save a huge amount of money, which can be then be put to better uses, along with bringing an improved and better quality of life for those who are at most risk.

## 6.2 Need for computational intelligence in health care

Computational intelligence provides us with a considerable opportunity for advancing many characteristics of healthcare practice, including clinical disease management, such as diagnosis, prevention, treatment, and follow-up, along with administrative management of the patient, such as the patient's personal information along with healthcare delivery. Computational intelligence can be thought of as a study of the design of intelligent agents, that is, a system or agent that acts intelligently and does what it thinks is appropriate for its own goals and circumstances.

It is also flexible to changing environments and goals. It learns from its experience and makes suitable choices given finite computation and perceptual limitations [10]. Nevertheless, computational intelligence is much more than the study of the design of intelligent agents in application domains such as health care. It is also inclusive of the study of problems for which there is no effective algorithm. Humans easily solve such problems on a day-to-day basis with various levels of aptitude: understanding language, extracting meaning from perception, and solving ill-defined computer vision problems.

The core engineering goals of computational intelligence are to illustrate the means for the design of intelligent and useful artifacts and the central scientific task of computational intelligence is to recognize the ideologies that make intelligent behavior possible, whether in artificial or natural systems. The core approaches of computational intelligence—like fuzzy systems, neural computing, and evolutionary computing—have recently emerged as promising tools for the application, development, and execution of intelligent agents/systems in health care. These computational intelligence tactics have offered many advantages in creating and automating an almost physician-like capability in healthcare practice. Advancements made in computational intelligence have significant latency to bring reforms to prevalent healthcare practice.

There is a huge need for computational intelligence in the field of health care and, because of this need only, computational intelligence has found its way into this area. Some of the applications of computational intelligence techniques, such as neural networks, in health are comprised of:

- Cancer prediction
- Clinical diagnosis
- Length of stay prediction
- Speech recognition
- Ophthalmology (tissue differentiation in MRI, glaucoma)
- Radiology (MRI, adaptive medical image visualization, ultrasound images)
- Neurology (aphasia, electroencephalogram—EEG, and EEG analysis)
- Cytology (pap-smear test)
- Image interpretation and analysis
- Development of drugs

Apart from clinical applications, there are some nonclinical applications, such as in the organizational management of health care, and some key indicator predictions, such as facility utilization or cost management.

Neural networks have been used as a part of the decision support models to provide healthcare system and healthcare providers with a cost-effective solution to manage their resources and time. The neural networks have the ability to solve highly complex problems within the area of the physical sciences, and also can be used by scholars to help them provide a digital tool to enable faster processing of data collection and processing. The advantage of neural networks lies in their ability to solve problems that have a complex available solution or do not have an algorithmic solution. Neural networks are well suited to tackle problems that people are good at solving. Neural networks have been applied within the medical domain for image analysis and interpretation, clinical diagnosis, drug development, and signal analysis and interpretation.

The fuzzy nature of making a decision in health care forces technology researchers and producers to employ smooth and creative solutions. Conversion from fuzzy ideas and concepts to hard values often causes the loss of precision and results in weakening of the output decisions. Soft computing is a fast-developing, promising, and popular area that helps meet this smooth and creative need in health care. Fuzzy logic can be used as a classifier, or in the selection process of diseased patients or a specific type of disease, or for determination of the ratio of the risk of a disease, or in constructing a decision support system or in data mining.

Screening mammography has emerged as the gold standard in the field of detection of breast cancer. However, since it has such a high failure rate, researchers have been trying to apply computational intelligent tools to improve the much-needed sensitivity of this system. Most of the applications of GAs in radiology have been performed on breast cancer screening, using primarily mammography. GAs have been applied for the selection of features for studies which aim to identify the area of interest in mammograms as either normal or containing a mass, and for differentiating between malignant and benign breast tumors during ultrasound imaging.

## 6.3 Need for hybrid computational intelligence in health care

Speaking of hybrid intelligent methodologies that can be found in the literature from the last decade, irrespective of the application area, one would find several approaches related to fuzzy control, function approximation, forecasting, knowledge discovery, decision making, scheduling, feature selection, system design, data classification, and image processing. The most popular application domains are those related to medical problems [11].

There are many scenarios where the relationships are not clear, and the fuzzy if–then rules cannot be defined in support of fuzzy reasoning. In such situations, techniques combine fuzzy logic methods with other methods like neural networks, GAs, wavelet transform, Bayesian reasoning, and ML. Like combining fuzzy Logic with another technique, cascading fuzzy logic with another technique is also a method of hybrid fuzzy methodology. In the cascading method, two methods are applied one by one in turn [12]. Neuro-fuzzy combinations are mostly used in medical image processing applications. Image processing is a wide area of research. Along with neuro-fuzzy combinations, cascade methods are also used, like fuzzy logic and classification and clustering methods. GAs capture the most optimal choice by elimination of defective possibilities. Using the optimal search of a GA, a GA–fuzzy hybrid approach is commonly used in a cascade model over a combination.

An adaptive fuzzy-leader clustering algorithm has been used for the segmenting procedure for magnetic resonance images (MRI) of the neural system and brain. This method has proved to be of superior performance as compared with the other prevailing dissection methods. An amalgamation of the neural networks and fuzzy logic is in use for the development of an adaptive switch system of arterial blood pressure. Fuzzy logic-based adaptive neural networks is aimed to reimburse for image dilapidation which occurs due to photon trickling and its infiltration through an altered gamma camera to allow more precise measurements of the radiotracers. Euro-fuzzy systems, along with adaptive learning capabilities, are needed for controlling the discerning stimulation of fat embolism syndrome (FES).

Chaos theory, in collaboration with a neuro-fuzzy network, is used for designing an intelligent and adaptive information scheme for the analysis of the time series, which is applicable in the case of heart rate inconsistency. During the stages of pregnancy, a neural and fuzzy classifier has been developed, to distinguish among normal and pathological fetal conditions that can occur during pregnancy. Both classifiers are based upon the nonlinear and linear indices that are withdrawn from the cardiotocographic fetal monitoring. The corresponding outcomes show very promising performance based on the set of collected fetal heart rate signals [13]. Also, a network-based predictor, along with an adaptive fuzzy controller, has been developed into a system for supervising the mean arterial blood pressure of seriously ill patients.

Other neuro-fuzzy hybrid computational techniques are used for:
- The study of glaucoma
- Electrocardiography (ECG) beat recognition
- Situation assessment of glaucoma
- Antenatal fetal risk assessment
- Adaptive control for selective stimulation of FES

A hybrid computational intelligent system with neural networks and evolutionary algorithms is widely used for breast cancer diagnosis. ECG R—R wave peak detection is done using the hybrid system of an evolutionary algorithm with a fuzzy inference system, to assess the brain—gut interaction [14]. The hybrid computational intelligent system with ML and fuzzy logic has found wide use in MRI and for the diagnosis of coronary stenosis. For cervical cancer, much progress has been made with the use of a hybrid intelligent system with ML and an evolutionary algorithm.

Health care is emerging as a prominent area for AI research and applications, and nearly every area across this industry will be impacted by the rise in technology. Image recognition, for example, is revolutionizing diagnostics. Recently, Google DeepMind's neural networks matched the accuracy of medical experts in diagnosing 50 sight-threatening eye diseases. Even pharma companies are experimenting with deep learning to design new drugs. For example, Merck partnered with startup Atomwise, and GlaxoSmithKline is partnering with Insilico Medicine. In the private sector, healthcare AI startups have raised $4.3B across 576 deals since 2013, topping all other industries in AI activity, as shown below in Fig. 6.3, as AI becomes a new approach in the healthcare sector. If we

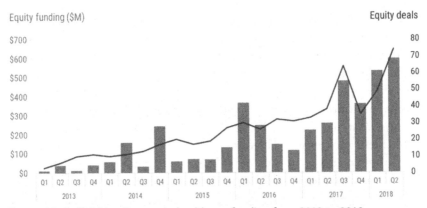

**Figure 6.3** Artificial intelligence in healthcare funding from 2013 to 2018.

combine the different technologies as mentioned above then computational intelligence may hit a healthcare sector in the upcoming years.

## 6.4 Use cases for hybrid computational intelligence in health care

### 6.4.1 Research and clinical decision support

CDS provides us with timely information to enable the support to make informed decisions about patients. The system and tools of CDS helps the concerned team by taking over routine tasks, by providing with basic suggestions for the team and the patient to consider, or by warning of the potential threats [15]. CDS was designed to provide timely updating of information regarding patients, clinicians, and other healthcare-related information. It has the potential to solve three most important issues currently:

- Cost reduction
- Better efficiency
- Reduction in patient inconvenience

CDS requires person-specific data, biomedical knowledge, and an inferencing and reasoning mechanism which combines data with knowledge for the presentation and generation of helpful information which the clinical expert can use in delivering health care [16]. The information collected needs to be organized, filtered, and presented in such a manner that it supports the workflow in the current situation and also allows the user to make informed decisions at a quicker pace and to take actions accordingly. Most CDS applications operate like a component of the comprehensive electronic health records (EHRs), though independent systems are also in use.

The cognitive computing decision support system has great benefit in terms of the adverse reaction of the ineffective treatments and those ineffective treatments in the first place can be minimized, which will result in improved outcomes, which also helps in the reduction of costs [17].

### 6.4.2 Medical imaging

A team involving the services provided by radiographers, radiologists, medical physicists, sonographers, biomedical engineers, nurses, and other support staff, working along with each other for imaging for medical purposes and to optimize and look out for the well-being of patients. Medical imaging requires a multidisciplinary approach.

Medical imaging includes distinctive imaging modalities and procedures to picture the human body for symptomatic and treatment purposes, and in this manner assumes a vital job in activities to improve the general well-being of all populations. Moreover, medical imaging is often used in the follow-up of an ailment previously analyzed or potentially treated.

Medical imaging, particularly X-ray-based examinations and ultrasonography, is vital in an assortment of medicinal settings and at all significant dimensions of social insurance. In general healthcare and preventive prescription, just as in both remedial and palliative considerations, viable choices rely upon the correct determinations. In spite of the fact that restorative/clinical judgment might be adequate before treatment of numerous conditions, the utilization of symptomatic imaging is principal in affirming, accurately surveying, and recording courses of numerous illnesses, just as in evaluating reactions to treatment.

With an improved medicinal services strategy and the expanding accessibility of medical equipment, the quantity of worldwide imaging-based methods is expanding extensively. Powerful, safe, and astounding imaging is critical for much restorative basic treatment and can decrease the amount of pointless procedures. For instance, some careful intercessions can be avoided if basic analytical imaging, for example, ultrasound, is accessible.

### 6.4.3 Voice to text transcription

Medical transcription tools have long been legacy products but, as vendors inject modern technologies, notably automation and voice recognition, new data suggest that hospitals are going to deploy more of these products and services amid broader digital transformation work.

Medical transcription is the process by which doctors and healthcare professionals process health records, which are then converted into a readable format from voice and text. Such data are used largely by healthcare organizations and EHR initiatives.

Medical transcription software (MTS) is a specialized speech recognition program that includes a database of medical terminology. An MTS is used to convert audio recordings made by physicians or other healthcare professionals into electronic text that can be transferred over a network and printed out.

Healthcare providers can implement speech recognition software in two ways. In a front-end implementation, the physician or nurse activates the software, reviews the notes that have been digitized to text, and signs it off. With a back-end implementation, the software automatically converts speech to text and routes both audio and text to a transcriptionist for review. In back-end systems, the person who originated the dictation still must review transcriptions for accuracy and sign them off.

MTS has changed the way medical transcriptionists do their jobs. Instead of creating documents, transcriptionists are now responsible for editing transcribed documents for medical accuracy. Adapting to this new role has been a challenge for some transcriptionists; for others, it has opened doors to new professional opportunities that support EHRs, including quality assurance and coding.

## 6.4.4 Fraud detection

Different fraudulent activities in other sectors as compared to the healthcare sector, the number of fraudulent behaviors in healthcare is more with respect to the other sectors. Different nations experience different type of fraud which need to be given attention to. There is not a particular or a specific type of fraudulent behavior, rather multiple types can be observed in this industry. A distinctive classification as per the individuals or groups involved in these activities has been done here.

- Fraud carried out by insurance subscribers:
  - Claiming for medical services which in reality were not received by subscribers who are filing for it.
  - To obtain a lower premium rate, the falsification of records of the eligibility or the employment done.
  - Use of another persons' insurance coverage or their insurance card to illegally claim those insurance benefits which they were not entitled to.
- Fraud by service providers:
  - Unbundling or the process where each and every stage of treatment is represented as an individual treatment and billing is done accordingly.
  - Billing for those services which in reality were not actually performed.
  - Performing unnecessary medical treatment so as to generate larger insurance payments.
  - Performing a cheaper medical treatment but charging for a much more expensive one.

- Performing those treatments which were not needed in the first place just to charge and claim higher insurance money, and the falsification of the patient's treatment history or the patient diagnosis reports.
- Conspiracy frauds:
  - Fraudulent activities carried out in collaboration with multiple parties, which can include the patient in collaboration with the doctor or the insurance providers, etc.
- Frauds by insurance carriers:
  - To misrepresent the service as well as the benefit statements.
  - Making fake reimbursements which should not be there.

### 6.4.4.1 Data for healthcare fraud

The basic data obtainable for fraudulent activities in the healthcare sector are mostly insurance claims which one can get from varied sources. Apart from insurance claim data which are used for the detection of healthcare fraud, other data which can be used are the data of prescriptions given by physicians, physician data, data from bills and transactions, and data of the medications or drugs prescribed. Every country has its own method for generating healthcare data and so, for the evaluation of fraud committed, one needs to consider those government data.

### 6.4.4.2 Methods for healthcare fraud detection

There are different unpredictable and convoluted examples with numerous minimal details involving fraud, whose information is assembled over a drawn-out time. It is incredibly difficult to distinguish these examples in current occurrences, where we have an immense collection of information and not many methods for assessing them. Customarily, a couple of examiners used to deal with a great many social insurance claims. In this way, normally, only experienced agents would oversee misrepresentation identification. Be that as it may, because of the extensive gathering of information, this technique was tedious and wasteful. Upgrades in information mining and AI instruments have indicated mechanized frameworks for misrepresentation identification. For inconsistent data and identification of extortion, different profiling strategies dependent on AI methods are utilized. For this reason, the standard of conduct for every individual associated with the human services framework is arranged to be watched and checked for any conclusion. Information mining strategies are grouped into two classifications, regulated and unsupervised learning, by the majority of scientists. However, at times, alongside these two methodologies, semiadministered learning is also associated with this characterization.

There are several steps to develop a model to mine healthcare claims to detect fraud and abuse as follows:

1. Initial preprocessing stage.
2. Analysis stage. To build a model in a hierarchy structure and evaluate the claims processing workflow. The basic experimental model which evaluates the dataset and identifies the important attributes of data which discriminates the behavior of the whole data set [18,19].
3. Development stage. Application of data mining algorithms and use of statistical measures to extract new features and which assists in mining abnormal or abusive behavior [20,21].
4. Recognizing unusual data with mined features, and then examining and labeling them as outliers [22,23].
5. We recommend that this model will help in finding fraudulent claiming behaviors for particular procedures which are suited to any size data sets, as applicable to medium- and high-income insurance companies.

The performance of the technique is determined by the type of data set and experimental model. As on no single computational approach will give dependable outcomes for all types of healthcare data, we need a hybrid approach (more than one) to detect fraud in the healthcare sector.

## 6.4.5 Cyber security

It has turned out to be progressively evident that cyber security is a hazard factor in medicinal services information. Information breaches cost the human services industry around $5.6 billion annually, as indicated by Becker's Hospital Review. The Breach Barometer Report: A Review in a Year also discovered that there was an average of one health data breach for each day in 2016, attacks that influenced in excess of 27 million patient records. As associations try to shield their patient data from these developing dangers, interest in well-being informatics experts who know about the present conditions of cyber security in human services is on the ascent.

### 6.4.5.1 Cyber security challenges in health care

The newest digital vulnerabilities are not really an association's greatest digital danger. Verizon's 2016 Data Breach Investigations Report found that most breaks are about cash and attackers more often than not take the least demanding course to get the data they need. Therefore, numerous regular dangers remain risky in human services, including:

1. *Cloud threats*: An expanding measure of secure well-being data is by putting it on the virtual cloud. Without appropriate encryption, this can be a weak spot for the security of human services associations.
2. *Malware and ransomware*: Cybercriminals use malware and ransomware to close down individual gadgets, servers, or even whole systems. At times, a payoff is then requested to correct the encryption.
3. *Phishing attacks*: This methodology conveys mass measures of messages from apparently respectable sources to get sensitive data from clients.
4. *Misleading websites*: Cunning cybercriminals have made sites with addresses that are similar to respectable destinations. Some essentially substitute.com for.gov, giving the unwary client the illusion that the sites are equivalent.
5. *Employee error*: Workers can leave medicinal services associations helpless to attack through powerless passwords, decoded gadgets, and different failures of consistency.
6. *Encryption blind spots*: While encryption is basic for securing well-being information, it can likewise create vulnerability where programmers can escape the devices intended to recognize breaks.

Another developing danger in medicinal services security is found in restorative gadgets. As pacemakers and other hardware become associated with the Web, they face vulnerabilities from other PC frameworks. To guarantee understanding well-being, the U.S. Nourishment and Drug Administration has prescribed that both the producer that makes the gadget and the medicinal services office that insert it take preventive safety efforts.

### 6.4.5.2 Strategies for improving cyber security

Because of the noteworthy monetary effect of information failures in medicinal services, well-being informatics and different experts are assuming an imperative job in guaranteeing that restorative associations stay secure.

As per HealthIT.gov, singular medicinal services associations can improve their cyber security by executing the following practices:

1. *Protection of mobile devices*: A growing number of human services suppliers are utilizing cell phones at work. Encryption and other defensive measures are basic to guarantee that any data on these gadgets are secure.

2. *Establishment of a security culture*: Due to increasing cybersecurity attacks, preparations and instructions from each individual for the association/organization is responsible for protecting patient data and creating a culture of security.

3. *Using a firewall*: Anything associated with the Web ought to have a firewall.

4. *Maintaining good computer habits*: New representative onboarding ought to incorporate preparing for best practices in PC use, including programming and working framework support.

5. *Planning for the unexpected*: Records ought to be supported for fast and simple information reclamation. Associations ought to considered putting away data from the fundamental framework if possible.

6. *Installing and maintaining antivirus software*: Installation of an antivirus program is insufficient. Nonstop updates are fundamental for guaranteeing healthcare frameworks have the most ideal assurance at all times.

7. *Using strong passwords and changing them regularly*: The Verizon report claimed that 63 percent of affirmed information breaks included exploiting passwords that were the default, powerless, or stolen. Healthcare workers ought to use solid passwords as well as guarantee they are changed from time to time.

8. *Controlling access to protected health information*: Access to secured data ought to be allowed only for individuals who need to view or utilize it.

9. *Controlling physical access*: Information can also be hacked when physical gadgets are stolen. PCs and different hardware that contain data ought to be kept in secured rooms in secure areas.

10. *Limiting network access*: Any product, applications, and different increments to existing frameworks ought not to be introduced by staff without earlier permission from the best possible authoritative specialists.

Notwithstanding these suggestions, healthcare experts are ceaselessly growing new techniques and best practices to guarantee the security of health-related information, shielding both the patient and association from financial misfortune and other types of mischief.

## 6.5 Conclusion

The advancements being made in the field of hybrid computational intelligence have great scope and potential to bring about a revolution in the field of healthcare practices. The main focus of this chapter has been to make the reader aware of the recent hybrid technology and the current research, along with their results regarding the applications of hybrid computational intelligence in the field of healthcare practices. This chapter gives a wide and clear perspective to readers regarding the advancements this field has made and how these advancements can be used. The chapter gives a detailed insight into how hybrid computational intelligent systems are much better than computational intelligent systems. The chapter first explains computational intelligence in detail followed by a detailed explanation of hybrid intelligence and then a comparative study between the two. A detailed insight into health care is also given which highlights the advancements which health care has made by implementing computational intelligence techniques. This was then followed by the need for both computational and hybrid computational intelligence in health care. Detailed insight into the various uses of hybrid intelligent systems were discussed, including medical imaging, fraud detection, etc.

In such a time of healthcare transformation at such a fast pace, healthcare organizations quickly adapt to the latest technologies and so regulate and meet consumer demands. The AI industry offers an incredible option of learning from the past and making better decisions for the future. GAs, neural networks, fuzzy logic, ML, and various forms of basic computational intelligence techniques and their hybrids are also discussed. The continued focus and attention on quality, cost, and care outcomes will ensure that there are further advancements in the field using different AI technologies to improve the quality of the services provided across various healthcare areas.

## References

[1] L. Ogiela, Cognitive computational intelligence in medical pattern semantic understanding, in: 2008 Fourth International Conference on Natural Computation, Jinan, 2008, pp. 245–247. Available from: https://doi.org/10.1109/ICNC.2008.714.

[2] H. Yoshida, S. Vaidya, L.C. Jain, Introduction to computational intelligence in healthcare, in: S. Vaidya, L.C. Jain, H. Yoshida (Eds.), Advanced Computational Intelligence Paradigms in Healthcare-2. Studies in Computational Intelligence, vol. 65, Springer, Berlin, Heidelberg, 2007.

[3] National Research Council (US) Committee on Engaging the Computer Science Research Community in Health Care Informatics, in: W.W. Stead, H.S. Lin (Eds.), Computational Technology for Effective Health Care: Immediate Steps and Strategic Directions, National Academies Press (US), Washington, DC, 2009. Available from: https://www.ncbi.nlm.nih.gov/books/NBK20640/. https://doi.org/10.17226/12572.

[4] L. Ogiela, Computational intelligence in cognitive healthcare information systems, in: I. Bichindaritz, S. Vaidya, A. Jain, L.C. Jain (Eds.), Computational Intelligence in Healthcare 4. Studies in Computational Intelligence, vol. 309, Springer, Berlin, Heidelberg, 2010.

[5] A.K. Mourya, P. Tyagi, A. Bhatnagar, Genetic algorithm and their applicability in medical diagnostic: a survey, Int. J. Sci. Eng. Res. 7 (12) (2016) 1143. ISSN 2229-5518. <http://www.ijser.org>.

[6] G. Dounias, Hybrid computational intelligence in medicine, Dept. of Business Administration Journal, Greece, 2003.

[7] A. Suresh, R. Kumar, R. Varatharajan, Health care data analysis using evolutionary algorithm, J. Supercomput. (2018). Available from: https://doi.org/10.1007/s11227-018-2302-0.

[8] G. Gürsel, Healthcare, uncertainty, and fuzzy logic, Digit. Med. 2 (2016) 101−112.

[9] S.G. Mishra, A.K. Takke, S.T. Auti, et al., Role of artificial intelligence in health care, Biochem. Ind. J. 11 (5) (2017) 120. Trade Science Inc.

[10] K.C. Tan, Q. Yu, C.M. Heng, T.H. Lee, Evolutionary computing for knowledge discovery in medical diagnosis, Artif. Intell. Med. 27 (2003) 129−154. Available from: https://doi.org/10.1016/S0933-3657(03)00002-2.

[11] A. Tsakonas, G. Dounias, Hybrid computational intelligence schemes in complex domains: a review of selected publications, in: I. Vlahavas, C. Spyropoulos, (Eds.), Int. Conf. SETN-02, Thessaloniki, Greece, also appeared in LNAI-2308, "Methods and Applications of Artificial Intelligence", Springer Publications, 2002, pp. 494−511.

[12] C. Chin Te, L.W. Li, et al., A combination of neural network and fuzzy logic algorithms for adaptive control of arterial blood pressure, Biomed. Eng. Appl. Basis Commun. 10 (3) (1998) 139−150.

[13] S. Osowski, T.H. Linh, ECG beat recognition using fuzzy hybrid neural network, IEEE Trans. Biomed. Eng. 48 (11) (2001) 1265−1271.

[14] G. Georg, Computerization of clinical guidelines: an application of medical document processing, in: B.G. Silverman, A. Jain, A. Ichalkaranje, L.C. Jain (Eds.), Intelligent Paradigms for Healthcare Enterprises. Studies in Fuzziness and Soft Computing, vol. 184. Springer, Berlin, Heidelberg.

[15] J.E. Tcheng, S. Bakken, D.W. Bates, H. Bonner III, T.K. Gandhi, M. Josephs, et al. (Eds.), Optimizing Strategies for Clinical Decision Support: Summary of a Meeting Series, National Academy of Medicine, Washington, DC, 2017.

[16] Clinical Decision Support Content last reviewed August 2018, Agency for Healthcare Research and Quality, Rockville, MD. http://www.ahrq.gov.in/professionals/prevention-chronic-care/decision/clinical/index.html.

[17] S. Brahnam, L.C. Jain, Intelligent decision support systems in healthcare, in: S. Brahnam, L.C. Jain (Eds.), Advanced Computational Intelligence Paradigms in Healthcare 5. Studies in Computational Intelligence, vol. 326, Springer, Berlin, Heidelberg, 2010.

[18] T. Hillerman, J.C.F. Souza, A.C.B. Reis, R.N. Carvalho, Applying Clustering and AHP Methods for Evaluating Suspect Healthcare Claims, vol. 19, Elsevier, 2017, pp. 97−111.

[19] M. Kumar, et al., Data mining to predict errors in health insurance claims processing, in: KDD'10, ACM, 2010, pp. 1−9.

[20] S. Kang, J. Song, Feature selection for continuous aggregate response and its application to auto insurance data, Expert Syst. Appl. 93 (2018) 104−117.

[21] R.A. Bauder, T.M. Khoshgoftaar, Medicare fraud detection using machine learning methods, in: IEEE Conference, 2017, pp. 858−865.

[22] C. Ngufor, J. Wojtusiak, Unsupervised labeling of data for supervised learning and its application to medical claims prediction, Comput. Sci. 14 (2) (2013) 191–214.

[23] M.J. Tang, B.S.U. Mendis, D.W. Murray, D. Sumudu, Y. Hu, A. Sutinen, Unsupervised fraud detection in Medicare Australia, Conf. Proc. 121 (2011) 103–110.

## CHAPTER 7

# Utility system for premature plant disease detection using machine learning

**B.J. Sowmya[1], Chetan Shetty[2], S. Seema[1] and K.G. Srinivasa[3]**
[1]Department of Computer Science and Engineering, Ramaiah Institute of Technology, Bangalore, India
[2]HCL Technologies, Bangalore, India
[3]Department of Information Management & Coordination, NITTTR, Chandigarh, India

## 7.1 Introduction

With the advancements and improvements in technologies, a huge amount of data is being generated and is described as big data, making it excruciatingly difficult to be handled by traditional databases. The fields of artificial intelligence (AI), cloud computing, and the Internet of Things (IoT) among others are aiding in the development of big data to a great extent. Analogous to the IoT is the cyber physical system (CPS), which combines the capabilities of physical components with computing and communicational components. There are numerous CPS applications, such as smart grids, unmanned aerial vehicle networks, smart cities, transportation networks, healthcare systems, and smart agriculture.

This chapter focuses on insights into smart agriculture or smart farming applications as the topic of discussion. In India, agriculture is the main source of income. Most of the population's works in agriculture, which contributes about 17% of the nation's GDP. Unpredictable changes in the climatic conditions, inadequate irrigation techniques, lack of experience in using modern technologies, and pesticides have caused an imbalance in farming that has caused improper cultivation of crops and unhealthy crops, thereby threatening food security. As agriculture strives to satisfy the growing demands of the current rapidly growing population, plant disease has proved to be detrimental to production as well as quality of crops. Farmers spend a substantial amount of money on managing plant diseases, usually due to a lack of knowledge, which results in an uncontrolled increase in plant disease. Increased improper farming can lead to degradation of ecosystems, aggravating environmental losses and leading to

*Hybrid Computational Intelligence*
DOI: https://doi.org/10.1016/B978-0-12-818699-2.00008-1
149

inferior land management. Pathogens, pests, and weeds altogether are responsible for between 20% and 40% of the total agriculture productivity losses. Apart from monetary loss, this has a tremendous impact on society, among which the most significant was the Irish Famine (1845), which affected the country immensely with about 1.5 million dying. Human illness and degradation of the environment are also caused by infected crops. Extreme crop losses lead to importing of foods, and thereby increasing the dependency on processed foods, thus harming the diet. Although many farmers have been able to achieve good crop yields and efficient crop health management, some farmers lack the necessary resources. Therefore, an adept and economical methodology to detect these plant diseases is an imminent need.

At times when the human eye is not able to detect the plant disease precisely, techniques such as image processing and classification would be useful. Early detection of disease in plants can lessen the risk of crop failure and increase yields. Reduced diseases would make crops more nutritious, and thereby decrease health issues for consumers. In this work, a plan is made to provide an efficient and precise method which could be used to identify infected plants and also to measure the intensity of infection in the crop. This could be utilized by farmers to detect the onset of a disease and take the necessary measures to stem the disease in its infancy, which would go a long way in stopping the disease from spreading and affecting other parts of the plants. The proposed system makes use of a support vector machine (SVM) and neural network to classify the image and give remedies accordingly.

The focal point of this work revolves around the tomato. The tomato is a food crop that is cultivated throughout the seasons. Temperature and light intensity affect the pigmentation, fruit-sets, and nutritive value of these fruits. Due to all these environmental norms, the plant is susceptible to diseases caused by fungi, bacteria, and viruses. Early detection can immensely help in preventing diseases and thereby increasing the yield.

The objectives of the illustrated system are:
- Implementation of leaf disease detection using SVM and AlexNet;
- The implemented system must be able to perform classification correctly;
- Provision of a solution with the least hardware requirement;
- Application of an image processing technique to analyze the pattern of tomato leaf disease.

## 7.2 Literature survey

Before diving into the implementation of the proposed system, there are some noteworthy works that have already made an impact across the world in the field of agriculture. Some of these are briefly described below to give a clear understanding of the system.

### 7.2.1 Related work

As the basis of this chapter is smart agriculture, and especially the prediction and detection of diseases in plants, image processing is one of the primary tasks that is carried out, wherein an image of the plant leaf under consideration is captured for analysis. This image processing can be on a standalone application or a remote database. The general flow of the technique to process an image is shown in Fig. 7.1. The first task is to preprocess the image samples wherein they are converted to the required format. The next task is to segment the obtained image samples to distribute the picture into different partitions. The essential features are acquired from the samples and classified accordingly. Infectious plants are identified by segmenting the image and soft computing, as described by Singh and Mishra [1] who provide a valuable insight into the techniques of image processing.

Petrellis [2] proposed a technique for processing the image which can be used as an app on cell phones for the recognition of plant diseases. The system segregates the visible that at different parts of the plant. The application has been tested for vineyard diseases based on images with grape

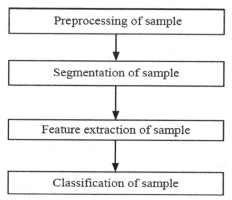

**Figure 7.1** Steps for processing the image.

leaves. The proposed method extracts the lesion features such as the number of spots, corresponding gray level area, and a histogram indicating pixels that have specific red, blue, green (RGB) levels. A global positioning system is also used to determine the specific rural regions where the plant may exist. The flow of the threshold algorithm used is depicted in Fig. 7.2. A threshold is maintained for a particular leaf disease. If the RGB value of a pixel falls below the threshold value, then the corresponding pixel value is blackened, otherwise it is whitened out. Thereby, the output will only consist of a pattern of black spots, which can be easily classified by comparing with the available data set and predicting whether the plant suffers from the disease or not. The suggested method was applied to a small training data set and attained an accuracy of over 80%.

The approach discussed above was straightforward and does not require any analytical algorithms. However, in the modern computerized world where analytics plays a major role, there is a necessity to apply them, and thereby increase the production rate. Tete and Kamlu [3] came up with a $K$-means clustering algorithm for detection of plant diseases. The flow of this algorithm is shown in Fig. 7.3.

After loading the image of the leaf, conversion of the image from RGB to $L^*a^*b$ color space takes place using the predefined conversion formulae. Using $K$-means clustering the classification of colors in $a^*b$ space follows. Subsequently, the results from the previous step are plotted in the

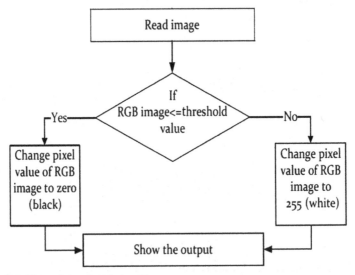

**Figure 7.2** Flow of threshold algorithm.

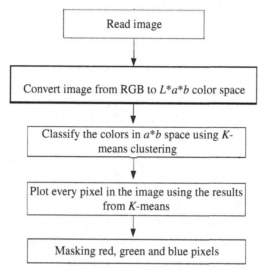

**Figure 7.3** Flow of the *K*-means clustering algorithm.

image, masking red, green, and blue pixels to obtain the spots or changes on the leaves that are clearly visible and are correlated with the existing data to detect the disease. The *K*-means clustering requires a prior condition of the number of clusters and this technique is more effective than the thresholding algorithm.

Varshney and Dalal [4] presented an approach using SVM classifier for the detection of plant diseases. SVM is a nonlinear classifier that is widely used in pattern recognition and texture classification. The RGB feature pixel-counting techniques are utilized for detecting plant leaf, stem, and fruit diseases, to quantify the affected area, and to determine the color and boundary of the affected area. The input data in SVM, which are nonlinear, are mapped to linearly separate the data in high-dimensional space. The infected area is calculated in terms of percentage (e.g., 30% infected) and the disease is detected based on the pattern with the SVM classifier. The entire process is illustrated in Fig. 7.4. The SVM classifier is used to enhance the features of the image to a large extent, following which the segmentation process is carried out to differentiate the region of interest. The authors claim that it achieves an accuracy of greater than 90%, which is very much better than the existing algorithm.

Keskar et al. [5] built up a leaf disease recognition and analysis framework for the assessment of leaves and to discover the disease type. The framework includes four phases: Stage 1—transformation of HSI shading

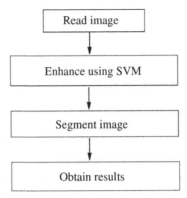

**Figure 7.4** Flow of approach involving a support vector machine classifier.

space and assessment of the histogram of power channel to get the edge. Stage 2—segmentation—a change of the fuzzy element calculation parameter to fit the application. Stage 3—feature extraction—isolation and spot distinguishing proof is carried out and three highlights (color, size, and shape) of spots are separated. Stage 4—classification with the assistance of an artificial neural network (ANN).

Sannakki et al. [6] proposed a framework that analyzed different diseases of pomegranate plants as well as depicting the phase of the disease. The technique of this framework is partitioned into four stages: Step 1—the pictures are procured utilizing a computerized camera. Stage 2—image preprocessing using procedures like segmentation, image resizing, morphological activities, filtering, etc. to upgrade the picture, which is increasingly helpful for analysis. Stage 3—image postprocessing and feature extraction, wherein the issues like cuts, void openings, and others are evacuated by applying area filling, morphological tasks. Further the highlights are extricated, including shading, shape, surface, etc. Stage 4—use of AI methods like ANN, decision tree, clustering, genetic calculation, SVMs, fuzzy rationale, Bayesian systems, and so on are used to decide the class or type of disease.

Phadikar et al. [7] built up a robotized arrangement framework that is shaped on the morphological changes instigated by dark-colored spots and the leaf shoot diseases of rice plants. To order the diseases, radial appropriation of the hue from the middle to the limit of the spot has been utilized as highlighted by utilizing naïve Bayes and SVM classifiers. The element extraction for rice leaf diseases is handled in these steps and procedures: at first, pictures of the unhealthy rice leaves are obtained from the fields.

These pictures are then prehandled to expel defects from the harmed leaf and then an upgraded picture is made utilizing the mean separating system. Otsu's segmentation calculation is then connected to siphon the infected portion of the picture, and after that spiral tint dissemination vectors of the segmented regions are processed and utilized as feature vectors.

The evolution and innovations in modern technology have led to the emergence of the field of artificial intelligence, wherein machine learning (ML) plays an important part. Patil and Thorat [8] exploited ML and the IoT for the detection of grape diseases that uses the hidden Markov model (HMM), wherein the states are hidden from the user and the probability of being in a state depends on the probability of its previous states. A Zig-Bee is used for the acquisition and transmission of sensor data and this system consists of S1, S2, and S3 as hidden forms having some initial condition for flow in and out of the states and seven observing states corresponding to six different types of disease observed in grapes (anthracnose, powdery mildew, rust, downy mildew, bacterial leaf spot, bacterial leaf cancer) plus one "no disease" (healthy) state. Finally, hypothesis testing is also conducted to conclude that the results obtained using HMM model give more accuracy than a statistical HMM model.

A broader classification of ML is deep learning (DL), which uses artificial neural network (ANN) algorithms. Park et al. [9] made use of these DL concepts by dynamically analyzing the images to detect and predict diseases in plants. It uses convolutional neural networks (CNNs) to classify healthy and disease-affected images with higher accuracy. The proposed system consists of two main components: a data aggregation module and a disease learning and testing engine to automate the process of classification and automation of strawberry plant diseases. The disease learning and testing engine is used to construct the model and perform disease identification by obtaining the data from a data aggregation module. It also makes use of Hadoop HDFS nodes for storing purposes. The feedback from the farmer or the user is also obtained and reflected in the model to improve the classification performance. The model performs with an accuracy of 89.7% on a CPU.

Other notable works on the detection and prediction of plant disease includes detection of leaf rot diseases in betel vine using a technique known as the image processing technique that observes the exterior disease features. After preprocessing of the captured image, segmentation is carried out, which is implemented by color analysis, and it was found that the hue component of the hue, saturation, and value (HSV) model gives neat discernment of rotted leaf and masks the background and rest of the leaf area. This technique gives a solution for smart agriculture using computer vision and computer intelligence [10]. Suresha et al. [11] presented the use of a k-nearest neighbor (kNN) for the recognition of different types of diseases in paddy, such as brown spots and blast diseases. It follows the same flow as general image processing, starting with preprocessing of the image followed by segmentation of the image, wherein they used the HSV model, and prominent features are extracted, such as the area, major axis length, minor axis length, and perimeter. With the kNN classifier an accuracy of 76.5% was obtained. Joshi and Jadhav [12] provided the monitoring and control of rice diseases using a minimum distance classifier (MDC) and the kNN. MDC with Manhattan distance and kNN with city-block distance metric have been implemented, giving an accuracy of 89.23%. Beulah and Punithavalli [13] demonstrates the prediction of diseases in sugarcane plants using data mining techniques such as a decision tree model and random forest model. They also calculated the area under the recall curve that produced 57% and 71%, respectively, for the decision tree model and random forest model.

MohamadAzmi et al. in their work [14] recommended a method for the detection of orchid diseases using image processing and fuzzy logic [15]. Methods like threshold segmentation, gray scaling, and noise removal are used for leaf image processing. The data are comprised of the number of diseased spots, centroid, and leaf area. The data are then processed through fuzzification [16], fuzzy inference, and defuzzification. Phadikar et al. [17] use image processing and soft computing technique on various diseased plants. They proposed a technique to classify rice images which were captured by digital camera using an SOM neural network. Revathi et al. [18] came up with a novel method based on image RGB feature-ranging techniques. The images are first enhanced and color image segmentation is done to identify the target regions. The edges are identified by homogenization techniques like Sobel and Canny filter. The diseases are then classified using the HPCCDD proposed algorithm.

Mohanty et al. [19] used a CNN to recognize plant leaf diseases. They utilized 54,306 pictures of diseased and healthy plant leaves to prepare a profound convolution neural system to indicate 14 crop species and 26 infections with the assistance of apparatuses, for example, AlexNet and GoogleNet. Rumpfa et al. [20] proposed early discovery of plant infections before the presence of side effects utilizing hyperspectral information which was recorded from healthy leaves and those mixed with different pathogens. The SVM algorithm is applied to classify the healthy and unhealthy leaves. where it is applied on the huge data set. Al-Bashish et al. [21] proposed a neural network classifier that depends on measurable grouping for the Al-Ghor zone data set. A K-means procedure is utilized here to fragment the picture, which then goes through a pre-prepared neural system. Meunkaewjinda et al. [22] presented a programmed plant infection analysis utilizing decision methods. A backspread neural network is utilized to perceive the shade of grape leaf, wherein SVM is utilized for arrangement. Divided pictures are separated through a Gabor wavelet which encourages the framework to dissect the highlights of leaf shading diseases. The framework can recognize three classes of grape leaves: scab, rust, and no infection. Arivazhagan et al. [23] created a technique for programmed identification and grouping of plant leaf diseases. Color change is accomplished for RGB pictures of leaf tests. Explicit limit worth is utilized for concealing and certain thresholds are set to divide the red, blue, green pixels pursued by a division process. Surface statistics are processed utilizing a shading co-event system and the highlights removed go through a classifier, where a neural system is used for recognition of plant leaf images.

### 7.2.1.1 Image processing
In software engineering, computerized picture handling is the utilization of computer algorithms to perform picture preparation on digital images. As a subcategory or field of digital signal processing, digital image processing has numerous favorable qualities over simple picture handling. It permits much more extensive scope of algorithms to be connected to the information and can avoid noises, for example, the development of commotion and signal distortion during processing. Since images are characterized in more than two dimensions (maybe progressively) digital image processing might be demonstrated as multidimensional frameworks. Efficient image processing techniques are connected to the image transferred to remove fundamental element vectors to help classification and clustering.

### 7.2.1.2 Feature extraction
Feature extraction from information images is where the highlights are removed. To do this, as opposed to picking the entire arrangement of pixels, we can pick just those which are important and adequate to depict the entire segment. The segmented picture is first chosen by manual

interference. The influenced territory of the picture can be found from ascertaining the zone associating the parts. In the first place, the associated parts with six neighborhood pixels are found. Later, the essential area properties of the info paired picture are found. We are interested in the extracted part of the image for further classification. The influenced region is discovered. The percent zone canvassed in this portion illustrates the nature of the outcome. The histogram of an element or picture gives data about the recurrence of an event in the entire picture. It is a significant apparatus for frequent analysis. The co-event takes this analysis to the next level wherein the force occurrences of two pixels together are noted in the network, making the co-event a gigantic instrument for analysis. From a gray-co-matrix, the highlights, for example, contrast, correlation, energy, and homogeneity are removed.

| No. | Features | Formula |
| --- | --- | --- |
| 1. | Contrast | $\sum_i \sum_j |i-j|^2 p(i,j,d,\theta)$ |
| 2. | Correlation | $\sum_{i,j} \frac{(i-\mu_i)(j-\mu_j)p(i,j)}{\sigma_i \sigma_j}$ |
| 3. | Energy | $\sum_i \sum_j p(i,j,d,\theta)^2$ |
| 4. | Homogeneity | $\sum_i \sum_j p(i,j,d,\theta)/(1+|i-j|)$ |

### 7.2.1.3 Classification and clustering

Once the techniques, such as image processing techniques, are applied, based on the feature vectors a set of images (cluster) representing the pattern of the disease is created. The user, who usually is a farmer, uses his intuition to select the image he thinks if the best fit. Based on this input from the user, the classifier (SVM) classifies the plant as infected by a different set of diseases. It also furnishes the stage of the disease.

## 7.2.2 Current system

Some of the existing systems obtain an RGB image of the leaf and then apply color transformation techniques. This is followed by the application of a $K$-means clustering algorithm through which identification of the infected clusters is carried out. In the next step the leaf is classified as healthy or diseased using a pretrained neural network. Other rudimentary methods include looking at the leaf and making assumptions on the disease and its stage.

### 7.2.3 Proposed system

The proposed system uses image preprocessing techniques like image enhancement and feature extraction followed by a *K*-means clustering algorithm. Then the SVM classification technique is carried out to identify the type and stage of the disease. The model can be trained to detect any number of diseases irrespective of the plant species. Methods to cure a particular disease can be added as an additional functionality.

## 7.3 Design and implementation

The proposed system will be primarily used by farmers, who will upload the pictures of affected leaves into the system, to obtain the type and stage of disease currently affecting the plant. The major tool used for the implementation is MATLAB. It is a multiparadigm numerical computing environment. A proprietary programming language developed by MathWorks, MATLAB allows matrix manipulations, plotting of functions and data, implementation of algorithms, creation of user interfaces, and interfacing with programs written in other languages, including C, C++, C#, Java, Fortran, and Python.

The major techniques used are image processing, clustering, and classification, which work in tandem to deliver the required result.

The image processing techniques include:

- *Image enhancement*: The process which makes the image suitable for further analysis. It is employed to bring out the features of the leaf that are essential to determine whether the leaf has been affected or not.
- *Image segmentation*: This refers to the partitioning of an image into regions. This technique will be used to isolate the parts of the leaf that have been affected by the disease.

  Clustering of images is done using the *K*-means algorithm. This clustering is done only after all the image processing techniques have been applied. Figs. 7.5 and 7.6 include the architecture and flow of the model.

  Classification is done using the SVM classifier.

- *SVM*: this is a formidable classifying technique which will be used to classify whether the leaf is healthy or not based on the parameters obtained in the above two steps.

To obtain the required results, the system needs to be trained so as to detect the diseased plants.

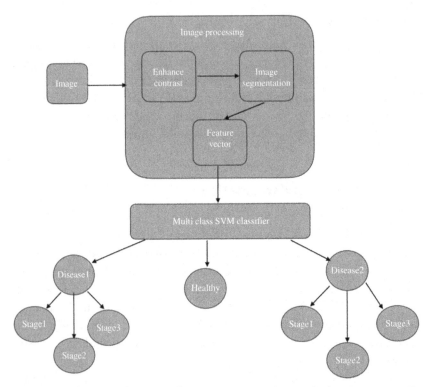

**Figure 7.5** System architecture for image processing and the support vector machine model.

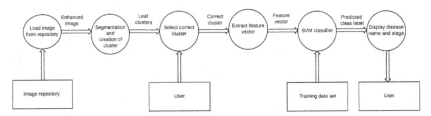

**Figure 7.6** Flow of the model.

*Training*

1. Start with images of which classes are known for sure.
2. Find the property set or list of capabilities for every one of them and afterward name them appropriately.
3. Take the following picture as information and discover the highlights of this one as a new input.

4. Next design and implement the binary SVM to a multiclass SVM procedure and method.
5. Train SVM using kernel function of choice. The yield will contain the SVM structure and data of help vectors, bias value, etc.
6. Find the class of the input image.
7. Depending on the result species, the mark is given to the following picture. Add the features set to the database.
8. Steps 3—7 are rehashed for every one of the pictures that are to be utilized as a database.

*Testing*
- The testing method comprises of stages 3—6 of the training strategy. The result species is the class of the input image.
- To discover the precision of the framework or the SVM, an arbitrary arrangement of information sources is picked for preparing and testing from the database.

The proposed procedure consists of different stages such as image acquisition, image preprocessing, and segmentation using *K*-means clustering method. Gray level co-occurrence matrix (GLCM) is used to extract the features. SVM algorithm, AlexNet, and naïve Bayes algorithm are used to train the system. The flow of the proposed approach is shown in Fig. 7.7.

The steps followed, as depicted above, include the following.

1. *Image acquisition*

Pictures are caught through a versatile camera and are put in the database for further activities.

2. *Image preprocessing*

Image prepreparing is done to improve the quality of the picture and to upgrade the image highlights for further handling. The gained pictures are resized, upgraded, and RGB is changed over to grayscale for making clusters in segmentation.

3. *Image segmentation*

Image segmentation is utilized to find the image and separate it from its experience. *K*-means clustering technique is utilized for partition of the images into groups/clusters. The classification is finished by changing over RGB shading space to $L^*a^*b$ color space. $L^*a^*b$ shading space comprises of "$L^*$" glow layer, "$a^*$" and "$b^*$" chromaticity layer. The shading data put in the "$a^*$" and "$b^*$" layers are characterized utilizing *K*-means grouping. From the aftereffects of *K*-means, every

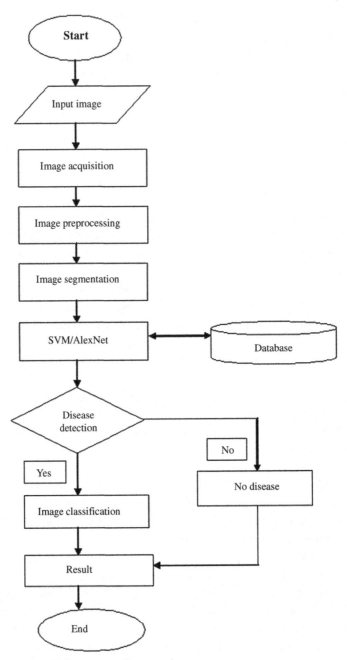

**Figure 7.7** Flow of the proposed approach.

pixel in the picture is marked and the divided pictures of the infected leaves are produced. The separation between each bunch is determined and a new centroid is relegated. The clusters are regrouped until the groups have low similitude between them. This algorithm likewise limits squared error function.

**4.** *Feature extraction*

Desired features, for example, texture, color, and structure can be obtained from the feature extracted. A GLCM formula is utilized for statistical textual features. The statistical texture features of GLCM incorporate entropy, contrast, mean, smoothness, skewness, and so on.

**5.** *Threshold*

The threshold image comprises of just binary pixels, where an article pixel is given a worth "1" (commented by white shading) while the background pixel is given an estimation of "0" (commented by dark shading).

```
I=imread('image.jpg');
I_Otsu = im2bw(I,graythresh(I));
```

Color vision can be processed using HSV color space. HSV color space describes colors in terms of the hue, saturation, and value.

I_HIS = rgb2hsv(I);

**6.** *Grayscale*

If the segmented image is in RGB then it is converted to a grayscale image.

img = rgb2gray(seg_img);

**7.** *Training and classification*

The data set was taken from a crowdAI plant village challenge which had 21,916 images. A total of 600 images of tomato plants of six classes was selected. The images were trained using (transfer-learning) AlexNet, SVM on f6 of AlexNet, and training from scratch using feature extraction with the aid of $k$-means clustering. Using the features extracted from the input leaf image SVM is used for classification. In another approach, features from AlexNet (f6) are taken and SVM is fit on the model. Classification on AlexNet is also done by fine tuning the fully connected layers.

**8.** *Algorithm explanation*

$K$-means clustering algorithm: This calculation is utilized to group/ separate the object dependent on the element of the leaf into $k$

number of gatherings. This is finished by utilizing the Euclidean separation metric.

The calculation of $k$ means:

- Initialization: The image is partitioned into $k$ number of bunches. Each pixel is relegated to its closest centroid ($k$).
- The position of the centroid is changed by methods for information being allotted to the gathering.
- The centroid moves to the focal point of its appointed focuses.

Of these three bunches, grouping is accomplished for just one group which has an influenced zone.

Classification: After extraction of all the important highlights, the values are contrasted and the predetermined data set put in a. mat document, wherein the SVM classifier is utilized for grouping the disease.

SVMs are associated supervised learning techniques used to classify and regress. Supervised learning includes breaking down a set of marked observations (the set of training) to anticipate the names of unlabeled future information (the set of tests). Specifically, the goal is to familiarize yourself with some feature that shows the link between observations and their labels. In a high-dimensional or infinite dimensional space, SVM develops a hyperplane or set of hyperplanes that can be used for classification, regression, or various errands. Instinctively, the hyperplane that has the greatest separation from the nearest training data purpose of any class, as a rule the greater the utilitarian edge the lower the classifier's speculation error, accomplishes an excellent detachment.

Use of a SVM in association with the multiclass SVM assigns labels, which are drawn from a finite set of numerous elements. By using the concept of SVM, multi classification is happening, better than the normal binary classification. using this algorithm, the best ouput we have got to detect the specific disease.

## 7.4 Results

The results are from a variety of inputs we have given to the system and provisional results of this job. Some of the differences can be observed in the same class pictures (Figs. 7.8–7.13).

This is the initial stage where the user uploads the image of the leaf. This image is resized to $512 \times 512$ and used for further processing.

The second stage is where the image is enhanced to bring out the necessary features of the leaf. Enhancing the contrast includes color thresholding.

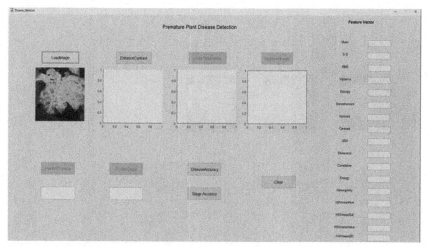

**Figure 7.8** Loading of the image.

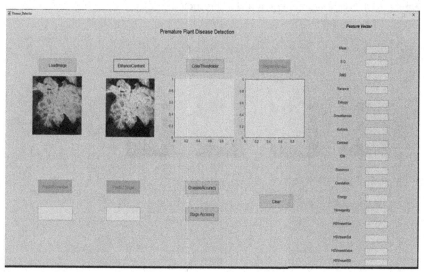

**Figure 7.9** Enhancement of the image.

Color thresholding is applied to make the image suitable for image segmentation. This is necessary to remove the background to eliminate unwanted noise and to extract the required information from the image.

In this step the user chooses the closest cluster which resembles the disease pattern. The chosen cluster is then used to extract the feature vector.

Formation of clusters is done using a K-means algorithm (one of which should be selected by the user). This cluster is converted into a feature vector and then fed to the SVM classifier for prediction of the disease and stage.

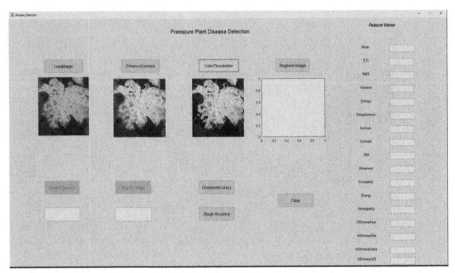

**Figure 7.10** Image segmentation (color threshold).

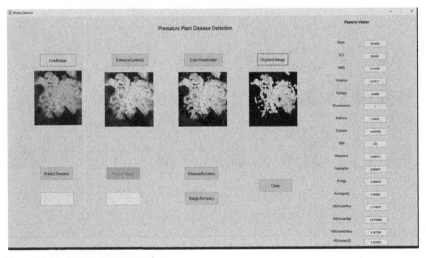

**Figure 7.11** Image segmentation.

After the feature vector is fed to the SVM, the classifier predicts the disease to which it belongs. The same is displayed to the user. After the disease is predicted and if the leaf is found to be infected with a disease, the same feature vector is fed to another SVM classifier to determine the stage of infection. The stage is then displayed to the user. We found the accuracy of the models using SVM, AlexNet, AlexNet-SVM, and

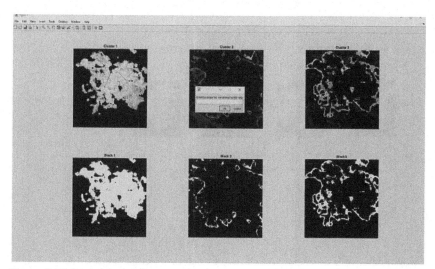

**Figure 7.12** Formation of clusters.

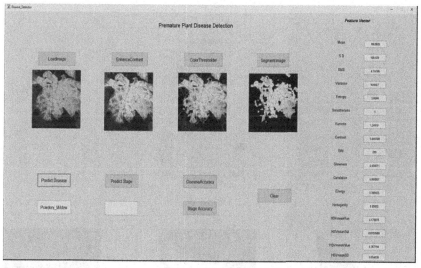

**Figure 7.13** Support vector machine classifier for predicting the disease.

AlexNet-Naive Bayes for our data set to be 75%, 92.44%, 87.3%, and 80%, respectively. Hence the accuracy of AlexNet was found to be the best among the classifiers. The remedies are thus given based on the classification result given by the AlexNet model (Figs. 7.14 and 7.15).

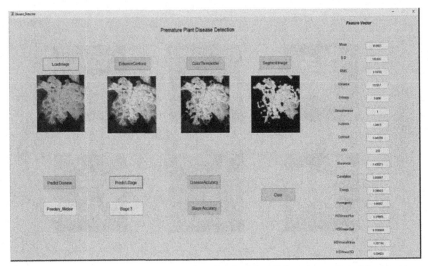

**Figure 7.14** Support vector machine classifier for identifying the stage of the disease.

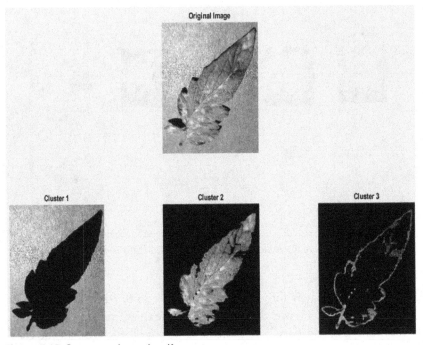

**Figure 7.15** Segmentation using *K*-means.

## 7.5 Conclusion

Efficient detection and suggestion of remedies for plant disease reduces the risk of crop failure, hence, higher yield increases farmers' economic benefits. Image processing and neural network algorithms, like AlexNet, can be used to build an efficient model that detects plant diseases. This chapter focuses on finding the best method to build an efficient model. According to this classification the remedial measures are notified. Using this method completely eliminates the requirement for consulting an expert to determine whether a plant is diseased or not.

The world is shifting toward an age based on technology. Farmers regularly face leaves that have been eaten away by multiple diseases, even after using expensive fertilizers (Fig. 7.16). India's most expensive and delicate treatment is for pomegranate leaf.

There is rarely expertise in this sector. Since an expert's view may differ from that of a novice, making the most of technology for diagnosis and treatment is advisable. ML techniques exemplify this by monitoring the database and assisting botanists in disease diagnosis with a great deal of accuracy. One of the techniques of ML, SVM, is used to classify leaf diseases. The precision gained is in a range between 95% and 100%. By enhancing the database, this can be improved further. The findings acquired from pictures directly taken from plants are very encouraging.

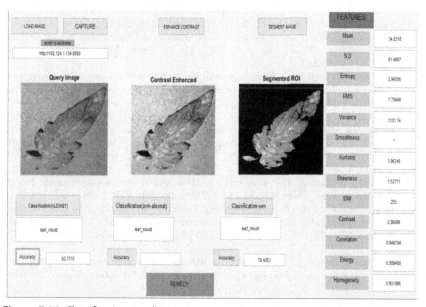

**Figure 7.16** Classification results.

# References

[1] V. Singh, A.K. Mishra, Detection of plant leaf diseases using image segmentation and soft computing procedia computer science, Inform. Process. Agric. 65 (2016).

[2] N. Petrellis, A smart phone image processing application for plant disease diagnosis, in: 2017 6th International Conference on Modern Circuits and Systems Technologies (MOCAST), Thessaloniki, 2017, pp. 1–4. https://doi.org/10.1109/MOCAST.2017.7937683.

[3] T.N. Tete, S. Kamlu, Detection of plant disease using threshold, k-mean cluster and ann algorithm, 2017 2nd International Conference for Convergence in Technology (I2CT), Mumbai, 2017, pp. 523–526. https://doi.org/10.1109/I2CT.2017.8226184.

[4] S. Varshney, T. Dalal, A novel approach for the detection of plant diseases, Int. J. Comput. Sci. Mobile Comput. 5 (7) (2016) 44–54. ISSN: 2320–088X.

[5] P.V. Keskar, S.N. Masare, M.S. Kadam, S.U. Deoghare, Leaf disease detection and diagnosis, Int. J. Emerg. Trends Electric. Electron. (IJETEE) 2 (2) (2013).

[6] S.S. Sannakki, V.S. Rajpurohit, V.B. Nargund, R. Arun Kumar, P.S. Yallur, A hybrid intelligent system for automated pomogranate disease detection and grading, Int. J. Mach. Intell. 3 (2) (2011). ISSN: 0975– 2927 and E-ISSN: 0975–9166.

[7] S. Phadikar, J. Sil, A.K. Das, Classification of rice leaf diseases based on morphological changes, Int. J. Inform. Electron. Eng. 2 (3) (2012).

[8] S.S. Patil, S.A. Thorat, Early detection of grapes diseases using machine learning and IoT, in: 2016 Second International Conference on Cognitive Computing and Information Processing (CCIP), Mysore, 2016, pp. 1–5. https://doi.org/10.1109/CCIP.2016.7802887.

[9] H. Park, J.S. Eun, S.H. Kim, Image-based disease diagnosing and predicting of the crops through the deep learning mechanism, in: 2017 International Conference on Information and Communication Technology Convergence (ICTC), Jeju, 2017, pp. 129–131. https://doi.org/10.1109/ICTC.2017.8190957.

[10] A.K. Deya, M. Sharmaa, M.R. Meshramb, Image processing based leaf rot disease detection of betel vine, in: International Conference on Computational Modeling & Security (CMS 2016), Procedia Comput. Sci. 85 (2016) 748–754.

[11] M. Suresha, K.N. Shreekanth, B.V. Thirumalesh, Recognition of diseases in paddy leaves using kNN classifier, in: 2017 2nd International Conference for Convergence in Technology (I2CT), Mumbai, 2017, pp. 663–666. https://doi.org/10.1109/I2CT.2017.8226213.

[12] A.A. Joshi, B.D. Jadhav, Monitoring and controlling rice diseases using Image processing techniques, in: 2016 International Conference on Computing, Analytics and Security Trends (CAST), Pune, 2016, pp. 471–476. https://doi.org/10.1109/CAST.2016.7915015.

[13] R. Beulah, M. Punithavalli, Prediction of sugarcane diseases using data mining techniques, in: 2016 IEEE International Conference on Advances in Computer Applications (ICACA), Coimbatore, 2016, pp. 393–396. https://doi.org/10.1109/ICACA.2016.7887987.

[14] Y. Nie, K.E. Barner, The fuzzy transformation and its applications in image processing, IEEE Trans. Image Process. 15 (4) (2006), pp. 910, 927.

[15] D. Al-Bashish, M. Braik, S. Bani-Ahmad, Detection and classification of leaf diseases using Kmeans-based segmentation and neural-networks-based classification, Inform. Technol. J. 10 (2011) 267–275. Available from: https://doi.org/10.3923/itj.2011.267.275.

[16] A. Meunkaewjinda, P. Kumsawat, A. Srikaew, Grape leaf disease detection from color imagery using hybrid intelligent system, in: IEEE 5th International Conference ECTI-CON, vol. 1, 2008, pp. 513–516.

[17] A.A. Bernardes, J.G. Rogeri, R.B. Oliveira, N. Marranghello, A.S. Pereira, A.F. Araujo, et al., Identification of Foliar Diseases in Cotton Crop, Springer, São Paulo, Brazil.

[18] V.A. Gulhane, A.A. Gurjar, Detection of diseases on cotton leaves and its possible diagnosis, IJIP 5 (5) (2011) 591−598.

[19] Y.C. Zhang, H.P. Mao, B. Hu, M. Xili, Features selection of cotton disease leaves image based on fuzzy feature selection techniques, in: IEEE Proceedings International Conference on Wavelet Analysis and Pattern Recognition, Beijing, China, 2007, pp. 124−129.

[20] A. Meunkaewjinda, P. Kumsawat, K. Attakitmongcol, A. Sirikaew, Grape leaf disease. Detection from color imaginary using hybrid intelligent system, in: Proceedings of ECTI-CON, 2008.

[21] M.T. bin MohamadAzmi, N.M. Isa, Orchid disease detection using image processing and fuzzy logic, in: 2013 International Conference on Electrical, Electronics and System Engineering.

[22] B.-T. Chen, Y.-S. Chen, W.-H. Hsu, Image processing and understanding based on the fuzzy inference approach, in: 1994 IEEE World Congress on Computational Intelligence, Proceedings of the Third IEEE Conference on Fuzzy Systems, vol. 1, 26−29 June 1994, pp. 254, 259.

[23] H. Al-Hiary, S. Bani-Ahmad, M. Reyalat, M. Braik, Z. ALRahamneh, Fast and accurate detection and classification of plant diseases, Int. J. Comput. Appl. 17 (1) (2011).

## Further reading

D.A. Bashish, M. Braik, S. Bani-Ahmad, A framework for detection and classification of plant leaf and stem diseases, in: 2010 International Conference on Signal and Image Processing.

A. Camargo, J.S. Smith, An image-processing based algorithm to automatically identify plant disease visual symptoms, Biosyst. Eng. 102 (1) (2009) 9−21.

A.B. Dheeb, M. Braik, B.-A. Sulieman, Detection and classification of leaf diseases using K-means-based segmentation and neural-networks-based classification, Inform. Technol. J. 10 (2) (2011) 267−275.

J. Du, D. Huang, X. Wang, X. Gu, Shape recognition based on radial basis probabilistic neural network and application to plant species identification, in: Proceedings of 2005 International Symposium of Neural Networks, ser. LNCS 3497, Springer, 2005.

H. Fu, Z. Chi, Combined thresholding and neural network approach for vein pattern extraction from leaf images, IEEE Proc. Vis. Image Signal Process. 153 (6) (2006).

R.C. Gonzalez, R.E. Woods, Digital Image Processing, Pearson Education, Delhi, 2007.

R.C. Gonzalez, R.E. Woods, S.L. Eddins, Digital Image Processing, second ed., Pearson Education, 2008.

C.-Y. Gwo, C.-H. Wei, Y. Li, Rotary matching of edge features for leaf recognition, Comput. Electron. Agric. 91 (2013) 124−134.

B.C. Heymans, J.P. Onema, J.O. Kuti, A neural network for opuntia leaf-form recognition, in: Proceedings of IEEE International Joint Conference on Neural Networks, 1991.

Z.B. Husin, A.H.B.A. Aziz, A.Y.B.M. Shakaff, R.B.S.M. Farook, Feasibility study on plant chili disease detection using image processing techniques, in: 2012 Third International Conference on Intelligent Systems Modelling and Simulation.

Image Processing ToolboxTM7 User's Guide, ©Copyright by The MathWorks Inc., 1993−2010.

J. Laaksonen, M. Koskela, E. Oja, Self-organizing maps for content-based image retrieval, in: International Joint Conference on Neural Networks, vol. 4, 1999, pp. 2470–2473.

N.B.A. Mustafa, K.A. Syed, A. Zaipatimah, W.B. Yit, A.Z.A. Aidil, A.M.S. Zainul, Agricultural produce sorting and grading using support vector machines and fuzzy logic, in: IEEE International Conference on Signal and Image Processing Applications, 2009, pp. 391–396.

Y. Qing, G. Zexin, Z. Yingfeng, T. Jian, H. Yang, Y. Baojun, Application of support vector machine for detecting rice diseases using shape and color texture features, in: International Conference on Engineering Computation, 2009, pp. 79–83.

P. Revathi, M. Hemalatha, Classification of cotton leaf spot diseases using image processing edge detection techniques, in: 2012 — International Conference on Emerging Trends in Science, Engineering and Technology.

H. Ritter, T. Kohonen, Self-organizing semantic maps, Biol. Cybern. 61 (1989) 241–254.

J. Sil, S. Phadikar, Rice disease identification using pattern recognition techniques, in: Proceedings of 11th International Conference on Computer and Information Technology (ICCIT 2008), 25–27 December 2008, Khulna, Bangladesh.

A.K. Singh, Precision Farming, Water Technology Centre, I.A.R.I., New Delhi, 2010.

A. Tellaeche, P. Xavier, A. Burgos, G. Pajares, A. Ribeiro, A vision-based classifier in precision agriculture combining bayes and support vector machines, in: IEEE International Symposium on Intelligent Signal Processing, 2007.

Y. Tian, L. Tianlai, Y. Niu, A Vision-based classifier in precision agriculture combining bayes and support vector machines, Conference: Intelligent Signal Processing, 2007. WISP 2007. IEEE International Symposium, 2007.

CHAPTER 8

# Artificial intelligence-based computational fluid dynamics approaches

**Vishwanath Panwar[1], Seshu Kumar Vandrangi[2] and Sampath Emani[3]**
[1]Department of Mechanical Engineering, Rai Technology University, Bangalore, India
[2]Department of Mechanical Engineering, Universiti Teknologi PETRONAS, Tronoh, Malaysia
[3]Department of Chemical Engineering, Universiti Teknologi PETRONAS, Tronoh, Malaysia

## 8.1 Introduction

During the investigation of product or material flows, computational fluid dynamic (CFD) plays a crucial role. Given the increasing presence of optimization algorithms, most product development processes have witnessed an increasing application of CFD-based optimization with the aim of steering improvements in the products' designs [1]. Whereas the approach has matured increasingly, the dilemma that arises is that CFD solvers are unlikely to respond to changes in design in situations such as those involving the batch mode [2]. Due to this limitation, most of the previous investigations contend that CFD-based optimization tends to be marred by incorrect optimization and simulation results [2–4]. It is also worth noting that the current state of research in material flows has witnessed the extensive application of CFD with the aim of analyzing flow fields and also governing improvements in product designs, but the process proves time-consuming and tedious and the method is unlikely to produce optimal product designs [4]. Therefore, artificial intelligence (AI)-based CFD has evolved to address these challenges and also ensure that based on CFD simulation outcomes, the optimum is established [5]. The increase in the adoption of AI-based CFD is also informed by documentation that when product designs experience significant changes that also prompt alterations in flow regimes, CFD solvers are unlikely to respond to the perceived alterations adequately [6]. The failed response poses the danger of yielding the wrong simulation results that are often associated with the wrong optimization results [3]. In this chapter, the main aim is

*Hybrid Computational Intelligence*
DOI: https://doi.org/10.1016/B978-0-12-818699-2.00009-3
173

to examine the use of AI-based CFD approaches and the extent to which they have been embraced to study material flows in different settings and with different parameters.

## 8.2 AI-based computational fluid dynamic approaches

### 8.2.1 The use of artificial neural networks in computational fluid dynamic expert systems

In Navier–Stokes equations, real problems fail to have analytical solutions due to the highly nonlinear nature of the equations [5]. Therefore numerical results are obtained mostly with the use of CFD solvers [6]. To ensure that the performance is optimized, high-level user knowledge is required by the CFD solvers. In relation to computational time, the CFD solvers also lead to expensive calculations, with nonexpert users forced to embark on various parameters of programs toward realization of the desired results [7]. Should the users gain adequate experience, selection of the right CFD parameters is based on the perceived experience.

The design of aircraft is associated with numerous calculations through which the performance of systems can be estimated. Given that the calculations are likely to take a great deal of computational time, artificial neural network (ANN) has emerged and proved to be a useful AI application responsible for the modeling of otherwise complex and unknown nonlinear systems [6,7]. The eventuality is that the recent past state of the CFD field has witnessed ANN gain increasing applications in solving selected problems in the field of aeronautics. Some of these problems include restricted flight dynamic models through which parameters of aircraft could be estimated, low Reynolds number airfoil optimization, and the modeling of high-speed turbulent boundary layers that induce optical distortions [7–9].

A specific CFD area that has witnessed the use of ANN is the tuning and analysis utilities (TAU) solver. In particular, TAU has been embraced as a CFD software, while ANN has been used as an AI application responsible for establishing expert systems for the CFD solver [9,10]. Inspired by the brain, ANN technology has been used as an AI application defining expert systems in CFD solutions targeting aircraft [11]. Particularly, the role of the ANN-led expert systems has been to estimate the number of iterations through which CFD simulation convergences could be developed [12], as well as the computation time [13]. Specific useful information with which this I-based CFD approach has been

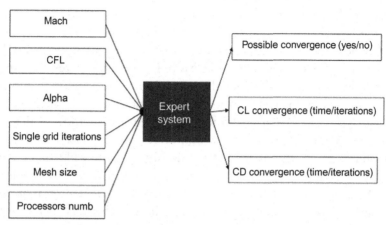

**Figure 8.1** Expert system development using artificial neural network technology. *Data from G. Rubio, E. Valero and S. Lanzan, Computational fluid dynamics expert system using artificial neural networks, World Acad. Sci. Eng. Technol. Int. J. Comput. Inform. Eng. 6 (3), 2012, 413—417 [14].*

associated involves estimation of the iteration numbers for convergence and advance estimation of the required time [11]. Also, ANN technology has gained application in aircraft to develop a CFD solver's expert system through which recommendations could be provided relative to parameter values through which the CFD solver could be improved [9]. The specific form of expert system that ANN has produced is indicated in Fig. 8.1.

In the expert system above, the most used ANN has been documented to be multilayer perceptron (MLP). In the results, many investigations contend that ANN's MLP reflects a perfect approach through which AI aids in analyzing and predicting the number of iterations and CFD convergence time relative to CFD solver convergence in the aeronautic setting [11,13,15].

## 8.2.2 Coupled artificial intelligence (via artificial neural network) and computational fluid dynamic in predicting heat exchanger thermal—hydraulic performance

Apart from the aircraft sector, another setting in which AI-based CFD approaches have gained application involves plate-fin-tube heat exchangers. Indeed, it is notable that heat exchangers have gained extensive application in areas such as refrigeration systems, process engineering, air conditioning, ventilating, and heating [12,13]. As fin dissipation wakes and interrupted channels form, the associated boundary layers and periodic starting yield significant enhancements in heat transfer [15]. The result is that the interrupted fins' finite thickness increases form-drag contribution and friction that, in turn, contribute to increased pressure drop [16]. Therefore, increasing research effort has been made, but extensive experimental databases are needed for the establishment of correlations through which the heat exchangers' friction characteristics and heat transfer can be predicted [17,18]. Compared to the experimental data, most of the proposed correlations, however, lie within more than 20% accuracy [13,19]. Therefore, combinations of AI-based ANNs and CFD have been employed as alternative approaches through which fluid flow could be modeled and predicted [18]. Also, the combinations have been motivated by the need to determine plate-fin-tube heat exchangers' heat transfer characteristics [20].

It is imperative to highlight that the main aim of the use of AI-based CFD simulations has been to discern the feasibility of the extent to which coupled ANNs and CFD in producing correlations of friction data and heat transfer in the context of selected heat transfers [18,20]. The experimental set-ups focusing on these combinations have been established in such a way that 3D-CFD analyses have aided in the development of ANN models, with this development aimed at playing a specific role of predicting the fin-tube heat exchangers' flow characteristics (Figs. 8.2 and 8.3).

Indeed, this combination of AI (ANNs) and CFD investigations has relied on heat exchangers that exhibit differences in pitches, transversal

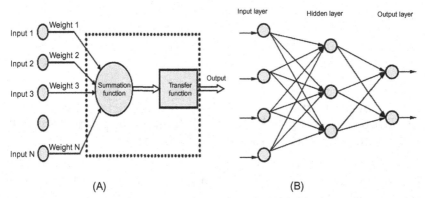

(A)                                              (B)

**Figure 8.2** Multilayer network schematic and artificial neuron. *Data from W. Yaici, E. Entchev, Coupled computational fluid dynamics (CFD) and artificial neural networks (ANNs) for prediction of thermal—hydraulic performance of plate-fin-tube heat exchangers, in: COMSOL Conference, 2016, Boston, 2016.*

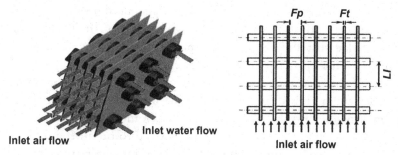

**Figure 8.3** Plate-fin-tube heat exchanger geometric model. *Data from W. Yaici, E. Entchev, Coupled computational fluid dynamics (CFD) and artificial neural networks (ANNs) for prediction of thermal–hydraulic performance of plate-fin-tube heat exchangers, in: COMSOL Conference, 2016, Boston, 2016.*

tube pitches, and longitudinal tube pitches [20,21]. Regarding the perceived thermal–hydraulic performance of the heat exchangers, CFD characteristics on focus have been identified as the efficiency index $j/f$, Fanning friction factor $f$-factor, and Colburn $j$-factor [13]. Notably, the efficiency index reflects a function of the Reynolds numbers [19], with the CFD data results aiding in the training of ANNs towards the prediction of $f$- and $j$-factors. A specific learning algorithm that has been applied to the realization of the latter objective entails back-propagation exhibiting variants of scaled conjugate gradient and Levenberg–Marquardt algorithm [22]. From the findings, many scholarly investigations claim that certain ANN architectures can be trained and modeled accurately using CFD data for the purposes of predicting heat transfer characteristics and the nature of fluid flow in the context of plate-fin-tube heat exchangers [15,20,22,23]. Specific results indicate that the AI-based CFD approach in the specific form of CFD–ANNs reflects a criterion through which the heat exchangers' thermal–hydraulic characteristics can be predicted robustly and effectively [23,24]. Hence, it can be inferred that such results point to and account for the recent increase in the combination of AI techniques with CFD approaches toward predicting or establishing and solving problems involving material flows and product designs [24,25].

## 8.2.3 Fluid flow optimization using artificial intelligence-based convolutional neural networks computational fluid dynamic

As mentioned earlier, improvements in product design and other product developments have experienced tremendous growth in the use of

CFD-based optimization, which has also experienced a dramatic increase in the incorporation of optimization algorithms [26]. It is important to acknowledge that the CFD process plays a crucial role in shaping the degree to which material flows in selected products are investigated [13]. However, the increasing maturity of the use of CFD-based optimization has been compromised by the inability of the CFD solver to respond to design changes correctly, especially under batch modes [3,27].

In aerodynamics, CFD solvers have proved to be time and memory demanding, and computationally expensive iterative processes [27−29]. Given these CFD solver-related drawbacks, opportunities through which space exploration could be designed have been limited [26]. Also, the drawbacks have compromised the quest to realize interactive designs [30,31]. Therefore, convolutional neural networks (CNNs) have been employed to support CFD solvers in assuring real-time predictions of steady, nonuniform laminar flows in contexts such as those involving 3D and 2D domains [32]. The results obtained have also been compared with the cases of central processing unit (CPU)-based CFD solvers and graphics processing unit (GPU)-based CFD solvers, especially regarding the capacity to estimate velocity fields accurately [33].

Notably, CFD analyses and their associated calculations seek to simulate real-world physical interactions of gases and liquids with the surfaces that they encounter; achieving these analyses through prescribed boundary conditions and target parameters [34]. Indeed, the increasing combination of AI and CFD in the form of ANNs has been informed by the desirable level of success with which CNNs are associated relative to learning geometry representations [34,35]. In images, CNNs have also been avowed to provide per-pixel predictions [35]. Therefore, the CNNs have been applied toward modeling nonlinear, large-scale general CFD analyses under restricted classes of flow conditions [36]. The practical use of CNNs in CFD analysis has been achieved by using arbitrary geometries immersed in flows under selected classes of flow conditions [37].

Regarding the AI-based CFD performance analysis relative to the use of CNNs, most of the results reported by previous scholarly studies suggest that as the batch size increases, CNN combination with CFD analysis yields significant reductions in the average time cost [38]. Also, the shared CNN−CFD coding has been reported to exhibit less time compared to the separated coding that is applied to various batch sizes [31,36].

Additional findings show that the separated and shared CNN—CFD coding architectures have closer prediction accuracies, but the shared architecture (as mentioned above) reflects a lower time cost, outperforming the separated coding architecture. The additional motivation behind the use of CNNs in CFD analyses concerns the AI technique's associated memory efficiency. For large geometry shapes, the realization of whole-velocity field surrogate models has been shown to be a bottleneck [33]. However, CNNs exhibit the property of weight-sharing and sparse connectivity and the result is that they yield significant reductions in GPU memory costs [37,38].

Based on the results demonstrated by many experimental studies, CNN as an AI technique has been combined with CFD analyses to compute system speedups and the results compared with those in which the lattice Boltzmann method (LBM) has been applied on GPU and CPU. From the speedup results, an AI-based CFD analysis that incorporates CNNs demonstrates that due to the capacity of the CNN to assure amortized overtime relative to the use of GPU, an increase in batch size correlates with increased speedup [39,40], pointing to the reliability of the use of CNN as an appropriate path for an AI/CFD combination toward accurate and optimal determination or prediction and solution of CFD problems [6,9]. The speedup results involving combinations of CNNs and CFD analyses demonstrate further that when compared to GPU-accelerated LBM solvers, the use of the CNN model yields up to 292-speedup [38,39]. When compared to the case of traditional LBM solvers that are linked to single CPU cores, CNN models that are employed to accelerate the GPU have been established to yield up to 12K speedup [11,23,25]. Therefore, it can be inferred that CNN-based CFD solvers are superior to GPU-accelerated CFD solvers because their estimation of the velocity magnitude is faster (two orders of magnitude) and that the CNN-led CFD solver achieves these superior outcomes at a lower cost. Also, the CNN-based CFD solver proves superior to the CPU-based CFD solver in such a way that the former exhibits four orders of magnitude compared to the latter. For real-time design iterations, it is evident that CNN-based CFD solvers promise immediate feedback at the initial design stages. For designers and engineers, the insight gained is that the CNN approximation model can be applied directly in various algorithm-based design space explorations with necessarily engaging in the training of perceivably extra lower-dimensional surrogate models [23,28] (Fig. 8.4).

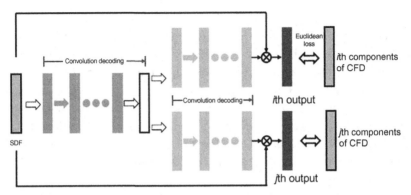

**Figure 8.4** Summary of the convolutional neural network-based computational fluid dynamic solver. *Data from X. Guo, W. Li, F. Lorio, Convolutional neural networks for steady flow approximation, in: KDD'16, August 13–17, 2016, San Francisco, CA, 2016.*

## 8.2.4 Genetic algorithm-based computational fluid dynamic multiobjective optimization

Emerging as a heuristic search method, a genetic algorithm (GA) has gained increasing application in computing and artificial intelligence [3]. In particular, the role of the GA is to establish optimized solutions through which problems can be searched relative to evolutionary biology and the theory of natural selection [4]. Given the complex and large sets of data, many studies concur that GAs are the most appropriate [5–7]. These affirmations are informed by the ability of GAs to solve constrained and unconstrained optimization issues [9,11]. To solve the perceived problems, GAs embrace techniques inspired by evolutionary biology, including recombination, inheritance, mutation, and selection [8].

In aerodynamics, the quest for an optimum shape design has attracted increasing research attention toward multiobjective optimization. Given this trend, GAs have been incorporated to enhance the operations of CFD solvers. For experimental studies that have strived to incorporate GAs into CFD multiobjective optimization, the motivation behind AI exploitation is that GAs reflect robust optimization algorithms that are better placed to support CFD solvers in various situations. Examples of these situations include cases where several local minima could be presented by the cost functional, the types of parameters to be optimized are different, and where the initialization is unlikely to be intuitive [10]. To ensure that Eulerian flow-based airfoil designs have their multiobjective shape optimization problems solved, GAs have gained increasing application toward supporting the CFD solver [12,13].

It is imperative to highlight that when system designs face multiobjective optimization problems, the implication is that there exist several objectives that require simultaneous optimization and that the multiobjective optimization problems are linked to several equality and inequality constraints [15]. When the GAs are used with CFD solvers (on both fine and coarse meshes), the findings suggest that the use of the GAs toward multiobjective optimization does not rely on decision makers and that GAs are well placed to establish Pareto optimal solutions simultaneously [16,18]. Based on these insights, it can be inferred that the adoption of GAs as AI techniques aimed at enhancing CFD solvers' identification and solution of optimization problems promises to steer improvements in optimal designs in situations where the key objective is to focus on different speeds and determine the airfoils' different shapes [29,30].

## 8.2.5 The use of an Elman neural network as an artificial intelligence in computational fluid dynamic hull form optimization

The wide use of CFD tools is seen as a response to rapid developments with which computational technology is associated. One of the areas or research settings that have received this increasing attention entails ship hydrodynamic performance, especially regarding optimization in hull forms [30]. Despite this promising trend, most CFD simulations have been documented to be time-consuming because the majority of those simulations tend to be applied to a single optimization at a time [31]. This gap has led to increasing demand for a highly effective approach through which the CFD tools' calculations could be enhanced. To improve the accuracy of optimization and ensure that the total resistance of the hull form is reduced (and also yield significant improvements in the accuracy of prediction of the total resistance of hull forms in calm water), an improved particle swarm optimization (IPSO)—Elman neural network (ElmanNN) has been proposed in many scholarly investigations [28–33]. Indeed, the Reynolds averaged Navier—Stokes (RANS) technique has been employed to calculate the hull forms' total resistance, while the sampling hull forms have been designed using optimal Latin hypercube design. In turn, the latter design has led to realization of the IPSO—ElmanNN model [31,33]. Having assumed a feedforward connection as its main structure, the ElmanNN constitutes output nodes, context nodes, hidden nodes, and input nodes [33–35]. Similar to the feedforward neural network are the output nodes, hidden nodes, and input nodes [34]. Also, the role of the neural networks' input networks entails signal transmission, while the process of linear weighting is associated with the output nodes.

In relation to the IPSO—ElmanNN as an AI approach supporting CFD-based hull form optimization, the output and input determine the training of samples. Also, the design of the note numbers associated with the output nodes, hidden nodes, and input nodes is conducted before defining the ElmanNN's topology structure [34,35]. Furthermore, the IPSO algorithm parameters are defined. The parameters include acceleration coefficients, inertia factor, number of iterations, and population size [31]. The particle evaluation function is also defined before the initial randomization of the particle sets' positions and velocities.

Indeed, promising outcomes are documented regarding the use of IPSO—ElmanNN as an AI technique supporting CFD solvers in hull form optimization. Specifically, comparisons between ElmanNN and IPSO—ElmanNN aimed at the prediction of total resistance coefficients indicate that IPSO—ElmanNN exhibits improved prediction accuracy [36,37]. Additional experimental studies have focused on some of the moderating factors that tend to account for the perceived improvements when IPSO—ElmanNN is used as an AI approach supporting CFD solvers that target hull form optimization processes. In such studies, results point to the affirmation that the IPSO algorithm exhibits sets of coefficients that are better placed to train ElmanNN, while ensuring that the challenge of relying on experience to choose the coefficients is avoided [37—39]. However, some studies report that the IPSO—Elman algorithm exhibits a preferable forecasting precision when compared to the case and performance of the Elman algorithm, but errors tend to arise between the prediction data and the CFD data [39,40]. These errors are associated with inadequacy in the number of samples. To ensure effective improvements in the network training outcomes, it becomes important to use more training samples [37].

Based on the results documented above and in relation to previous scholarly investigations, it is evident that the evaluation of convergence and a random weighting method aimed at achieving hull form optimization can be realized using the IPSO algorithm as an AI approach seeking to support CFD solvers. This algorithm is associated with improved results and is also seen to overcome some of the drawbacks or shortcomings with which the PSO algorithm is associated. Based on four mathematical functions that are tested, the results suggest that the IPSO algorithm yields significant improvements in optimization accuracy. Also, the IPSO algorithm aids in training ElmanNN parameters, with the proposed prediction model emerging in the form of IPSO−ElmanNN. When IPSO−ElmanNN and ElmanNN are applied toward hull resistance prediction, CFD results suggest that better stability and precision accrue from the use of IPSO−ElmanNN. Given that CFD-based approximation approaches employing IPSO−ElmanNN are observed to be rational and feasible relative to the optimizing of hull forms, it is worth inferring that the AI/CFD approach could offer relevant technical support regarding the design of ship types.

## 8.3 Conclusion

In conclusion, the last few decades have witnessed increasing research attention whose aim has been to apply AI in CFD solvers. This trend has led to the evolution of the AI/CFD concept. The central motivation behind the growing use of AI in CFD problems involves scholarly assertions that when AI approaches are embraced in CFD-related problems, pre-enumerated solutions are likely to be selected and classified effectively. Despite the promising nature of AI adoption in CFD solvers (as contended by many scholarly studies documented in this chapter), it is worth noting that poor understanding or formalization of CFD tasks could attract large investment efforts in AI technology and also translate to long system development times. As such, the assertion points to the criticality of considering the manner in which CFD tasks are understood and formalized before embracing AI technology toward system optimization in contexts such as hull forms, aeronautic, and other fluid and gaseous material flow situations where they (the materials) interact with surfaces such as those of heat exchangers. Should the understanding and formalization of CFD tasks be poor, this chapter has established that payoff is unlikely to be guaranteed. Hence, the central purpose of the study has been to examine some of the AI techniques that have continually been used to support the identification and solution of optimization problems among CFD solvers; focusing on different CFD tasks in different environments and different parameters. The chapter has also examined some of the moderating factors that determine the type of AI technology selected to help achieve the task of CFD solvers, as well as the manner in which those factors shape the degree of success of integrating AI techniques into CFD-based optimization.

Imperatively, computational efforts striving to incorporate AI techniques into CFD problems have focused on two broad sets of activities. These activities include those that demand human perception, reasoning, and knowledge and those that call for high-speed computer-based numerical processing. Indeed, the incorporation of AI techniques has been motivated by the growing need to enhance humans' decision making via high-speed color graphics and also the need to streamline computation using improved algorithms, solutions methods, and grid generators. It is also worth noting that there remains traditional labor separation between computers and humans in such a way that computers aid in number computation while humans make decisions. As CFD solutions are established, most of the human reasoning concerning aspects such as intermediate solution assessment, graphical display, code execution, data format, parameter adjustment, discretization, and geometry definition has been observed to be rate-limiting and also remains prone to errors.

Given the limitations above, there is an increasing trend in the use of AI-based CFD approaches to enhance the automation of tasks among CFD solvers, as well as assure improvements in accuracy. Specifically, AI incorporation into CFD tasks has emerged due to the need for reduction in CFD solution turnaround time, consistency in application, the distribution, preservation, and codification of expertise, and relief from tedium. Some of the specific AI techniques that have gained increasing application in CFD tasks include the use of Elman neural network (ElmanNN) as an AI in CFD's hull form optimization, the use of the GA-based CFD multiobjective optimization, the implementation of fluid flow optimization using AI-based CNNs CFD, the use of coupled AI (via ANN) and CFD in predicting heat exchanger thermal—hydraulic performance, and the use of ANNs in CFD expert systems. From these insights, this study has established that different AI technologies are suitable for different CFD tasks. Regardless of the experimental settings, research materials, and parameters on focus, the majority of AI techniques are seen to improve the performance of CFD solvers regarding the determination and solution of computational problems. The implication for the field of fluid dynamics and the rest of the engineering arena is that AI incorporation into CFD tasks is a promising trend that is likely to dominate the future of system, material, or design optimization and that more accurate results might be achieved if AI technology or algorithms are incorporated into CFD solvers, rather than embracing the latter (for purposes of system optimization) solely.

# References

[1] L. Li, F.L. Carlos, M. Yongsheng, Association of design and computational fluid dynamics simulation intent in flow control product optimization, Proc. Inst. Mech. Eng. B J. Eng. Manuf. 232 (13) (2018) 2309−2322.

[2] G.M. Antonova, Pattern recognition methods as applied to optimize systems represented by simulation models, Pattern Recognit. Image Anal. 22 (1) (2012) 69−81.

[3] L. Li, C.F. Lange, Z. Xu, P. Jiang, Y. Ma, Feature-based intelligent system for steam simulation using computational fluid dynamics, Adv. Eng. Inform. 38 (2018) 357−369.

[4] B. Julien, M. Walter, C.L.F. Ricardo, M. Nathan, Intelligent co-simulation: neural network vs. proper orthogonal decomposition applied to a 2D diffusive problem, J. Build. Perform. Simul. 11 (5) (2018) 568−587.

[5] R.Z. Freire, L.C. dos Santos, G.H. dos Santos, V.C. Mariani, Predicting building's corners hygrothermal behavior by using a fuzzy inference system combined with clustering and Kalman filter, Int. Commun. Heat Mass Transf. 71 (2016) 225−233.

[6] K. Kuniar, M. Zajkac, Some methods of pre-processing input data for neural networks, Comput. Assist. Methods Eng. Sci. 22 (2) (2015) 141−151.

[7] M. Wetter, Co-simulation of building energy and control systems with the building controls virtual test bed, J. Build. Perform Simul. 4 (3) (2011) 185−203.

[8] H.C. Chang, B.W. Feng, Z.Y. Liu, C.S. Zhan, X.D. Cheng, Research on application of approximate model in hull form optimization, Shipbuild China 53 (1) (2012) 88−98.

[9] H. Garg, A hybrid PSO-GA algorithm for constrained optimization problems, Appl. Math. Comput. 274 (11) (2016) 292−305.

[10] Y.H. Hou, F. Liu, X. Liang, Minimum resistance hull form optimization design based on IPSO-BP neural network, J. Shanghai Jiaotong Univ. 50 (8) (2016) 1193−1199.

[11] F. Huang, L. Wang, C. Yang, Hull form optimization for reduced drag and improved seakeeping using a surrogate-based method, Int. Soc. Offshore Polar Eng. (2015).

[12] F.X. Huang, C. Yang, Hull form optimization of a cargo ship for reduced drag, J. Hydrodyn. Ser. B 28 (2) (2016) 173−183.

[13] J.K. Qian, X.F. Mao, X.Y. Wang, Q.Q. Yun, Ship hull automated optimization of minimum resistance via CFD and RSM technique, J. Ship Mech. 16 (1) (2012) 36−43.

[14] G. Rubio, E. Valero, S. Lanzan, Computational fluid dynamics expert system using artificial neural networks, World Acad. Sci. Eng. Technol. Int. J. Comput. Inform. Eng. 6 (3) (2012) 413−417.

[15] Z.Z. Song, Y.Q. Zhao, Suspension test system based on modified Elman neural network, China Mech. Eng. 27 (1) (2016) 1−6.

[16] W. Yaïci, M. Ghorab, E. Entchev, 3D CFD analysis of the effect of inlet air flow maldistribution on the fluid flow and heat transfer performances of plate-fin-and-tube laminar heat exchangers, Int. J. Heat Mass Transf. 74 (2014) 490−500.

[17] W. Yaïci, M. Ghorab, E. Entchev, 3D CFD study of the effect of inlet air flow maldistribution on plate-fin-tube heat exchanger design and thermal−hydraulic performance, Int. J. Heat Mass Transf. 101 (2016) 527−541.

[18] A. Younis, Z. Dong, Trends, features, and tests of common and recently introduced global optimization methods, Eng. Optim. 42 (8) (2010) 691−718.

[19] H.S. Park, X.P. Dang, Structural optimization based on CADCAE integration and metamodeling techniques, Comput. Des. 42 (10) (2010) 889−902.

[20] L. Luo, D. Liu, M. Zhu, J. Ye, Metamodel-assisted design optimization of piezoelectric flex transducer for maximal biokinetic energy conversion, J. Intell. Mater. Syst. Struct. 28 (18) (2017) 2528−2538.

[21] W. Wang, F. Gao, Y. Cheng, C. Lin, Multidisciplinary design optimization for front structure of an electric car body-in-white based on improved Collaborative Optimization method, Int. J. Automot. Technol. 18 (6) (2017) 1007−1015.

[22] A. Ayancik, E. Acar, K. Celebioglu, S. Aradag, Simulation based design and optimization of Francis turbine runners by using multiple types of metamodels, Proc. Inst. Mech. Eng. C J. Mech. Eng. Sci. 231 (8) (2017) 1427−1444.

[23] A. Younis, Z. Dong, Global optimization using mixed surrogates and space elimination in computationally intensive engineering designs, Int. J. Comput. Methods Eng. Sci. Mech. 13 (4) (2012) 272−289.

[24] M. Diez, E.F. Campana, F. Stern, Design-space dimensionality reduction in shape optimization by Karhunen−Loève expansion, Comput. Methods Appl. Mech. Eng. 283 (2015) 1525−1544.

[25] A. Younis, Z. Dong, Metamodelling and search using space exploration and unimodal region elimination for design optimization, Eng. Optim. 42 (6) (2010) 517−533.

[26] S.E. Fang, R. Perera, Damage identification by response surface based model updating using D-optimal design, Mech. Syst. Signal Process 25 (2) (2011) 717−733.

[27] L. Liu, Y. Ma, A survey of manufacturing oriented topology optimization methods, Adv. Eng. Softw. 100 (2016) 161−175.

[28] L. Liu, Y.S. Ma, 3D level-set topology optimization: a machining feature-based approach, Struct. Multidiscip. Optim. 52 (3) (2015) 563−582.

[29] L. Liu, Y. Ma, A new multi-material level set topology optimization method with the length scale control capability, Comput. Methods Appl. Mech. Eng. 329 (2018) 444−463.

[30] K. Yonezawa, R. Ogawa, K. Ogi, et al., Flow-induced vibration of a steam control valve, J. Fluids Struct. 35 (2012) 76−88.

[31] J. Schmidhuber, Deep learning in neural networks: an overview, Neural Netw. (2015).

[32] J. Liu, H. Yu, Concurrent deposition path planning and structural topology optimization for additive manufacturing, Rapid Prototyp. J. 23 (5) (2017) 930−942.

[33] D. Eigen, C. Puhrsch, R. Fergus, Depth map prediction from a single image using a multi-scale deep network, Adv. Neural Inf. Process Syst. (2014).

[34] S. Gupta, R. Girshick, P. Arbeláez, J. Malik, Learning rich features from RGB-D images for object detection and segmentation, in: Computer Vision (ECCV), 2014.

[35] N. Umetani, Y. Koyama, R. Schmidt, T. Igarashi, Pteromys: interactive design and optimization of free-formed free-ight model airplanes, ACM Trans. Graph. 33 (4) (2014) 65.

[36] I. Ebtehaj, H. Bonakdari, A.H. Zaji, H. Azimi, A. Sharifi, Gene expression programming to predict the discharge coefficient in rectangular side weirs, Appl. Soft Comput. 35 (2015) 618−628.

[37] A. Kaveh, A. Nasrollahi, Charged system search and particle swarm optimization hybridized for optimal design of engineering structures, Sci. Iranica Trans. A: Civ. Eng. 21 (2014) 295−305.

[38] M. Najafzadeh, A.M. Sattar, Neuro-fuzzy GMDH approach to predict longitudinal dispersion in water networks, Water Resour. Manag. 29 (7) (2015) 2205−2219.

[39] M. Najafzadeh, A. Zahiri, Neuro-fuzzy GMDH-based evolutionary algorithms to predict flow discharge in straight compound channels, J. Hydrol. Eng. 20 (2015) 12.

[40] A. Ramamurthy, S. Han, P. Biron, Three-dimensional simulation parameters for 90° open channel bend flows, J. Comput. Civ. Eng. 27 (3) (2013) 282−291.

[41] W. Yaici, E. Entchev, Coupled computational fluid dynamics (CFD) and artificial neural networks (ANNs) for prediction of thermal−hydraulic performance of plate-fin-tube heat exchangers, in: COMSOL Conference, Boston, MA, 2016.

[42] X. Guo, W. Li, F. Lorio, Convolutional neural networks for steady flow approximation, in: KDD '16, August 13−17, 2016, San Francisco, CA, 2016.

# Appendix

| Serial no. | CFD approach | Materials used/studied | Results | Turbulence models/algorithms/associated equations | References |
|---|---|---|---|---|---|
| 18 | The loop of design–analysis–redesign in the optimization process | Computer aided designing (CAD)–computer aided engineering (CAE) computer-aided tools | The proposed model was found to yield significant reductions in monotonous repetitive tasks, as well as the time required to solve computation-intensive design optimization problems | Commercial CAD–CAE software | [19] |
| 19 | A novel piezoelectric flex transducer based on the Cymbal device | Energy-harvesting devices | From the optimal piezoelectric flex transducer harvesting device, findings indicated that an application of 2.0 as a safety design factor implies that the electrical power generated can be in the magnitude of up to 6.5 MW | Sequential quadratic programming on metamodels | [20] |
| 21 | A metamodel-based optimization approach employing several metamodels | Francis type turbine runner | From the results, it was reported that the proposed model reduces the design process time significantly. The reduction was found to be a factor of 9.2. It was also established that when optimization via the proposed approach is employed, there is a significant increase in turbine performance and also a reduction in the turbine blades' cavitation (often associated with lifespan reduction and harm to the turbine) | Metamodel-based optimization | [22] |

| Serial no. | CFD approach | Materials used/studied | Results | Turbulence models/ algorithms/associated equations | References |
|---|---|---|---|---|---|
| 30 | Concurrence performance of the structural topology optimization and the deposition path planning | Additively manufactured parts | With most of the planned deposition paths aligned to principle stress directions, the combination was observed to enhance structural performance | Level set topology optimization algorithm and the iso-value level set contours | [32] |
| 35 | A data-driven method aimed at the efficient and combat representation of glider aerodynamics | Hand-launched free-flight glider airplanes | The proposed technique was found to be better placed to gain application in the inexpensive and easy design or creation of hobby-grade hand-launched gliders exhibiting creative shapes | Aerodynamic model | [35] |
| 36 | Gene expression programming (GEP) | Side weir discharge coefficient in rectangular sharp-crested side weirs | The best performance was found when the model with ratio of weir height to its length ($p/\gamma_1$) parameters of $R^2 = 0.947$, $RMSE = 0.037$, $MARE = 0.05$, $SI = 0.067$, and $BIAS = 0.01$, ratio of weir length to depth of upstream flow ($b/\gamma_1$), Froude number ($F_1$), dimensionless weir length ($b/B$) was used. Hence, GEP could be used to estimate the rectangular sharp-crested side weirs' discharge coefficient | Coefficient determination ($R^2$), BIAS, scatter index ($SI$), mean absolute relative error ($MARE$), and root mean square error ($RMSE$) | [36] |
| 37 | Charged system search (CSS) | Structural optimization problems | The hybrid CSS and PSO exhibited higher convergence and better performance | Hybrid charged system search and particle swarm optimization (HCSSPSO) | [37] |

| Serial no. | CFD approach | Materials used/studied | Results | Turbulence models/algorithms/associated equations | References |
|---|---|---|---|---|---|
| 38 | Adaptive neuro fuzzy group method of data handling | Pipe flows | Major parameters that were examined included the pipe diameter, the pipe friction coefficient, the average velocity, and the Reynolds number. Findings indicated that when compared to previous numerical solutions, the proposed relations proved simpler in terms of the effective evaluation of pipe flows' longitudinal dispersion coefficients | Particle swarm optimization-based evolutionary algorithm | [38] |
| 39 | The adaptive learning network used was a neuro-fuzzy-based group method of data handling (NF-GMDH) | With the central aim being the prediction of flow discharge, focus was on straight compound channels | The accuracy of prediction associated with NF-GMDH−GSA network was found to be superior to the case of the NF-GMDH−PSO network | Gravitational search algorithm (GSA) and particle swarm optimization (PSO) | [39] |
| 40 | Large eddy simulation (LES), Reynolds stress model (RSM), and k-epsilon renormalization group (RNG) | Water surface treatments [volume of fluid (VOF), porosity, and rigid lid] | The software embracing VOF and RSM depicted the best results regarding representation of counter-rotating secondary flow cells | Domain representations in terms of body-fitted coordinate (BFC) and Cartesian grids | [40] |

| Serial no. | CFD approach | Materials used/studied | Results | Turbulence models/algorithms/associated equations | References |
|---|---|---|---|---|---|
| 41 | Coupled computational fluid dynamic (CFD) and artificial neural networks (ANNs) | Plate-fin-tube heat exchangers. Study parameters included efficiency index $j/f$ as a function of Reynolds (Re) numbers, Fanning friction $f_0$ factor, and Colburn $j$-factor | The main aim was to predict flow characteristics in the targeted heat exchangers. Results suggested that coupled CFD–ANNs prove robust and effective toward the plate-fin-tube heat exchangers' prediction of thermal–hydraulic performance | COMSOL Multiphysics software | [41] |
| 42 | The authors focused on CPU–based CFD solver and GPU–based CFD solver | 2D and 3D nonuniform steady laminar flow in domain based on convolutional neural networks | CNN estimates velocity fields faster than CPU–based CFD solvers and GPU–accelerated CFD solvers in four and two orders of magnitude, respectively, assuring further a cost of low error state | Convolutional neural network (CNN)–based surrogate model | [42] |

# CHAPTER 9

# Real-time video segmentation using a vague adaptive threshold

**Hrishikesh Bhaumik[1], Siddhartha Bhattacharyya[2] and Susanta Chakraborty[3]**
[1]Department of Information Technology, RCC Institute of Information Technology, Kolkata, India
[2]Department of Computer Science and Engineering, CHRIST (Deemed to be University), Bangalore, India
[3]Department of Computer Science & Technology, Indian Institute of Engineering Science and Technology, Howrah, India

## 9.1 Introduction

There has been a boundless growth of multimedia content in the online repositories available over the Internet. Of the available media types, video is the most challenging as it engulfs the three other types, namely text, audio, and image. Therefore video analysis has emerged as an extensive field of research and deals with many problems related to computer vision. Video analysis can be accomplished by extracting low-level, mid-level, and high-level features. While video properties, such as frame rates, resolution, color model, and statistical features of pixels are treated as low-level features, mid-level features include extraction and description of interest points from video frames in order to identify and track objects, perform scene detection, etc.

Many algorithms, such as SIFT [1], SURF [2], DAISY [3], GIST [4], BRIEF [5], ORB [6], and BRISK [7] have been developed for the detection and description of these feature points. High-level features, such as the shapes of objects [8,9], active contours [10], curvelets [11], edges of objects in the frames [12−14], optical flow [15], and motion vectors [16] are used for semantic analysis of videos, such as event detection [17], scene modeling [18], object description [19], etc. However, in order to analyze a video, it is of paramount importance that the video be temporally disintegrated into its constituent shots. Though shot boundary analysis has been a topic of research over the last two decades, there has been limited work in the domain of real-time video segmentation. This provides the necessary motivation for this work.

*Hybrid Computational Intelligence*
DOI: https://doi.org/10.1016/B978-0-12-818699-2.00010-X
191

Detection of shot boundaries in real time holds importance in the domain of video surveillance [20], object tracking [21], video indexing [22], dynamic video summarization [23], and many other related fields. Real-time shot boundary analysis involves a Boolean decision on an incoming frame of the video to determine whether it is a part of the cut-set ($CS$) or not. At the lowest level, a video ($V$) may be represented as a set of frames, that is, $V = f_1 \Theta f_2 \Theta f_3 \Theta \ldots \Theta f_n$, where $f_i$ is the $i$th time-sequenced frame and $\Theta$ is a coalition operator. These frames may be grouped together to form a shot such that the frames in each shot represent a time-continuous sequence captured from a camera without any break. At a higher level, the semantically similar and time-sequenced shots may be combined together to form a scene. The video hierarchy has been represented in Fig. 9.1.

In order to perform real-time detection of shot boundaries, extraction of features from the incoming frames and setting a dynamic threshold based on the features extracted from the new frames is necessary. The distance between the incoming successive frames is computed using the

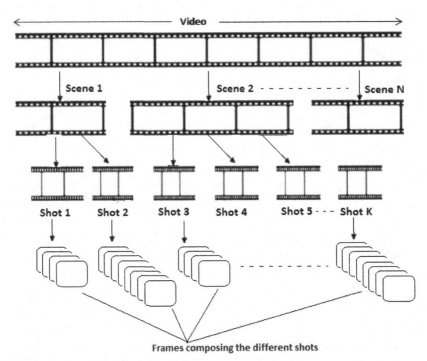

**Figure 9.1** Granularity levels in a video.

features extracted from these frames and the dynamic threshold is continuously updated to detect the shot transitions. In this work, vague set modeling has been used to determine the dynamic threshold, called vague adaptive threshold (VAT), which is used for on-the-fly shot detection. Thus, the major contributions of this work are as follows:

1. To devise a method for on-the-fly detection of shot boundaries from live streaming videos.
2. To determine a dynamic threshold for shot boundary detection based on extracted features from the buffered frames of the video.

The remainder of this chapter is structured as follows. A brief survey of the recent works on shot boundary detection is presented in Section 9.2. The basic concepts related to the present work including the preprocessing steps like fuzzy hostility map generation, pixel intensification, fuzzy hostility map similarity, vague set modeling, computation of VAT, and look-back technique are described in Section 9.3. The proposed methodology for real-time shot boundary detection along with an explanation of the different steps of the proposed approach is enumerated in Section 9.4. The experimental results, analysis, and comparison with other state-of-the-art methods is elaborated in Section 9.5. Concluding remarks and future directions are discussed in Section 9.6.

## 9.2 Temporal video segmentation (shot boundary detection)

A video is a conglomeration of a set of frames, arranged in a time-sequenced manner. Temporal video segmentation or shot boundary analysis is the process of determining meaningful segments in a video such that the frames composing a segment, which have been captured by a single camera in a time-continuous manner can be isolated. In order to detect shot transitions, it is necessary to extract features from the frames and identify points of discontinuity. Shot transitions are the effects which are introduced during the editing stage of a video. The two main categories of shot transitions are abrupt and gradual transitions. Over the past two decades, researchers in this field have been engaged in developing methods which could be used reliably for detecting the different types of shot transition in videos. However, in recent years the focus in this field has shifted to developing algorithms that could be used for fast detection of the shot transitions present in videos. Thus, the total time required for extracting features from the video frames and identifying the points of shot transition is comparable with the duration or length of the video. In this section, a review of the recent works is presented which includes approaches pivoted around the classical as well as soft computing methods. Some of the techniques discussed here focus on real-time scenarios and are discussed in a separate subsection.

## 9.2.1 Shot transition detection methods based on classical approaches

A shot boundary detection (SBD) technique based on a histogram of the intensity images, taken from video frames was devised by Liu and Dai [24]. A set sequence is constructed with the adjacent sampled histograms and a Grey model is used to analyze the sampled histogram. Absolute mean error (AME) and regulative AME with thresholds is used to detect the shot boundaries. Tippaya et al. [25] developed a shot boundary detection method based on multimodal visual features. The work employs a cumulative moving average and, using a discontinuity signal, the algorithm identifies the position of shot boundaries. In a work by Hannane et al. [26], an SIFT point distribution histogram (SIFT-PDH) was extracted from the video frames. Shot boundaries are detected using an adaptive threshold on the distances computed on these SIFT-PDHs. Pal et al. [27] compared a few algorithms based on discrete cosine tranform (DCT), motion vector, and histogram for shot boundary detection and derived the pros and cons of these methods. In a three-stage method, Li et al. [28] used multilevel difference of color histograms (MDCH) to detect abrupt and gradual boundaries. In order to deal with the gradual transitions in the same way as abrupt transitions, the former type is converted to the latter type in the first stage using two self-adapted thresholds. The second stage is used to filter noise caused by object motion, flash, and camera zoom by using local maximum difference of MDCH. In the third stage a voting mechanism is used to make a final decision on the shot boundaries. Moeglein et al. [29] demonstrated that shot boundary detection can be used to identify the points of crystal growth. Shot boundary detection has also been applied for endoscopic surgery to signify the appearance of a different surgical scene by Loukas et al. [30]. The work is based on a variational Bayesian algorithm using a spatiotemporal Gaussian mixture model. Verma and Raman [31] used a color histogram in order to detect the abrupt transitions. Youssef et al. [32] used Frobenius norm of low-rank approximation matrices for adaptive feature extraction. In this work, double thresholding is used for detecting abrupt transitions and singular value decomposition (SVD) updating is used for gradual transition detection. A review of several SBD techniques is presented by Gupta et al. [33], in which some recent SBD techniques have been compared on the basis of performance metrics such as precision, recall, $F1$ score, and time complexity. Abdulhussain et al. [34] presented a comprehensive review of the advantages and disadvantages of several SBD algorithms and discussed the challenges faced and proposed recommendations for the same. Thounaojam et al. [35] proposed a three-step mechanism for detection of shot boundaries. In the first step clusters of frames are formed by computing the correlation of GIST features between the consecutive frames of a video. Abrupt transitions are detected in the second step using maximally stable extremal regions (MSERs) and a threshold. Triangular pattern matching is used to detect gradual transitions. In the approach by Cyganek and Woźniak [36], the video frames are represented as tensors of order consistent with signal dimensions. A tensor model is built from the signal stream using dynamic tensor analysis. A drift detector is used to compare the stream data to the model in order to detect the shot boundaries. Singh and Aggarwal [37] presented a survey of the major SBD methods over the past two decades. Another review is presented by SenGupta et al. [38], which discusses the different approaches for SBD. Kar and Kanungo [39] take up the problems faced in detection of shot transitions due to illumination change and complex object/camera motion. The shot boundary detection algorithms are unable to achieve satisfactory performance for video sequences which consist of flash light and complex object/camera motion. For this purpose the absolute sum gradient orientation feature difference is matched in order to detect the abrupt boundaries. Liu et al. propose an approach [40] for event detection in soccer videos based on temporal action localization and play-break (PB) rules. In this work, action localization is performed using 3D convolutional networks. PB rules are then employed to organize actions into events. The semantic classes of events are determined according to principal actions which contain key semantic information highlights. A deep feature distance is used to increase the precision of detection and improve the performance of localization. The approach adopted by Benni et al. [41] uses eigenvalues as a dissimilarity measure for detecting the shot boundaries. The covariance matrix is dynamically updated and analyzed for detecting the shot transitions. The updating process also reduces the computational time for SBD and further extracting the keyframes. Tippaya et al. [42] represent the temporal characteristics of a video based on global and local feature descriptors. Further, the possible candidates for shot transition and pattern analysis are performed on a dissimilarity score between video frames. An adaptive threshold is used to select the actual shot transitions. A two-step method is proposed by Shao et al. [43] for the detection of shot boundaries. In the first step, the dissimilarity between two consecutive frames is computed using hue, saturation, and value (HSV) color histogram difference. Using an adaptive threshold, the possible points where shot transition might be present are detected. In order to eliminate false candidates and also detect missed shot boundaries, an HOG feature is used. Dynamic mode decomposition (DMD) was used by Bi et al. for SBD [44]. In this work, DMD was used to extract temporal foreground and background features such that sharp changes in amplitude could be detected using the DMD coefficient. This method is useful for detection of shot boundaries, especially when there are rapid changes in background illumination or swift motion of objects or camera. The approach has reported high accuracy in situations where either the foreground objects are occluded, there is a slow change in illumination, or color changes are not perceivable. Using the concept of sparse coding, Li et al. [45] devised an approach for SBD in which a dictionary is created through learning from a given video. Piramanayagam et al. [46] devised a shot transition detection technique in which the dissimilarity between 2D segmentations of each frame is computed. The 2D segments are propagated in both spatial and temporal directions over a window of frames in order to detect shot boundaries. The window is moved across the video to obtain all the shot boundaries.

## 9.2.2 Soft computing-based approaches for shot transition detection

Xu et al. [47] designed a framework for shot transition detection based on convolutional neural networks (CNNs). The motivation for this work revolved around the fact that many recent methods often miss detection of shot transitions due to small changes in background. CNN is used to extract features which are used to detect both abrupt and gradual transitions using pattern analysis. A combined approach using genetic algorithm (GA) and fuzzy logic was devised by Thounaojam et al. [48]. In this approach GA is used to compute the membership functions of the fuzzy system. Shot transitions are classified using this fuzzy system. In another work by Fan et al. [49], a fuzzy color distribution chart based on spatial color distribution is used to compensate for noise, illumination, and in-frame insertions like text and logos. A hybrid method was devised by Shen et al. [50] by integrating a high-level fuzzy Petri net (HLFPN) model with keypoint matching. In the initial stage, a HLFPN model with histogram difference is used to identify possible candidates for shot transition. SURF is then applied to detect the false shots and gradual transitions from the candidate shot transitions given by the HLFPN model. Hassanien et al. [51] presented a method for shot transition detection using spatiotemporal CNNs. This method is evaluated over a large data set and reports a great improvement in speed over the state-of-the-art methods. Tong et al. [52] used CNNs to learn the interpretable TAGs from a WordNet tree in order to detect cut and gradual transition in the candidate segments within a video. The semantic labels extracted by the framework can be used to portray the contents of a shot. A SBD technique based on basis pursuit denoising (BPDN), which is a sparse representation of the video frames was used by Pingping et al. [53] for detection of shot transitions. The BPDN of the frames was given as input to make the support vector machine (SVM) learn to enable the shot detection task. Another CNN model was proposed by Liang et al. [54] which was used to extract features from a video sequence. Local frame similarity and dual-threshold sliding window similarity mechanisms were used to enhance recall and precision for shot detection. Lee and Kolsch [55] developed a method for extracting frame information based on color histograms with key point feature matching. Two similarity metrics based on graph cuts are defined for individual frames as well as set of frames. Temporal feature vectors are formed with these metrics for training an SVM in order to detect the shot transitions. Mondal et al. [56] devised a unified framework for the detection of both abrupt and gradual transitions. The approach is based on multiscale geometric analysis of nonsubsampled contourlet transform, which is used for feature extraction from the frames composing the video. Dimensionality reduction is done using principle component analysis and a least squares SVM classifier is used to categorize the frames into either no-transition, abrupt, or gradual transition types.

## 9.2.3 Methods for real-time shot boundary detection

In a work by Boussaid et al. [57], the authors modified two methods in order to reduce the time complexity and satisfy the real-time constraints. The two algorithms modified were the one by Nagasaka et al. [58], which was based on a local histogram and the edge change ratio algorithm developed by Zabih et al. [59]. In a further work, Boussaid et al. [60] achieved the hardware implementation of a real-time shot cut detector in which a local histogram was used for detecting abrupt transitions in real-time applications. A field–programmable gate array (FPGA)-based platform was used to implement the detector. A motion activity-based method was devised by Amel et al. [61] for shot boundary detection using an adaptive rood pattern search algorithm. This work was aimed at real-time implementation and achieved a reasonable performance in detecting shot boundaries. Motion vectors were also extracted for video segmentation by Youness and Abdelalim [62]. Using a fully convolutional neural network, Gygli [63] devised a very fast method for shot boundary detection which is trained with a data set containing one million frames and various types of shot transitions which are automatically generated from it. Calic and Izquierdo [64] devised a method for cut detection on the principle that the information useful for shot boundary detection can be extracted from the moving picture experts group (MPEG) compressed stream. The algorithm developed for the purpose was based on analysis of features extracted from MPEG compressed stream such as macroblock, resulting in fast and robust detection of abrupt transitions. Gauch et al. [65] developed a pipelined architecture for digital video processing which can digitize, process, index, and compress videos in real-time. The client-server-based graphical user interface (GUI) is capable of searching an archive and presenting to the user the video segments under different bandwidth constrained scenarios.

Amer et al. [66] developed a system for high-level representation of a video in real time which is targeted for video surveillance applications. The core of the system is based on four video-processing layers whose function is to estimate and reduce noise, stabilize, extract meaningful objects through analysis. and interpret in order to extract context-independent semantic features. The framework is shown to be effective and real-time compliant using different indoor and outdoor video shots having different attributes.

Apostolidis and Mezaris [67] developed a method for shot transition detection in which SURF and HSV histograms are used to compute the frame similarity. In this approach, graphics processing unit (GPU)-based processing is used for real-time analysis. There is a sharp change in the similarity score for abrupt transitions and a gradual change in the similarity score for soft transitions. The method is reported to be capable of faster than real-time analysis.

In another work, Ma et al. [68] developed a method for detection of shot transitions in videos with MPEG compression. The DC images are computed from the I frames of the video and the difference values of histogram of these images are used to detect the approximate shot boundaries. The B frames are used to detect the abrupt transitions accurately. The gradual changes are detected by using the difference values of consecutive N number of I frames. The change in the number of intracoding macroblocks in P frames is used for classification of the gradual shot changes.

A fast method to search and identify shot transitions was devised by Amini and Jassbi [69] using a divide and conquer approach. A global dissimilarity function is used to compare the first and last representative frames between specific parts of a video. In case there is low dissimilarity, the algorithm skips searching inside the segment as the possibility of finding a shot transition is minimal. This saves time and ensures faster identification of shot boundaries. A local dissimilarity function is used to detect shot boundaries in a local region.

## 9.3 Basic concepts and preliminaries

### 9.3.1 Fuzzy hostility map generation using spatio-temporal fuzzy hostility index

A color image $(C)$ is conceptually a three-dimensional matrix of size $M \times N \times 3$, where each pixel is represented by three values from the RGB planes. The color image may be converted to a grayscale image $(G)$, represented by a matrix of size $M \times N$ using the following equation:

$$G(i,j) = 0.2126C(i,j,1) + 0.7152C(i,j,2) + 0.0722C(i,j,3) \qquad (9.1)$$

where $G(i, j)$ is the resultant grayscale intensity at pixel $(i, j)$ of the grayscale image and $C(i, j, 1)$, $C(i, j, 2)$, and $C(i, j, 3)$ are the red, green, and blue intensities of the color image at the point $(i, j)$ in the RGB planes, respectively. The pixel values in $G$ lie in the range [0,255]. The fuzzy hostility index (FHI) [70] is a dissimilarity measure which indicates the contrast of a pixel in relation to its neighborhood using the following formula:

$$\xi = \frac{3}{2^{n+1}} \sum_{i=1}^{2^{n+1}} \frac{|\mu_p - \mu_{q_i}|}{|\mu_p + 1| + |\mu_{q_i} + 1|} \qquad (9.2)$$

where $\mu_p$ is the membership value of the pixel under consideration and $\mu_{q_i}$; $i = 1, 2, 3, \ldots, 2^{n+1}$ are the membership values of its fuzzy neighbors in an $n$-order neighborhood fuzzy subset. A high value of FHI signifies greater heterogeneity between the candidate and its adjacent pixels. In other words, the high-frequency regions can be visualized using the fuzzy hostility map (FHM) generated from the matrix of values obtained by computing the FHI of all the pixels in the image, as shown in Fig. 9.2. The FHM generated from an image resembles the spatial stretch of heterogeneous regions within it.

Since a video is composed of time-sequenced images, the spread of heterogeneity across the images is also temporal in nature. The spatio-temporal fuzzy hostility index (STFHI) ($\gamma$) of a pixel in the $i^{th}$ frame of a video is a function ($\omega$) of the FHI of the candidate pixel in the present frame ($f_i$) (*centre pixel* in Fig. 9.3B) and the corresponding pixels in the previous and post frames, that is, $f_{i-1}$ and $f_{i+1}$ (*centre pixels* in Fig. 9.3A and C), can be expressed as follows:

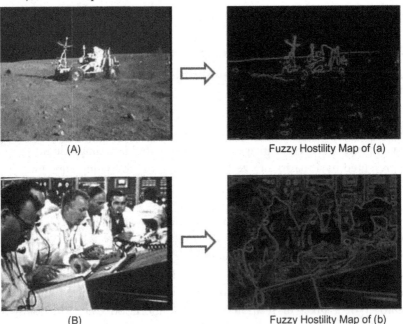

(A)

Fuzzy Hostility Map of (a)

(B)

Fuzzy Hostility Map of (b)

**Figure 9.2** Fuzzy hostility maps generated from images of the NASA 25th anniversary video.

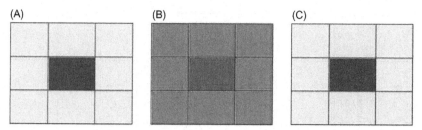

**Figure 9.3** Spatio-temporal fuzzy hostility index.

$$\gamma_{f_i} = \omega(\xi_{f_{i-1}}, \xi_{f_i}, \xi_{f_{i+1}}) \qquad (9.3)$$

In other words, $\gamma$ of a pixel is a function of the second-order neighborhood of its corresponding pixels (*pixels* other than centre pixel in Fig. 9.3A and C) and itself [*pixels* other than centre pixel in Fig. 9.3B]. $\gamma$ is computed as the average of $\xi_{f_{i-1}}$, $\xi_{f_i}$, and $\xi_{f_{i+1}}$ except for the first and last frames of a video, where $\xi_{f_{i-1}}$ and $\xi_{f_{i+1}}$ are not present, respectively. The edge map representing all the pronounced edges of the objects present in the image is obtained from the $2D$ matrix created by calculating the $\gamma$ of each pixel in the frame as portrayed in Fig. 9.2.

## 9.3.2 Pixel intensification and fuzzy hostility map dilation

The image corresponding to the FHM of a video frame is a grayscale image in which the regions having higher homogeneity are represented by shades close to black and the heterogeneous regions having high discontinuity in pixel values are represented with shades of white. The FHM image is thus able to distinctly portray the edges of objects or high-frequency regions. However, the FHM image may not be prominent and may undergo pixel intensification using an intensity scaling function ($\phi$) represented as:

$$\begin{aligned} \phi \quad &= (\lambda_{ij})^2, \quad \text{if } \lambda_{ij} < 0.5 \\ &= (\sqrt{\lambda_{ij}}), \quad \text{if } \lambda_{ij} \geq 0.5 \end{aligned} \qquad (9.4)$$

as shown in Fig. 9.4. In order to compensate for object and camera movement, the intensified edge map image is dilated using morphological operations. This ensures that there is overlap among the high-frequency regions between consecutive frames of a shot. Thus, the similarity values computed for images with the same content will be higher, even if there is object or camera movement.

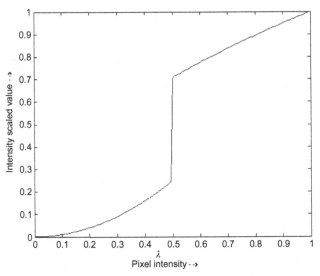

**Figure 9.4** Intensity scaling function.

### 9.3.3 Fuzzy hostility map similarity

As discussed in Section 9.1, the FHM is a matrix, of the same size as the image containing the STFHI values corresponding to each of the pixels. For computing the similarity between two FHM matrices $P$ and $Q$, the Pearson's correlation coefficient ($\rho_{P,Q}$) is applied as follows:

$$\rho_{P,Q} = \frac{\sum (x_{ij} - \bar{x})(y_{ij} - \bar{y})}{\sqrt{\left\{\sum (x_{ij} - \bar{x})^2\right\}\left\{\sum (y_{ij} - \bar{y})^2\right\}}} \quad (9.5)$$

where $x_{ij}$ and $y_{ij}$ are the elements in the $i^{th}$ row and $j^{th}$ column of matrices $P$ and $Q$, respectively, $\bar{x}$ is the mean value of the elements in $P$, and $\bar{y}$ is the mean value of the elements in $Q$. It should be noted here that the similarity values computed between consecutive images of a shot will be higher than the similarity values computed between frames of two different shots. This is depicted in Fig. 9.5.

### 9.3.4 Vague set modeling for video segmentation

Vague sets serve as an extension of fuzzy sets, where elements have a membership range rather than a fixed membership value. The membership range of an element to a vague set depends upon two factors, that is, true membership and false membership. The true membership or "for"

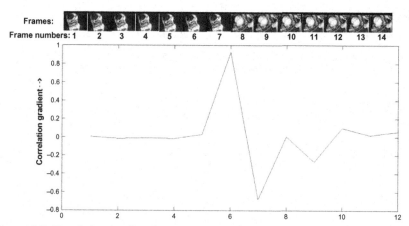

**Figure 9.5** Correlation gradient between FHMs of consecutive frames.

membership of an element to a vague set is computed from the instances which are in support of the element being part of the set. On the other hand, the false or "against" membership is computed from the evidences which are not in favor of the element being a part of the vague set. Given a video $V = f_1 \oplus f_2 \oplus f_3 \oplus \ldots \oplus f_n \oplus f_{n+1}$, where $f_i$ is the $i^{th}$ frame, the distance between two frames $f_i$ and $f_j$ may be given by $d_i = \Phi(f_i, f_j)$. Here $\Phi$ represents the distance function. In order to perform temporal segmentation of the video, the distance between consecutive frames needs to be computed. Thus, in a video consisting of $N + 1$ frames, it is possible to compute $N$ distances from the consecutive frames, using the distance function ($\Phi$) given by the set $D = \{d_1, d_2, d_3, \ldots, d_{n-1}, d_n\}$. If the distance between two consecutive frames exceeds a certain threshold, a hard cut is detected. The problem is elevated in real-time detection of hard cuts, where an initial threshold may not be available and the threshold needs to be updated continuously. In other words, the threshold needs to be adaptive to the present situation .

The modeling required for detection of hard cuts or abrupt transitions using vague sets is subject to fulfilling constraints which form the basis of such representation. In the case of vague sets, the membership range of an element is given by $[t_x, 1 - f_x]$, where $t_x$ represents the true membership and $f_x$ denotes the false membership, subject to the constraint $0 \leq t_x + f_x \leq 1$. The accuracy of the hard-cut detection process may be lower when the distance set $D$ is used. In order to portray the problem, a set of 15 distances, $D = \{d_1, d_2, d_3, \ldots, d_{15}\}$, generated from a video clip consisting of 16 frames is considered as shown in Tables 9.1. Let the

**Table 9.1** Arbitrary distances between consecutive frames generated by $\Phi$.

| Distances | $d_1$ | $d_2$ | $d_3$ | $d_4$ | $d_5$ | $d_6$ | $d_7$ | $d_8$ | $d_9$ | $d_{10}$ | $d_{11}$ | $d_{12}$ | $d_{13}$ | $d_{14}$ | $d_{15}$ |
|---|---|---|---|---|---|---|---|---|---|---|---|---|---|---|---|
| Values | 0.71 | 0.78 | 0.73 | 0.82 | 0.79 | 0.83 | 0.34 | 0.9 | 0.92 | 0.95 | 0.91 | 0.87 | 0.94 | 0.93 | 0.91 |

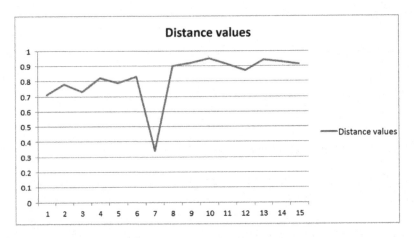

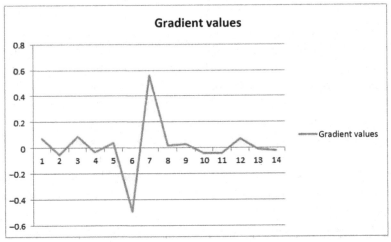

**Figure 9.6** Distance and gradient values.

gradient of the distances be denoted by the set G. Thus, the elements of the gradient set are denoted by $G = \{g_1, g_2, g_3, \ldots, g_{14}\}$, where $g_i = d_i - d_j$ and $j = i - 1$. The plot of the distance and gradient values is shown in Fig. 9.6. It is evident that the gradient is a better indicator of hard cuts than the distance between frames as the amount of change in gradient is more than the change in distance, and hence detection is easier. The problem is elevated when a shot change occurs while preserving the same background and objects. In such cases, the distance value at the point of shot transition may not be appreciable but the change in distance value (gradient) may be significant enough to detect the change. From the values of $G$, it is possible to trace back to the frames between which the shot boundary occurs. The gradient set $G$ is to be modeled as a vague set in order to determine the elements which denote an abrupt transition. The true membership of an element in the set $G$ denotes the affinity of that element to the hard-cut set $(H)$. Likewise, the false membership of an element portrays the resistance toward the membership of that element to the set $H$. In order to determine the membership value of each element in set $G$ to set $H$, the true and false membership values of each element need to be computed. The true membership of an element $g_i$ in $G$ is denoted by $t_{g_i}$ and is computed as follows:

$$t_{g_i} = \frac{g_i}{\max(G)} \tag{9.6}$$

Here, $g_i$ is the gradient of the $i^{th}$ element of set $G$ and $i = 1, 2, 3, \ldots, k$. The false membership $(f_i)$ is determined as:

$$f_{g_i} = \max(g_1, g_2, g_3, \ldots\ldots\ldots, g_k) - g_i \tag{9.7}$$

Thus,

$$f_{g_i} = M - g_i \tag{9.8}$$

Here, $M = \max(G)$. However, Eqs. (9.6) and (9.8) must follow the important postulate of vague sets, that is,

$$t_{g_i} + f_{g_i} \leq 1 \tag{9.9}$$

Substituting the values of $t_{g_i}$ and $f_{g_i}$ from Eqs. (9.6) and (9.8), respectively, in Eq. (9.9) and factorizing it, the following is obtained:

$$(M - g_i)(M - 1) \leq 0 \tag{9.10}$$

In Eq. (9.4) the term $(\max(G) - g_i)$ is always positive or zero as max $(G)$ will always be greater than or equal to any element in $G$, that is, $g_i$, and $\max(G)$ is always less than or equal to 1. Thus, the constraint given by Eq. 9.9 is satisfied. The actual membership $(\lambda)$ can be computed for each of the elements using the defuzzification formula:

$$\lambda = \frac{t_{g_i}}{t_{g_i} + f_{g_i}} \tag{9.11}$$

Thus, the membership value of each element in the set $G$ can be represented by $G_\lambda = \{\lambda_1, \lambda_2, \lambda_3, \lambda_4, \ldots, \lambda_k\}$

## 9.3.5 Computation of vague adaptive threshold (VAT) in real-time

Threshold selection forms a very important part of the shot boundary analysis task. In fact, the efficacy of the transition detection task is highly dependent on determining an appropriate threshold. As discussed in the previous subsection, $G_\lambda$ represents the set of membership values corresponding to each gradient value in the set $G$. The selected threshold will help to identify the gradient points which qualify as a hard cut. The membership values in the set $G_\lambda$ indicate the possibility of hard cuts being present at the different points of the video. A high membership value ($\lambda_i$) is indicative of a large distance gradient, as evident from Eq. (9.6).

In order to compute an adaptive threshold in a real-time scenario, let us consider that $k$ frames have been received by the destination at a particular instant of time. Thus, the number of inter-frame distances between the consecutive frames may be given as $D = \{d_1, d_2, d_3, \ldots, d_{k-1}\}$. Normalization of these distances may be performed as follows:

$$d_i^* = \frac{d_i - \min(D)}{\max(D) - \min(D)} \tag{9.12}$$

The normalized distance set may be represented as $D_{\text{norm}} = \{d_1^*, d_2^*, d_3^*, \ldots, d_{k-1}^*\}$. The membership values for each of the points ($\lambda_{d_i^*}$) may be computed in accordance with Eqs. (9.6), (9.8), and (9.11). As new video frames are buffered, the corresponding $\lambda_{d_i^*}$ are computed. For detection of video segments, the three-sigma rule is employed over the set $G_\lambda$ in order to compute a threshold. According to the three-sigma rule, for a normal distribution, 68.2% of the values lie in the range $[\mu - \sigma, \mu + \sigma]$, 95.4% of values in $[\mu - 2\sigma, \mu + 2\sigma]$ and 99.6% of values lie in the range $[\mu + 3\sigma, \mu - 3\sigma]$. Here $\mu$ denotes the arithmetic mean and $\sigma$ denotes the standard deviation of the data set. Considering the values in set $G_\lambda$ as a normal distribution, the values beyond the range $[\mu - 3\sigma, \mu + 3\sigma]$ are considered as the points of shot transition. However, as new video frames are buffered, the set $G_\lambda$ is updated and consequently a new mean ($M_{\text{new}}$) and standard deviation ($\sigma_{\text{new}}$) over the elements of $G_\lambda$ must be computed. The membership value is computed from the correlation gradient of the stream of consecutive correlation values obtained at a particular instant. The mean and standard deviations of the correlation gradient values are the parameters used for computing the threshold using the three-sigma rule. As new video frames are buffered in, these parameters are updated in real-time as new video frames are streamed in. The new mean ($M_{\text{new}}$) and standard deviation ($\sigma_{\text{new}}$) are computed from the present mean ($M$), present standard deviation ($\sigma$), and new membership value ($\lambda_{d^*_{k+1}}$) may be obtained as follows:

$$M = \frac{\sum_{i=1}^{k} \lambda_{d^*_i}}{k} \tag{9.13}$$

$$M_{new} = \frac{\sum_{i=1}^{k+1} \lambda_{d^*_i}}{k+1} = \frac{\left(\sum_{i=1}^{k} \lambda_{d^*_i}\right) + \lambda_{d^*_{k+1}}}{k+1} = \frac{Mk + \lambda_{d^*_{k+1}}}{k+1}$$

$$\therefore M_{new} = \left(\frac{k}{k+1}\right)M + \left(\frac{1}{k+1}\right)\lambda_{d^*_{k+1}} \tag{9.14}$$

Since,

$$\sigma = \sqrt{\frac{\sum (d^*_i - M)^2}{N}}$$

$$\Rightarrow N\sigma^2 = \sum (d^*_i - M)^2$$

$$\Rightarrow (N+1)\sigma^2_{\text{new}} = \sum_{i=1}^{N+1} (d^*_i - M_{\text{new}})^2$$

$$\Rightarrow (N+1)\sigma^2_{\text{new}} = \sum_{i=1}^{N+1} (d^{*2}_i - 2d^*_i M_{\text{new}} + M^2_{\text{new}})$$

$$\Rightarrow (N+1)\sigma^2_{\text{new}} = \sum_{i=1}^{N+1} d^{*2}_i - 2\sum_{i=1}^{N+1} d^*_i M_{\text{new}} + \sum_{i=1}^{N+1} M^2_{\text{new}} \tag{9.15}$$

$$\Rightarrow (N+1)\sigma^2_{\text{new}} = \sum_{i=1}^{N+1} d^{*2}_i + 2(N+1)M^2_{\text{new}} + (N+1)M^2_{\text{new}}$$

$$\Rightarrow (N+1)\sigma^2_{\text{new}} = \sum_{i=1}^{N+1} d^{*2}_i + (N+1)M^2_{\text{new}}$$

$$\Rightarrow \sigma^2_{\text{new}} = \frac{1}{N+1}\left[\sum_{i=1}^{N} d^{*2}_i + d^*_{i+1}{}^2\right] - M^2_{\text{new}}$$

$$\Rightarrow \sigma_{\text{new}} = \sqrt{\frac{1}{N+1}\left[\sum_{i=1}^{N} d^{*2}_i + d^*_{i+1}{}^2\right] - M^2_{\text{new}}}$$

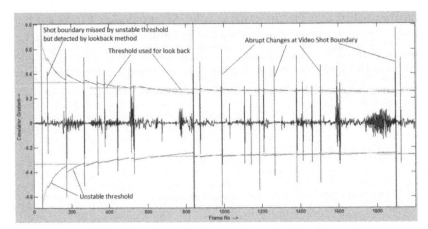

**Figure 9.7** Missed shot boundaries detected using the look-back technique.

Thus, the new VAT is:

$$\tau_{\mathrm{vat}} = M_{\mathrm{new}} + 3 \times \sigma_{\mathrm{new}} \tag{9.16}$$

Using this threshold, the elements in set $G_\lambda$, which are greater than $\tau_{\mathrm{VAT}}$, are identified as hard-cut points.

## 9.3.6 Look-back technique for detection of missed video segments

During initial buffering of video frames, the threshold ($\tau_{\mathrm{VAT}}$) fluctuates a lot as $\tau_{\mathrm{VAT}}$ is computed on a small number of points in $G_\lambda$. As more frames are buffered in, $\tau$ gradually stabilizes. The problem here is that the adaptive threshold based on vague set theory takes a little time to stabilize and, during this time, a few shot transition points may go undetected due to this unstable threshold. In order to enhance the efficacy of the detection process, a look-back technique is essential which will revisit the covered points so that no undetected shot transitions are left out. Look-back occurs after every $P$ frames and in this work $P$ is set to 300. From Fig. 9.7, it is observed that the shot transition points missed initially are detected using the look-back technique. For videos with frame rates 25 fps and 30 fps, the look-back will occur every 12 and 10 seconds, respectively.

## 9.4 Approach for real-time video segmentation

The sequence of steps composing the proposed method for real-time VAT is shown in Fig. 9.8. The set of steps constituting the shot detection process is described in later subsections.

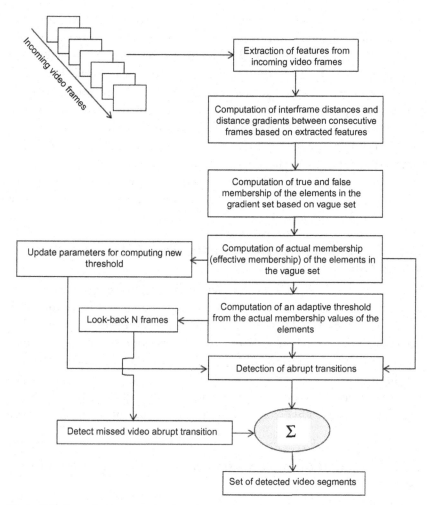

**Figure 9.8** Flow diagram.

## 9.4.1 Extraction of features from buffered frames

The frames of the incoming video are buffered in order to extract features for the detection of shot transitions. The interframe distances are computed between consecutive frames by taking into account the extracted features from the frames. In this work, a FHM is generated from each buffered frame using the spatio-temporal FHI as described in Section 9.1. The FHM extracted from each frame serves as a high-level feature for the detection of shot transitions. As described in Section 9.2, the process of pixel intensification causes the FHM to enhance the sharpness of the edges through a pixel intensification function. This is followed by the process of edge dilation in which the edges corresponding to the high-frequency regions of the image are dilated in order to compensate for object and camera movements. The correlation between the dilated FHMs is computed to arrive at an inter-frame distance between consecutive incoming frames. The gradient of these distances is determined and the set of such gradients is labeled as the gradient set $G$, which is modeled as a vague set for determining the shot boundaries as explained in Section 9.4. The membership of each element in set $G$ to the hard-cut set $(H)$ is determined from the true and false memberships using Eq. (9.11). The membership values of all elements in $G$ are represented by the set $G_\lambda$ as discussed in Section 9.4.

### 9.4.2 Computation of VAT for detection of shot boundaries in real-time

As new video frames are buffered, new membership values are computed in accordance with the vague set modeling as discussed in Section 9.4. Thus new values are added to $G_\lambda$ as time elapses. Since the shot boundary detection task is done in real-time, it is necessary to compute a new threshold referred to as the VAT ($\tau_{VAT}$) with the newly added values in $G_\lambda$. In order to compute $\tau_{VAT}$, the new mean ($M_{new}$) and standard deviation ($\sigma_{new}$) are computed in accordance with Eqs. (9.14) and (9.15). Using the three-sigma rule, $\tau_{VAT}$ is computed in accordance with Eq. (9.16).

### 9.4.3 Detection of missed video segments using the look-back technique

Due to the unstable value of $\tau_{VAT}$ initially, some of the shot boundaries may remain undetected. This situation may also arise at other points of the time-sequenced frames since the detection of the shot boundaries is attempted on the fly. In order to mitigate the chances of missed detection, a look-back technique is adopted in which look-back occurs after every $N$ frames with the present threshold value computed by Eq. (9.16). In this work, the value of $N$ is set at 300 as explained in Section 9.3.6.

### 9.5 Experimental results and analysis

The video test set used for evaluating the proposed method of real-time shot boundary detection comprised of 15 videos with varied features

(Tables 9.2−9.4). Apart from this, the proposed method was compared with other state-of-the-art methods on a subset of the benchmark TRECVID 2001 dataset (Table 9.5). All the videos considered in the test datasets of Tables 9.2−9.4 have a resolution of 640 × 360 at 25 fps in MP4 format, while the videos in the TRECVID 2001 data set have a resolution of 320 × 240. The proposed method for real-time shot boundary detection was evaluated on the test video datasets by considering two commonly used parameters, recall $(R)$ and precision $(P)$ defined as follows:

**Table 9.2** Test video dataset I.

| Video | V1 | V2 | V3 | V4 |
|---|---|---|---|---|
| Duration (mm:ss) | 02:58 | 02:42 | 04:10 | 03:27 |
| No. of frames | 4468 | 4057 | 6265 | 4965 |
| No. of hard cuts | 43 | 70 | 172 | 77 |
| Average no. of frames in each shot | 101.54 | 57.14 | 36.21 | 63.65 |

**Table 9.3** Test video dataset II.

| Video | V6 | V7 | V8 | V9 | V10 | V11 |
|---|---|---|---|---|---|---|
| Duration (mm:ss) | 30:30 | 25:27 | 25:01 | 26:33 | 25:03 | 28:40 |
| No. of frames | 54,846 | 45,771 | 44,991 | 39,843 | 37,597 | 43,018 |
| No. of hard cuts | 835 | 386 | 309 | 321 | 123 | 406 |
| Average no. of frames in each shot | 66.60 | 118.27 | 145.13 | 123.73 | 303.20 | 105.69 |

**Table 9.4** Test video dataset III.

| Video | V12 | V13 | V14 | V15 |
|---|---|---|---|---|
| Duration (mm:ss) | 51:20 | 58:06 | 59:29 | 111:19 |
| No. of frames | 74,020 | 87,150 | 89,225 | 166,990 |
| No. of hard cuts | 941 | 807 | 1271 | 2807 |
| Average no. of frames in each shot | 78.57 | 107.85 | 70.14 | 59.46 |

**Table 9.5** Videos from TRECVID 2001 dataset.

| Video | Length (mm:ss) | FPS | Resolution | No. of frames | Abrupt transitions |
|---|---|---|---|---|---|
| Anni005 | 6:19 | 30 | 320 × 240 | 11,364 | 38 |
| Anni006 | 9:13 | 30 | 320 × 240 | 16,588 | 41 |
| Anni009 | 6:50 | 30 | 320 × 240 | 12,306 | 38 |
| BOR08 | 28:07 | 30 | 320 × 240 | 50,569 | 380 |

$$\text{Recall} = \frac{B_d - B_f}{B_t} \qquad (9.17)$$

$$\text{Precision} = \frac{B_d - B_f}{B_d} \qquad (9.18)$$

where

$B_d$, shot transitions detected by algorithm;

$B_f$, false shot transitions detected;

$B_t$, actual shot transitions present in the video.

A comparison with other state-of-the-art methods in terms of $F_1$ score is also presented in Section 9.5.3. The $F_1$ score serves as a reliable metric for determining the effectiveness of an information retrieval system and is computed as the harmonic mean of precision and recall as follows:

$$F_1 = 2\frac{\text{Precision} \times \text{Recall}}{\text{Precision} + \text{Recall}} \qquad (9.19)$$

where the $F_1$ score varies between 0 (worst score) and 1 (best score).

## 9.5.1 Video dataset used for experimentation

The video test set comprised of 15 videos divided into three sets according to length. In order to establish the usefulness of the real-time video segmentation method, videos of varied characteristics were taken into consideration. Five videos of short duration form the first dataset and are listed in Table 9.2. The second set consists of six videos of medium length and are listed in Table 9.3. The third dataset consists of four long-duration videos as given in Table 9.4. The first video is a highlights clip taken from the Wimbledon semi-final match of 2013 between Del Potro and Djokovic (labeled as V1 in Table 9.2). The motivation behind choosing this video is that being a tennis match clip, apart from small-duration shots, the video has quick object movement. Video V2 in Table 9.2 is a

Hindi movie song called "Dagabaaz" from the film "Dabangg 2." This video comprises sequences which are mostly shot outdoors in daylight. Another Hindi film song called "Chammak Challo" from the movie "Ra. One" is selected as the third video and is labeled as V3 in Table 9.2. The significant feature of this video is that it has real-life shots intermingled with digitally created frames. The average shot duration of this video is the least among all the videos in the first data set. The fourth video (marked V4 in Table 9.2) is a music video on a violin track played by Lindsey Stirling and is characterized by simultaneous camera and object movement. This video was shot outdoors in a backdrop of trees and mountains and comprises swift zoom-out and zoom-in sequences. The 2010 FIFA World Cup official song called "Waka Waka" (This time for Africa) is taken as the fifth video in the dataset and marked as V5 in Table 9.2. In this video, match clips taken from FIFA World Cup history are intermingled with the song performance. The shots are taken against varied backgrounds and illuminations. This served as the motivation for including this video in the dataset. The videos V6 to V11 (listed in Table 9.3) are of moderate length having duration close to half an hour, whereas the videos V12 to V14 (listed in Table 9.4) are of long duration, having average length close to 1 hour. Video V15 is the longest video of the dataset having duration close to 2 hours. The videos V6 to V14 are documentaries taken from different TV channels, while video V15 is the highlights of the cricket final match between India and Sri Lanka, taken from the Cricket World Cup 2011.

In order to compare the proposed method with other state-of-the-art methods, five commonly used videos of the TRECVID 2001 benchmark collection are used. The characteristics of the five videos chosen from TRECVID 2001 are detailed in Table 9.5.

## 9.5.2 Experimental results

The proposed method for real-time detection of hard cuts works in two parallel phases. In one of the phases, hard cuts are detected by using a VAT which is computed on the elements of $G_\lambda$ using the three-sigma rule as explained in Section 9.3.5. It is observed that due to an unstable threshold during the initial part of the video, there is a possibility of missing the actual hard cuts. This is also true for situations where there is a change of shot with a similar background or objects. In order to mitigate the possibility of missed detection, a look-back method is employed as explained in Section 9.3.6, which works in parallel with the basic detection process and checks after certain intervals if some hard cuts have been missed. Experiments on the test set of videos are presented in Tables 9.6—9.8, which portray the efficacy of the method.

Table 9.6 Results of proposed real-time shot boundary detection method on dataset I.

| Video | V1 | V2 | V3 | V4 | V5 |
|---|---|---|---|---|---|
| Hard cuts present | 43 | 70 | 172 | 77 | 138 |
| Hard cuts detected | 43 | 68 | 168 | 76 | 132 |
| Detected by look-back | 0 | 2 | 5 | 2 | 8 |
| Falsely detected hard cuts | 0 | 0 | 1 | 1 | 3 |
| Recall | 1.0 | 1.0 | 1.0 | 1.0 | 0.992 |
| Precision | 1.0 | 1.0 | 0.994 | 0.987 | 0.978 |
| F1 score | 1.0 | 1.0 | 0.997 | 0.993 | 0.985 |

Table 9.7 Results of proposed real-time shot boundary detection method on dataset II.

| Video | V6 | V7 | V8 | V9 | V10 | V11 |
|---|---|---|---|---|---|---|
| Hard cuts present | 835 | 386 | 309 | 321 | 123 | 406 |
| Hard cuts detected | 826 | 380 | 303 | 300 | 108 | 405 |
| Detected by look-back | 16 | 11 | 7 | 31 | 21 | 3 |
| Falsely detected hard cuts | 8 | 6 | 2 | 11 | 7 | 4 |
| Recall | 0.998 | 0.997 | 0.996 | 0.996 | 0.991 | 0.995 |
| Precision | 0.990 | 0.984 | 0.993 | 0.966 | 0.945 | 0.990 |
| F1 score | 0.994 | 0.990 | 0.995 | 0.981 | 0.968 | 0.992 |

Table 9.8 Results of proposed real-time shot boundary detection method on dataset III.

| Video | V12 | V13 | V14 | V15 |
|---|---|---|---|---|
| Hard cuts present | 941 | 807 | 1271 | 2807 |
| Hard cuts detected | 940 | 805 | 1266 | 2801 |
| Detected by look-back | 1 | 3 | 6 | 8 |
| Falsely detected hard cuts | 5 | 1 | 3 | 6 |
| Recall | 0.994 | 1.0 | 0.998 | 0.998 |
| Precision | 0.994 | 0.998 | 0.997 | 0.997 |
| F1 score | 0.994 | 0.999 | 0.998 | 0.998 |

Table 9.9 Comparison with existing methods.

| Videos | Edge strength ext. [71] | | | Bitwise XOR [72] | | | Adaptive edge [73] | | | Localized edge [74] | | | Proposed method | | |
|---|---|---|---|---|---|---|---|---|---|---|---|---|---|---|---|
| | R | P | F1 | R | P | F1 | R | P | F1 | R | P | F1 | R | P | F1 |
| Anni005 | 0.95 | 0.9 | 0.92 | 0.92 | 1.0 | 0.96 | 0.91 | 0.87 | 0.89 | 0.79 | 0.73 | 0.76 | 0.947 | 0.923 | 0.935 |
| Anni006 | 0.93 | 0.83 | 0.88 | 0.71 | 0.81 | 0.76 | 0.89 | 0.82 | 0.85 | 0.73 | 0.63 | 0.68 | 0.926 | 0.950 | 0.938 |
| Anni009 | 0.92 | 0.92 | 0.92 | 0.79 | 0.91 | 0.85 | 0.93 | 0.87 | 0.9 | 0.79 | 0.71 | 0.75 | 0.894 | 0.918 | 0.906 |
| BOR08 | 0.93 | 0.95 | 0.94 | 0.82 | 0.9 | 0.86 | 0.91 | 0.86 | 0.88 | 0.91 | 0.91 | 0.91 | 0.973 | 0.984 | 0.978 |
| NAD53 | 0.96 | 0.89 | 0.92 | 0.86 | 0.89 | 0.87 | 0.97 | 0.81 | 0.88 | 0.9 | 0.8 | 0.85 | 0.927 | 0.950 | 0.939 |

**Table 9.10** Comparison with other real-time methods.

| Videos | Classical STFHI [75] | | | Proposed method | | |
|---|---|---|---|---|---|---|
| | *R* | *P* | *F1* | *R* | *P* | *F1* |
| Anni005 | 0.842 | 0.888 | 0.864 | 0.947 | 0.923 | 0.935 |
| Anni006 | 0.853 | 0.921 | 0.886 | 0.926 | 0.950 | 0.938 |
| Anni009 | 0.815 | 0.885 | 0.849 | 0.894 | 0.918 | 0.906 |
| BOR08 | 0.944 | 0.978 | 0.961 | 0.973 | 0.984 | 0.978 |
| NAD53 | 0.855 | 0.910 | 0.881 | 0.927 | 0.950 | 0.939 |

### 9.5.3 Comparison with other existing methods

The proposed method for real-time shot boundary detection was compared with four other existing methods including edge strength extraction [71], Bitwise XOR [72], adaptive edge [73], localized edge [74]. Five videos from the TRECVID 2001 dataset were chosen for evaluation and the results are presented in Table 9.9. The present work, which is based on vague set modeling was also compared with another real-time SBD approach [75] using the same videos in the TRECVID 2001 dataset. The comparison results are presented in Table 9.10. The results presented in Tables 9.9 and 9.10 show that the proposed method outperforms the existing methods.

### 9.6 Future directions and conclusion

The real-time video segmentation approach based on vague set modeling discussed in this chapter was evaluated on two sets of videos. The first set of videos is a test set divided into three subsets and another set is taken from the TRECVID 2001 benchmark videos. This approach outperforms the other existing methods in terms of both precision and recall. In this work, the automatic adaptive threshold is used, which eliminates the need to set an arbitrary threshold for detecting the shot transition points. It is also observed that the total number of false hits is also much less.

The problem of gradual transition detection has not been addressed in this chapter and remains an area of research where more efficient algorithms can be developed. The performance of existing gradual transition detectors is less than satisfactory, as reported in the literature. Also, the problem of detecting gradual transitions in real-time would pose new challenges to researchers. Hence, a robust shot boundary detection

algorithm would encompass detection of all important types of video edits
for advancement of research in the domain of video analysis.

## References

[1] D.G. Lowe, Object recognition from local scale-invariant features, in: The Proceedings of the Seventh IEEE International Conference on Computer Vision, 1999, vol. 2, IEEE, 1999, pp. 1150−1157.

[2] H. Bay, T. Tuytelaars, L. Van Gool, Surf: speeded-up robust features, Computer vision−ECCV 2006, Springer, 2006, pp. 404−417.

[3] E. Tola, V. Lepetit, P. Fua, Daisy: an efficient dense descriptor applied to wide-baseline stereo, IEEE Trans. Pattern Anal. Mach. Intell. 32 (5) (2010) 815−830.

[4] A. Oliva, A. Torralba, Building the gist of a scene: the role of global image features in recognition, Prog. Bra Res. 155 (2006) 23−36.

[5] M. Calonder, V. Lepetit, C. Strecha, P. Fua, Brief: binary robust independent elementary features, European Conference on Computer Vision, Springer, 2010, pp. 778−792.

[6] E. Rublee, V. Rabaud, K. Konolige, G. Bradski, Orb: an efficient alternative to sift or surf, in: 2011 IEEE International Conference on Computer Vision (ICCV), IEEE, 2011, pp. 2564−2571.

[7] S. Leutenegger, M. Chli, R.Y. Siegwart, Brisk: binary robust invariant scalable keypoints, in: 2011 IEEE International Conference on Computer Vision (ICCV), IEEE, 2011, pp. 2548−2555.

[8] V. Ferrari, F. Jurie, C. Schmid, From images to shape models for object detection, Int. J. Comput. Vis. 87 (3) (2010) 284−303.

[9] A. Toshev, A. Makadia, K. Daniilidis, Shape-based object recognition in videos using 3d synthetic object models, in: 2009 IEEE Conference on Computer Vision and Pattern Recognition, IEEE, 2009, pp. 288−295.

[10] T.F. Chan, L.A. Vese, Active contours without edges, IEEE Trans. Image Process. 10 (2) (2001) 266−277.

[11] E. Candes, L. Demanet, D. Donoho, L. Ying, Fast discrete curvelet transforms, Multiscale Model. Simul. 5 (3) (2006) 861−899.

[12] M.-T. Pham, Y. Gao, V.-D.D. Hoang, T.-J. Cham, Fast polygonal integration and its application in extending haar-like features to improve object detection, in: 2010 IEEE Computer Society Conference on Computer Vision and Pattern Recognition, IEEE, 2010, pp. 942−949.

[13] C.G. Harris, M. Stephens, et al., A combined corner and edge detector, in: Alvey vision conference, vol. 15, Citeseer, 1988, pp. 10−5244.

[14] L. Ding, A. Goshtasby, On the canny edge detector, Pattern Recognit. 34 (3) (2001) 721−725.

[15] S. Liu, L. Yuan, P. Tan, J. Sun, Steadyflow: spatially smooth optical flow for video stabilization, in: Proceedings of the IEEE Conference on Computer Vision and Pattern Recognition, 2014, pp. 4209−4216.

[16] A. Akutsu, Y. Tonomura, H. Hashimoto, Y. Ohba, Video indexing using motion vectors, in: Visual Communications and Image Processing'92, vol. 1818, International Society for Optics and Photonics, 1992, pp. 1522−1531.

[17] G. Medioni, I. Cohen, F. Brémond, S. Hongeng, R. Nevatia, Event detection and analysis from video streams, IEEE Trans. Pattern Anal. Mach. Intell. 23 (8) (2001) 873−889.

[18] S.A. Ay, R. Zimmermann, S.H. Kim, Viewable scene modeling for geospatial video search, in: Proceedings of the 16th ACM International Conference on Multimedia, ACM, 2008, pp. 309−318.

[19] O. Steiger, A. Cavallaro, T. Ebrahimi, Mpeg-7 description of generic video objects for scene reconstruction, in: Visual Communications and Image Processing 2002, vol. 4671, International Society for Optics and Photonics, 2002, pp. 947—959.

[20] R.T. Collins, A.J. Lipton, T. Kanade, H. Fujiyoshi, D. Duggins, Y. Tsin, et al., A System for Video Surveillance and Monitoring VSAM Final. Rep., 2000, pp. 1—68.

[21] D. Comaniciu, V. Ramesh, P. Meer, Kernel-based object tracking, IEEE Trans. Pattern Anal. Mach. Intell. (5)(2003) 564—575.

[22] S.W. Smoliar, H. Zhang, Content based video indexing and retrieval, IEEE Multimed. 1 (2) (1994) 62—72.

[23] Y. Gao, W.-B. Wang, J.-H. Yong, H.-J. Gu, Dynamic video summarization using two-level redundancy detection, Multimed. Tools Appl. 42 (2) (2009) 233—250.

[24] X. Liu, J. Dai, A method of video shot-boundary detection based on grey modeling for histogram sequence, Int. J. Signal Process. Image Process. Pattern Recognit. 9 (4) (2016) 265—280.

[25] S. Tippaya, S. Sitjongsataporn, T. Tan, M.M. Khan, K. Chamnongthai, Multi-modal visual features-based video shot boundary detection, IEEE Access 5 (2017) 12563—12575.

[26] R. Hannane, A. Elboushaki, K. Afdel, P. Naghabhushan, M. Javed, An efficient method for video shot boundary detection and keyframe extraction using sift-point distribution histogram, Int. J. Multimed. Inf. Retr. 5 (2) (2016) 89—104.

[27] G. Pal, D. Rudrapaul, S. Acharjee, R. Ray, S. Chakraborty, N. Dey, Video shot boundary detection: a review, Emerging ICT for Bridging the Future — Proceedings of the 49th Annual Convention of the Computer Society of India CSI, vol. 2, Springer, 2015, pp. 119—127.

[28] Z. Li, X. Liu, S. Zhang, Shot boundary detection based on multilevel difference of colour histograms, in: Multimedia and Image Processing (ICMIP), 2016 First International Conference on, IEEE, 2016, pp. 15—22.

[29] W. Moeglein, R. Griswold, B. Mehdi, N.D. Browning, J. Teuton, Applying shot boundary detection for automated crystal growth analysis during in situ transmission electron microscope experiments, Adv. Struct. Chem. imaging 3 (1) (2017) 2.

[30] C. Loukas, N. Nikiteas, D. Schizas, E. Georgiou, Shot boundary detection in endoscopic surgery videos using a variational bayesian framework, Int. J. Comput. Assist. Radiol. Surg. 11 (11) (2016) 1937—1949.

[31] M. Verma, B. Raman, A hierarchical shot boundary detection algorithm using global and local features, in: Proceedings of International Conference on Computer Vision and Image Processing, Springer, 2017, pp. 389—397.

[32] B. Youssef, E. Fedwa, A. Driss, S. Ahmed, Shot boundary detection via adaptive low rank and svd-updating, Computer Vis. Image Underst. 161 (2017) 20—28.

[33] S. Gupta, S. Dhiman, A. Makkar, D. Khanna, A. Arora, A review of video shot boundary detection (sbd) technique, J. Image Process. Pattern Recognit. Prog. 5 (2) (2018) 59—70.

[34] S. Abdulhussain, A. Ramli, M. Saripan, B. Mahmmod, S. Al-Haddad, W. Jassim, Methods and challenges in shot boundary detection: a review, Entropy 20 (4) (2018) 214.

[35] D.M. Thounaojam, V.S. Bhadouria, S. Roy, K.M. Singh, Shot boundary detection using perceptual and semantic information, Int. J. Multimed. Inf. Retr. 6 (2) (2017) 167—174.

[36] B. Cyganek, M. Woźniak, Tensor-based shot boundary detection in video streams, New Gener. Comput. 35 (4) (2017) 311—340.

[37] R.D. Singh, N. Aggarwal, Novel research in the field of shot boundary detection — a survey, Advances in Intelligent Informatics, Springer, 2015, pp. 457—469.

[38] A. SenGupta, D.M. Thounaojam, K.M. Singh, S. Roy, Video shot boundary detection: A review, in: 2015 IEEE International Conference on Electrical, Computer and Communication Technologies (ICECCT), IEEE, 2015, pp. 1—6.

[39] T. Kar, P. Kanungo, A motion and illumination resilient framework for automatic shot boundary detection, Signal, Image Video Process. 11 (7) (2017) 1237–1244.
[40] T. Liu, Y. Lu, X. Lei, L. Zhang, H. Wang, W. Huang, et al., Soccer video event detection using 3d convolutional networks and shot boundary detection via deep feature distance, International Conference on Neural Information Processing, Springer, 2017, pp. 440–449.
[41] V. Benni, R. Dinesh, P. Punitha, V. Rao, Keyframe extraction and shot boundary detection using eigen values, Int. J. Inf. Electron. Eng. 5 (1) (2015) 40.
[42] S. Tippaya, S. Sitjongsataporn, T. Tan, K. Chamnongthai, M. Khan, Video shot boundary detection based on candidate segment selection and transition pattern analysis, in: 2015 IEEE International Conference on Digital Signal Processing (DSP), IEEE, 2015, pp. 1025–1029.
[43] H. Shao, Y. Qu, W. Cui, Shot boundary detection algorithm based on hsv histogram and hog feature, in: 2015 International Conference on Advanced Engineering Materials and Technology, Atlantis Press, 2015.
[44] C. Bi, Y. Yuan, J. Zhang, Y. Shi, Y. Xiang, Y. Wang, et al., Dynamic mode decomposition based video shot detection, IEEE Access 6 (2018) 21397–21407.
[45] J. Li, T. Yao, Q. Ling, T. Mei, Detecting shot boundary with sparse coding for video summarization, Neurocomputing 266 (2017) 66–78.
[46] S. Piramanayagam, E. Saber, N.D. Cahill, D. Messinger, Shot boundary detection and label propagation for spatio-temporal video segmentation, Image Processing: Machine Vision Applications VIII, vol. 9405, International Society for Optics and Photonics, 2015, p. 94050D.
[47] J. Xu, L. Song, R. Xie, Shot boundary detection using convolutional neural networks, in: Visual Communications and Image Processing (VCIP), 2016, IEEE, 2016, pp. 1–4.
[48] D.M. Thounaojam, T. Khelchandra, K. Singh, S. Roy, A genetic algorithm and fuzzy logic approach for video shot boundary detection, Comput. Intell. Neurosci. 2016 (2016) 14.
[49] J. Fan, S. Zhou, M.A. Siddique, Fuzzy color distribution chart-based shot boundary detection, Multimed. Tools Appl. 76 (7) (2017) 10169–10190.
[50] R.-K. Shen, Y.-N. Lin, T.T.-Y. Juang, V.R. Shen, S.Y. Lim, Automatic detection of video shot boundary in social media using a hybrid approach of hlfpn and keypoint matching, IEEE Trans. Comput. Soc. Syst. 5 (1) (2017) 210–219.
[51] A. Hassanien, M. Elgharib, A. Selim, S.-H. Bae, M. Hefeeda, W. Matusik, Large-scale, fast and accurate shot boundary detection through spatio-temporal convolutional neural networks, arXiv preprint arXiv:1705.03281.
[52] W. Tong, L. Song, X. Yang, H. Qu, R. Xie, Cnn-based shot boundary detection and video annotation, in: 2015 IEEE International Symposium on Broadband Multimedia Systems and Broadcasting, IEEE, 2015, pp. 1–5.
[53] C. Pingping, Y. Guan, X. Ding, Z. Yu, Shot boundary detection with sparse presentation, in: 2016 IEEE 13th International Conference on Signal Processing (ICSP), IEEE, 2016, pp. 900–904.
[54] R. Liang, Q. Zhu, H. Wei, S. Liao, A video shot boundary detection approach based on cnn feature, in: 2017 IEEE International Symposium on Multimedia (ISM), IEEE, 2017, pp. 489–494.
[55] K. Lee, M. Kolsch, Shot boundary detection with graph theory using keypoint features and color histograms, in: 2015 IEEE Winter Conference on Applications of Computer Vision, IEEE, 2015, pp. 1177–1184.
[56] J. Mondal, M.K. Kundu, S. Das, M. Chowdhury, Video shot boundary detection using multiscale geometric analysis of nsct and least squares support vector machine, Multimed. Tools Appl. 77 (7) (2018) 8139–8161.

[57] L. Boussaid, A. Mtibaa, M. Abid, M. Paindavoine, Real-time algorithms for video summarization, J. Appl. Sci. 6 (8) (2006) 1679—1685.
[58] A. Nagasaka, Y. Tanaka, Automatic video indexing and full video search for object appearances, in: Proceedings of the IFIP TC2 WG 2.6 Second Working Conference on Visual Database Systems II, North Holland Publishing Co., 1992, pp. 113—127.
[59] R. Zabih, J. Miller, K. Mai, A feature-based algorithm for detecting and classifying scene breaks, in: Proceedings of the third ACM international conference on Multimedia, ACM, 1995, pp. 189—200.
[60] L. Boussaid, A. Mtibaa, M. Abid, M. Paindavoine, A real-time shot cut detector: hardware implementation, Comput. Stand. Interfaces 29 (3) (2007) 335—342.
[61] A.M. Amel, B.A. Abdessalem, M. Abdellatif, Video shot boundary detection using motion activity descriptor, arXiv preprint arXiv:1004.4605.
[62] T. Youness, S. Abdelalim, Shot boundary detection in videos sequences using motion activities, Adv. Multimed. Int. J. (AMIJ) 5 (1) (2014) 1—7.
[63] M. Gygli, Ridiculously fast shot boundary detection with fully convolutional neural networks, in: 2018 International Conference on Content-Based Multimedia Indexing (CBMI), IEEE, 2018, pp. 1—4.
[64] J. Calic, E. Izquierdo, Towards real-time shot detection in the mpeg compressed domain, in: Proceedings of the 3rd Workshop on Image Analysis for Multimedia Interactive Services, 2001.
[65] J.M. Gauch, S. Gauch, S. Bouix, X. Zhu, Real time video scene detection and classification, Inf. Process. Manag. 35 (3) (1999) 381—400.
[66] A. Amer, E. Dubois, A. Mitiche, A real-time system for high-level video representation: application to video surveillance, in: Image and Video Communications and Processing 2003, vol. 5022, International Society for Optics and Photonics, 2003, pp. 530—542.
[67] E. Apostolidis, V. Mezaris, Fast shot segmentation combining global and local visual descriptors, in: 2014 IEEE International Conference on Acoustics, Speech and Signal Processing (ICASSP), IEEE, 2014, pp. 6583—6587.
[68] C. Ma, J. Yu, B. Huang, A rapid and robust method for shot boundary detection and classification in uncompressed mpeg video sequences, Int. J. Comput. Sci. Issues 5 (2012) 368—374.
[69] E. Amini, S.J. Jassbi, A quick algorithm to search and detect video shot changes, Int. J. Comput. Appl. 115 (3) (2015).
[70] S. Bhattacharyya, U. Maulik, P. Dutta, High-speed target tracking by fuzzy hostility-induced segmentation of optical flow field, Appl. Soft Comput. 9 (1) (2009) 126—134.
[71] G.L. Priya, S. Domnic, Edge strength extraction using orthogonal vectors for shot boundary detection, Procedia Technol. 6 (2012) 247—254.
[72] B. Rashmi, H. Nagendraswamy, Shot-based keyframe extraction using bitwise-xor dissimilarity approach, in: International Conference on Recent Trends in Image Processing and Pattern Recognition, Springer, 2016, pp. 305—316.
[73] D. Adjeroh, M. Lee, N. Banda, U. Kandaswamy, Adaptive edge-oriented shot boundary detection, EURASIP J. Image Video Process. 2009 (1) (2009) 859371.
[74] H.-W. Yoo, H.-J. Ryoo, D.-S. Jang, Gradual shot boundary detection using localized edge blocks, Multimed. Tools Appl. 28 (3) (2006) 283—300.
[75] H. Bhaumik, S. Bhattacharyya, S. Chakraborty, An unsupervised method for real time video shot segmentation, in: Proceedings of International Conference on Digital Image Processing and Pattern Recognition, 2014, pp. 307—318.

# Index

*Note*: Page numbers followed by "*f*" and "*t*" refer to figures and tables, respectively.

Linear regression, 3
LingPipe tool, 12
Local Dissimilarity Function (LDF), 199
Local polynomial approximation (LPA), 110
Long short-term memory (LSTM), 9, 75–77, 79
  components of, 76
  memory cell, 76
Look-back technique, 193
  for missed video segment detection, 208, 208*f*, 210

# M

Machine learning (ML), 2, 7–8, 12, 21, 109–110, 118, 124, 126, 128, 133, 169*f*
  classification and clustering, 158
  classification of, 155
  design and implementation, 159–164
    algorithm explanation, 163–164
    clustering of images, 160*f*
    feature extraction, 163
    grayscale, 163
    image acquisition, 161
    image preprocessing, 161
    image processing techniques, 159
    image segmentation, 161–163, 166*f*
    *K*-means, 168*f*
    SVM classifier, 159, 164, 166–167, 167*f*
    threshold image, 163
    training and classification, 163
  enhancement of image, 165*f*
  feature extraction, 157–158
  formation of clusters, 167*f*
  image processing, 157
  image segmentation, 166*f*
  loading of image, 165*f*
  proposed system, 159
  support vector machine classifier, 166–167, 167*f*, 168*f*
Magnetic resonance imaging (MRI), 102–104, 108–110, 115, 119–121, 137–138
Map reduction approach, 118
Markov fields for modeling, 110

MathWorks, 159
MATLAB, 159
Maximally Stable Extremal Regions (MSER), 194–196
Meaning-based data interpretation, 125
Medical diagnosis, 111
Medical image classification, 102–110
  hybrid approach, based on, 105–108
  neural expert systems, 107–108, 107*f*
  neuro fuzzy system, 106–107
  supervised classification, 105
  unsupervised classification, 105
Medical image processes, 102–103, 103*f*, 139–140
Medical image segmentation, 102–110
  Edge-based segmentation, 104
  pixel classification, 104
  purpose of, 103–104
  region-based segmentation, 104
  thresholding, 104
Medical transcription software (MTS), 140–141
Medical transcription tools, 140
Memory cell, 76
Metaheuristic algorithms, 110
MICCAI brain cancer segmentation (BRATS 2013) challenge database, 119–120
Minimum distance classifier (MDC), 155–156
Mobiles application, 25
Modern artificial file, 117
Modified National Institute of Standards and Technology (MNIST) data, 85–88
Monte Carlo search, 90–92, 101
Motion activity based method, 197–198
Motion query, 53–54
  by clip, 54
  by faces and texts, 54
  JACOB, 54
  by shot, 54
  VideoQ, 54
MPEG, 197–199
Multilayer perceptron (MLP), 175
Multilevel Difference of Colour Histograms (MDCH), 194–196

Printed in the United States
By Bookmasters